Italian Style   *Forms of Creativity*

Scientific Committee

Carlo Bertelli
Umberto Colombo
Umberto Eco
Vittorio Gregotti
Omar Calabrese (editor)

Italian Style
Forms of Creativity

Edited by Omar Calabrese

SKIRA

Design
Marcello Francone

Coordination
Marzia Branca

Editing
Giorgio Bigatti

Layout
Evelina Laviano

Iconographic research
Marco Pierini

First published in Italy in 1998
by Skira Editore S.p.A.
Palazzo Casati Stampa
via Torino 61, 20123 Milano, Italy

Printed and bound in Italy.
First edition

ISBN 88-8118-522-9

Distributed in North America
and Latin America by Abbeville
Publishing Group, 22 Cortlandt
Street, New York, NY 10007, USA.
Distributed elsewhere in the world
by Thames and Hudson Ltd.,
181a High Holborn, London WC1V
7QX, United Kingdom.

Contents

Omar Calabrese

Introduction

It is possible to single out a character, a distinctive trait, or a certain quality, that we can use to define "Italian style" as it is known the world over? A special something—called by sociologists "lifestyle" and philosophers "style of existence"—that succeeds in transcending artistic and literary style? The question is not of mere academic interest, for under the banner of Italian style the most varied of products have sought out their niches far and wide, making their presence felt in all corners of the world, both economically and—of no lesser importance—culturally.

In truth, the origins of the expression "Italian style" in itself do not instil us with brimming pride. As popular custom would have it, it may have been used to describe the creations of Italian hairdressers who had emigrated to America and England at the beginning of the twentieth century. Without dwelling on the accuracy of this version, the term was certainly applied progressively to a host of different products in areas such as fashion, design, furnishing and architecture. And from there it moved on to be applied to more abstract things which were more anthropological and cultural, like music, literature, theatre, cinema. Even a certain style in behaviour was added, which everyone recognised as being to some degree "aesthetic", "creative" or "inventive". By this we do not, of course, want to say that, from the outside looking in, Italy is always seen in a favourable light. Italian style is also applied euphemistically to the Italian way of conducting politics, public administration, business and other aspects relating to social behaviour. And unfortunately "the Italian way" is also used negatively to describe approximation, roguery or slovenliness and shallowness. Yet there are some sectors in which, unjustifiably, no tradition is assigned at all, nor any trust or credit, such as in the fields of science and technology. But let us return to Italian style, and get down to understanding what it is really about. Of all the things acknowledged as being Italian, can we say that they are a random mass? Or do all the products mentioned briefly above really have something in common? And if so, from what does this common trait arise? From the special ways we make things, from our historic tradition, or perhaps from our way of approaching business?

This book brings together the reflections of many specialists from the fields of arts, applied sciences, and the work of a small yet illustrious Scientific Committee. It sets out to provide an initial, working answer to these questions. An underlying idea emerges that was perhaps not apparent or precisely formulated when we set out on our project: that Italy's consumer-oriented production can be defined as inspired by a model—whether conscious or not—of blending features that are strangely opposite but not contradictory. As linguists teach us, the union of two different features does not lead to cancellation or neutrality; rather, it brings about what we call a "complex". Our intellectual output may therefore belong to complexity. But let us see in more detail how this concept is born. A first pair of opposites can be highlighted from the fact that while production is regulated by industrialisation which shuns individuality and craftsmanship, Italy has a way of uniting the standardisation with unique craftsmanship. This is very clear in the case of fashion, especially for the everyday-wear market, where garments are made industrially yet we call their designers "stylists"—a term and a characteristic that has influenced the whole fashion world.

Industrialised production also entails certain consequences in terms of aesthetics. In the fashion industry, it leads to putting the creation's subjectivity to one side, since cost reductions and large-scale distribution require goods to be simplified. The effect of reducing individuality through the "mass culture" has been the subject of criticism—at times ideological—and of an attempt to found new rationalist aesthetics, such as those born in connection with the so-called "Modernism" which started in the '30s. Also, in the German debate at the beginning of the century it referred to the concepts of "technique and culture" and, in the controversy of the post Second World War years, on "art and industry". Here, then, is another pair of apparent opposites: *standardisation* and *individuality*, words that go with *repetition* and *originality,* and which seem to determine the areas of *mass production* versus *avant garde*. But Italian production always seems to have found an original path in uniting those opposites, launching modern society towards what some have called "social aesthetics". It is by no mere coincidence, though, that if Postmodernism was born philosophically in France with Jean-François Lyotard, it saw its first productive manifestations in the architecture and design of Italy at the Venice Biennial Exhibition of 1979.

At this point, other pairs of opposites appear almost as secondary. Our social aesthetics indeed make provision that the anonymity of industrial standardisation is at least embellished with the notion of authorship: and indeed it was Italy that created products which were *firmati*—literally "signed"—as prestigious brand names. This feature can be seen not only in fashion and design but also in literature. In the '90s, the sector has witnessed the boom of mass publishing, often reproduced abroad, which started not so much from the notion of "genre" as from that of "author": Umberto Eco, Antonio Tabucchi, Susanna Tamaro, Alessandro Baricco, Oriana Fallaci and many others are to some degree exemplary.

The same principle also holds true for another pair of opposites, which stems from the existence of cultural, élite objects that are usually considered a luxury. The Italian model instead is one that combines *luxury* with *economy,* as if the dispute over luxury, born in the eighteenth century with Etienne Bonnot de Condillac, finds its natural solution in this day and age. And again, the aesthetic accent on our applied arts involves *sensitivity* and *sensoriality* (words having the same roots as "aesthetics"), which were excluded or reduced by research into industrial materials that could bear the large numbers of standard production and which instead return successfully in all that which is "Italian".

Social aesthetics had neither a quick nor a painless birth. By resulting from a long gestation in history and tradition, this is perhaps the last piece in that deceptive jigsaw that depicts Italian-ness: the introduction into mass production of elements that came from a century-old sedimentation of our culture. A culture that perhaps lies with good reason also in the mind-set of Italian companies which, as a model of existence, could be defined as "humanistic" (as described by Giovanni Agnelli Jr shortly before his premature death). In Italy for at least a century, the humanistic company has been at work: the company which tries to measure itself at times not only in terms of monetary, but also of cultural profit.

These are the lines along which the essays in this book will develop. They will not try to give final solutions nor attempt to maintain that in everything Italy is characterised as industrially humanistic. We know the defects of modern Italy and are often the first to do ourselves down. At the same time, we can also acknowledge—and hopefully convey in this volume—some of the originality of Italian style around the world.

Umberto Colombo

Specific Features of the Italian Industrial Manufacturing Model

When speaking about the Italian model, I believe that one of its most characteristic and significant aspects is to be found precisely in the manufacturing system, and especially, but not only, in that of small and medium-sized concerns and the industrial estates. It is a system which, all in all, sums up a number of the specifics of the Italian socio-economic model so aptly described in this book, and represents the support structure of a healthy, competitive economy that, all things considered, is among the first in the world.

Italy, despite having some substantial imbalances, is an industrialised country and henceforth engaged in a post-industrial stage, with a high per capita income, possessing the requisite experience and structures for dealing with a number of problems. The growth of industry came about later than in the other major European countries, with concerns and structures copied on their model. However, increasingly significant and experienced sectors of industry turn out to consist in a system of businesses run according to methods of their own, and in any case different from those of conventional industrial firms.

This "manufacturing model", specific to our country, is typified by small and medium-sized concerns, including those of the industrial estates, as well as by a remarkable number of medium and medium-large concerns using a highly entrepreneurial rationale stimulated by individuals or family groups, who often urge their employees not to consider themselves as such, but as potential entrepreneurs themselves. Such a system is frequently adverse to rules and models, which deny them the degree of freedom they want and need, this being also one of the many reasons encouraging, in certain circumstances, a shadow economy; at the same time it leads to competition between businesses working in a certain sector—and frequently in a specific area—and widespread collaboration aiming at strengthening the entire group of concerns and the area where they operate. In time such a collaboration leads to connecting, first of all, the producers of consumer goods to those of the related investment goods, then to the providers of the services necessary for improving the entire system, and lastly to the manufacturers of other goods allowing for the creation of market synergies so as to guarantee a combined series of products and services. The Italian system does very little research, even though it is able to innovate on the technical, organisational and market level with timeliness and efficiency, taking advantage of the synergies of the collaboration networks that characterise it. Although, especially in the past, it privileged the direct technical, productive aspects (machines, processes), the system did not set up an organisation for manufacturing, warehousing and then selling, but instead sought to identify the demands of the market, so as to sell, and therefore manufacture. In short, the system is characterised by the search for aesthetically attractive solutions, well-adapted to the functions and the quality of the products; it is highly creative and frequently boasts a high-level, professional design; these features have become increasingly important with time, as the markets grew and became more sophisticated and more demanding.

Ours is a highly dynamic manufacturing system, in constant evolution and exposed to growing international competition; periodically this "instability" creates strains and crises that, in the past, it has been able to overcome, and even become stronger through them, more competitive and aggressive. We need only think of the many studies, both Italian and foreign, announcing the collapse of the model, and the prominent international economic reviews highlighting the crisis in our industry and wondering if and how we would ever be able to overcome it.

But it is equally true that foreign scholars, economic and social analysts have taken the Italian manufacturing model quite seriously, striving to understand it, to identify the specific factors that give it such strength and vitality, to see if, and to what degree, it could be applicable to other socio-economic realities, to demonstrate that it is a complex phenomenon involving aspects closely bound to production, technology, organisation, and market. A decisive role is also played by aspects such as social structures, individual and collective behaviour, values sedimented by a long, rich history, civic virtues and the sense of belonging, solidarity and the tradition of competition, the immersion in a society and an environment culturally and aesthetically outstanding, not an end in itself, but made to respond to functional demands, expressing itself in extremely livable urban centres, provided with a number of shops in proportion to the population, in a wealth of housing, in the culture of beautiful objects, in clothing that is not shabby, in a city and rural environment thought out down to the last detail. We are familiar with the works of the Americans, Charles Sabel and Michael Piore on the manner of producing in Italy, those of Michael Porter on the complex substratum of skills and traditions (the so-called "clusters") characterising this manner of producing, those of Robert Putnam on the historical roots of the civic tradition permeating this substratum; but recently the topic has been taken up by the Japanese, who also in their country—feature the presence of countless small and medium concerns, with many serious studies—we refer to the one carried out by JETRO, with the intention of adapting to Japan the extraordinary success of the Italian manufacturing system. Even in Europe, French, German, English industrialists often wonder how the system of the Italian firms, apparently so disorderly and inefficient, can be so competitive, so ready to adopt and invent new technical solutions and set up such an efficient international presence.

The Italy of Small Concerns and Industrial Estates

About twenty-five years ago, at the time of the first energy crisis, the worldwide economic-industrial system went through a deep recession, owing to the end of the era of Ford-Taylor-inspired standardised mass production, that had worked for a century and a half, ever since the advent of the industrial revolution. This way of manufacturing had been able to offer the entire population an impressive amount of durable consumer goods, as well as services; but now society demanded diversified goods, more care given to the aesthetic aspects and to fashion, function also taking into account tastes and traditions, the possibility of changing goods and solutions without too much expense, and also a regard for the issues of environment, ressources, health, safety, quality of life and fairness. The nimble, flexible, adaptable systems—to be found above all in the small and medium concerns—were largely prepared to provide sound answers to these market demands, whereas large concerns, with their heavy machinery, found it much more difficult to adjust to the new paradigms.

Small concerns and traditional sectors were a basic part of the Italian industrial background. They represent very substantial activities; we need only think of the fact, shown in a recent study performed by the Montedison Study Unit, collaborating with the Catholic University of Milan CRANEC, that the combined Italian sectors of textile, clothing, leather goods and shoes have a value added equal to that of the entire German automobile industry, and that, as a general rule, "Made in Italy" sectors are comparable as to turnover, value added, employment, export, to significant foreign sectors—considered to be higher-tech—such as pharmaceutics, office equipment, oil refineries in the U.S.A. Although "Made in Italy" does include medium-large concerns, which we shall talk about briefly in paragraph 5, in the regions of the centre and the north-east of the peninsula (but equally in the north-west and also increasingly scattered throughout the south, where the industrial estates are growing at an exceptional rate both numerically and in size, although still partly "hidden"), the economic structure is essentially characterised by networks of small concerns, specialised in the manufacturing of textile, clothing, leather, shoes, ceramics, furniture, articles in metal, machine tools and others, taps and fittings and valve equipment, other traditional industrial goods, with the formation of geographically well-localised systems: the so-called "industrial estates". Traditional industries, and particularly small concerns, are vital for employment and export, as opposed to what occurs in other industrialised countries, where they tend to respond instead to the national market.

Each small Italian concern operates like a part of a cycle of combined manufacturing—with connections upstream, downstream and on the sides, and presenting a very high degree of specialisation—and, for that very reason, does not spring up or expand in isolation. This model, having become essential for the local economies, results from the combination of various factors, often including a pluri-secular tradition of artisan manufacturing, combined with the de-verticalisation of the Italian industrial structure of the seventies and the strong dynamism of the industrial base. A key factor to the success of the networks of small concerns is the social context in which they operate, consisting in socially integrated communities, having a great individual mobility, and few devastating inequalities: such a social structure provides a solid base of cooperation, solidarity and intense flows of information representing, on the whole, an indispensable condition for the concerns to feel the incentive to take risks and introduce innovations.

The result is a manufacturing system which at first sight may appear highly fragmented and uncoordinated, but which is actually extremely integrated in a widespread network and has profound roots in inter-company and interpersonal relationships. This situation gives rise to a very high degree of flexibility of the manufacturing cycle—easily adapting itself to the shifting demands of the market, the request for new articles and the arising of new opportunities—but also permits an easy flow of information, a creative application of technological innovation to the manufacturing process—with its rapid spreading throughout the context of the industrial estate, and an availability to experiment new forms of productive organisation inside and outside the individual concerns—above all propitious to swift and responsible decision making. The success of this model is confirmed by the high quality of the articles of Italian fashion, and of a series of traditional consumer and industrial goods that, from mere standardised products, became quality articles, original in their conception and innovative in their execution, and adapted to their use.

In the network of small Italian concerns, the innovation of products and processes usually occurs following the same pattern and with the same synergy: the introduction of new technologies, in the form of new equipment for making traditional articles, stimulates the designing of innovative articles; the launching of new articles in turn stimulates the research for new machinery, processes and ways of organising production within the network of small concerns. Actually, the networks are constantly changing shape, developing new specialisations and giving up others, when the pressure of international competition, coming from countries technologically more advanced or from recently industrialised economies, becomes unbearable. In particular, the manufacturing of machines or equipment used by the local concerns provides a striking example of the broadening of the specialisation of Italian networks. Thanks to the success of the rejuvenated Italian textile industry, a new industry of textile equipment has blossomed, increasingly using electronics; but the same can be said of machines for processing wood or plastics, for machine tools and other equipment of high-level manufacture specialisation. All this implies that technological change in Italy is above all brought about by the intelligent application of "high technologies" to manufacturing in traditional sectors, rather than by the autochthonous development of a new, separate advanced technology sector.

All in all, in the estates there was a swift technological innovation of an incremental type, usually not brought about by actual research, but encouraged by a high level of social control and the coexistence of lively competition between concerns, in terms of prices, services and quality (with the consequent incentive to innovate), and by a close collaboration between the concerns themselves when they need to put together the various parts of the manufacturing cycle, with a constant flow of information regarding the new manufacturing technologies, the new organisational systems and the new market opportunities. The result of this combination of competition and cooperation is the improvement of the entire status of the local industry on the international markets, which goes with a constant increase in efficiency and swift technical and organisational innovation, with expenses generally relatively low for the industrial network as a whole, and in particular for the individual concerns. In other words, innovation, in the networks of small concerns, is not a zero-sum game between rival firms, in which the growth of one must necessarily imply the decline of the other; the benefits add up and do not annul each another, and the entire system benefits by it.

Such a way of innovating requires a horizontal managerial style leaving a wide margin of decision to the lowest levels; ties between concerns; the association, during the stage of development and prototypes, of research (or similar activities), production and commercial services; a high degree of flexibility in design; a good integration of the organisation and the systems and attentiveness to logistics. All these managerial instruments are typical of so-called "lean production", which is therefore a solution well-suited to the estates.

The Evolution of the Estates

As occurs for any system subjected to inside and outside pressures, industrial estates also are modified according to an evolutionary process tending to preserve competitiveness and to benefit by those opportunities that arise and which can be easily exploited.

Whereas the evolution of the various Italian industrial estates can be observed and described, its interpretation in global and consequently, in a certain sense, strategic terms, is highly dependent on the point of view used for analysing it, in order to draw conclusions as regards the future (their role, strength, vulnerability) of these estates. Besides, whereas analysis is relatively easy for the past, it is far more complicated to grasp what is relevant in what is happening at the moment, since this kind of analysis is strongly influenced by the characteristics (networks, territorial factors, dominance of artisan-industrial manufacturing) attributed to the estates, especially when they are based on numerous scholarly studies.

The evolution of industrial estates in Italy, beginning with their obvious success during the late seventies, therefore leaving aside the complex roots and earlier vicissitudes of the independent city states in the Middle Ages, appears to present four essential stages:

1. The estate is centered around its primary activity of production of the sector characterising it, generally traditional consumer goods aimed at ever-broader markets.

2. Within the estate several industrial and complementary service activities develop, first of all the production of investment goods, for the sector itself, with swift feed-back.

3. The existence or the emergence of one or several strong points leads to exploiting them by starting up all the related activities (production, availability of goods, services), so as to have an integrated and complete package allowing the estate to become a reference on a worldwide scale.

4. The less interesting and profitable activities, if not onerous, are exported (or emigrate) to other regions of the country or abroad, in countries where the cost of labour or other ressources is cheap; usually these are manufacturing activities of components or goods, whereas the more immaterial and strategic ones stay in the estate.

Stages 1 and 2 feature a "natural" evolution, meaning they exploit skills accumulated in the estate and circumstances appearing locally and on world markets. Thus, for instance, stage 1 is the natural response to a saturated market, that can no longer grow quantitively as in the two preceding decades, requiring an accrued differentiation and personalisation of the goods and, gradually, more quality. In stage 2 on the other hand, the association between traditional goods produced in the estate and related investment goods is "natural", in the sense that Italy as a country is characterised by the widespread presence of a strong engineering industry that is adaptable, capable of significant marginal innovation and seeks new activities and markets: this symbiosis entails conspicuous reciprocal benefits, with improved processes, but also articles, from the production originating in the estates, which are coupled with machinery and implements. The same is true of the development of a number of shared services the market structures inevitably bring about.

The estates are known to be characterised by their attentive catering to the demands of their customers: besides, they have multiple "instruments" and points of contact with the market (as is the case of the historically significant "textile workers" in Prato); nevertheless, we can say that stages 1 and 2 are typically "stimulated" by products and aligned on the tradition of small and medium-sized concerns, particularly Italian ones.

The two following stages, 3 and 4, reverse the traditional evolutive approach to adopt a more strategic one, meaning no longer relying nearly solely on the consolidated inside and local energies and the obvious market developments, but imagining and pursuing new solutions capable of creating competitive advantages in a market that not only is becoming global, but which offers outstanding opportunities to those who are able to conceive them. These stages, of which we can find a growing number of examples, are typically "drawn from the market".

To give an example as regards stage 3, an estate specialised in processing leather (for shoes, handbags, or other uses) can make up its mind to become the world reference for supplying leather and its manufactured articles, machines for its processing (studs, buckles, handles, laces, dyes, etc.) and all the connected services. The point is to guarantee a sufficiently varied and complex assortment of activities, some which the estate can directly carry out and other that it can commission or acquire from others estates (for instance, brass elements from an estate that processes that metal alloy) or other manufacturers, either in Italy or anywhere in the world. The point is that the customer working with the estate and going to visit it can find all he needs there, even if in the long run the foundation of the success of the estate still lies in the demonstration of its competitiveness on global markets.

A fundamental aspect of stage 3 is therefore the capacity to entirely integrate the activities and the products needed by a customer operating in the sector in which the estate is involved, the customer who has a hard time, or even does not succeed in finding them where he is based: the estate thus guarantees, anywhere in the world, all that (components, goods, services) is required for performing a certain business activity. The offer of the estate becomes complex and requires the creation of a very demanding network, less linked to territory and more immaterial than the conventional one typical of the estates. Ultimately, in the industrialised countries with high-cost labour, only complex, and truly high-tech activities will remain.

Stage 4 is an obvious outgrowth of stage 3, even if it can directly stem from stage 2. Henceforth the estate, even if it is still bound to its traditional production and its territory, has developed, vital links with a varied outside world, and is no longer product-oriented, but decidedly market-oriented, with a real world market. Run-of-the-mill activities and those with a low value added "evaporate", especially the industrial ones, disappearing or migrating where it is more convenient to perform them (low cost of labour, of resources, of infrastructures); those activities that are truly strategic remain, such as design, technological innovation, logistics; all the activities contributing to the success of the estate are controlled; the combination of skills, productive structures, specific features of the manufactured products, services of the sector the estate has chosen to operate are managed. The estate's activity becomes increasingly immaterial and strategic.

It is interesting to observe how, and over what length of time, this evolution in four stages of Italian estates comes about and, especially, which ones are entering stage 3, or even 4. Besides, it is interesting to grasp if one might imagine agile instruments of economic policies, on behalf of the state and the regions, to stimulate the most profitable evolution, and if the estates avail of conditions for a positive, more strategic change, since everything leads us to assume that, left on its own to evolve spontaneously, the traditional estate model is condemned, sooner or later, to wither away. Globalisation, constant technological innovation which, through globalisation, ends up by quickly permeating the entire economic and productive world system, the arrival of new operators, the rapid changes in behaviours and situations, tend to indicate that, in the coming years, the estates will be involved in an intense process of renewing and improving their technical, organisational, and market capacities.

A Key for Interpreting the Italian Specifics

Studies and analyses carried out on the Italian phenomenon of small concerns agree that it did not come about haphazardly, all of a sudden, with such a widespread growth and such substantially identical features—notwithstanding the typical differences of each area—but that it must be based on deep roots inherent to culture and tradition, roots perhaps dulled, but never quite dead—that at a certain moment in history found the conditions for rapidly developing a type of economy and production congenial to the country and responding to the demands of the world market.

Whereas it is easy to identify the decline of the society born with the industrial revolution—requiring huge, intricate, rigid productive systems, conceived to profit by economies of scale—as the primary condition for the emerging of productive systems that would be more unconnected, ready, flexible, adaptable like those of the Italian small concerns, it is more difficult to fully grasp how these systems could have appeared so swiftly in Italy, and of which technical, organisational bases they might have taken advantage. There is widespread agreement in placing the roots of this "culture" in the medieval traditions of the independent city states and the following developments during the Renaissance, whereas a secondary role might have been played by the industrialisation process that took place in the second half of the last century, at least at the start, brought about by businessmen and technical experts coming from the more developed part of Europe in order to take advantage of conditions offered by an emerging, low-cost economy, and which led to the gradual formation of businessmen, managers, and labour typical of conventional industry.

Michael Porter has sought to relate the "skills" of a country, sedimented throughout its history, to its present-day performances on world markets, and has convincingly shown that one should not refer to single (even if there are many) specific factors as much as to "clusters" of interacting factors that are at once technical, behavioural, and organisational, regarding needs, social structure, underlying traditions, demands of local markets: all in all, something that is characteristic of the type of "culture" inherent to the country, something of which even certain specific skills can be lost, because—as soon as the occasion appears—they could easily be re-acquired, since they actually intrinsically belong to its culture and its civilisation. Porter has dealt at length with the Italian case, pointing out that its complex technical-economic-financial-aesthetic-organisational-entrepreneurial market culture, stemming from the independent city states of the Middle Ages and later enriched during the Renaissance, demonstrates the very same traits belonging to the typical culture of the industrial estates and the successful areas of the Italian economy.

Robert Putnam, looking at the Italian case from an entirely different angle—that of civic traditions, of substantial democracy implying citizens' direct intervention in running things and the tendency to form associations—reaches conclusions similar to Porter's, i.e. above all that culture and civilisation in Italy today have their strongest roots in the experience of the independent city states. It is worthwhile observing the different histories of the regions having had the experience of communal freedom (that is, of a participant society, of a "bottom-up" type) from those—especially in the South, and from where precisely the Southern problem might arise—which are characterised instead by feudal structures (that is, of a "top-down" type). Putnam also examines how these characteristics, accumulated since these remote experiences, have bearing on their economic situation: during the Middle Ages, the level of well-being was the same in the two parts of Italy, becoming different with the industrial development. But he disagrees with the simplistic hypothesis of a democracy requiring industrial development, observing how, more even than wealth, what counts is the efficiency with which the local governments manage public affairs to offer greater conditions of effective democracy, and therefore of quality of life, and how this efficiency is more closely related to civic traditions than to wealth. All in all, civic traditions (and, we should add, cultural ones) may be a more powerful strength than any other, be it scientific, technical, or economic, and may contain the capacity to unleash—giving the general circumstances—socio-economic development itself: this would explain the country's success, as described by Porter, and that of "Made in Italy", the Italy of the estates and of fashion; the sudden appearing of very lively economies such as those of the Adriatic coast and of the North-East; the fact that, even more than technical skills, what counts is the social fabric which, for instance, makes the individual small concerns of the estates become systems of highly integrated networks, as they have been described above with all their positive synergies.

Bright and Dark Sides of the Italian Industrial System

Italian industrialisation came about in a way that was alien to the country's culture and society—except perhaps in Piedmont, where the cultural ties with France and Switzerland had created conditions for the development of large-scale undertakings (we refer to Fiat, Olivetti, broadcasting and the EIAR). A number of scholars wondered whether Italian culture was adjustable to modern industry and its capitalist structure, if its Catholic tradition were antithetical to the modern entrepreneurial conception, as it appeared to be bound on the other hand to the ethics of Protestantism; the work by Giovanni Federico and Gianni Toniolo, quoted in our bibliography, reflects this issue, henceforth superseded on the historical level, if we realise that capitalism was actually born in Italy in the late Middle Ages with its own ideas and own structures, as well as on the factual level, with the aggressive explosion of the "Italian Model", and on the behavioural level with the work ethics emblematically expressed by the development in the North-East. Lombardy too, where nonetheless major industries developed, was and is more prone to flexible small concerns, to industrial activities closely tied to commercial, economic and service ones, and even more to the latter as such. On the whole it was a "belated" industrialisation, as Giorgio Fuà defined it, with the problems that implies, having never been entirely "digested" by Italian society, owing also to the widespread presence of a very lively cultural tradition which, as soon as circumstances allowed, broke loose and prevailed over the imported solutions, which in the meantime however had led to the country's prosperity, therefore also creating favourable conditions for the unleashing of the typical Italian model, emblematically represented by the industrial estates.

The latter do not encompass all the "Made in Italy"—which is far more varied, articulate and complex and is characterised by those attitudes succinctly outlined in the introduction—these being undoubtedly more suited to the small and medium-sized concerns of the estates, but can be—and it does occur—the operating modes of even medium-large sized concerns, which draw on the cultural tradition of Italian entrepreneurship, although not belonging to the estates. Besides, the system of the Italian small and medium-sized concerns itself is highly diversified: near Milan, Bergamo, Brescia, in Brianza, next to estates, meaning areas specialised in production of a specific industrial sector, there is a blossoming of countless concerns producing machinery and implements on a wider scale, processing metals and other materials, and which nonetheless benefit by all the advantages inherent to the estates, owed mainly to the capillary network of available services, but also to the exploiting of all the synergies the neighbourhood allows.

The fashion industry too, which has outdone the traditional French one, is an example of the Italian industrial model, with its flexibility, its proneness to broaden its markets, to constantly innovate, including technologically and, at the same time, the limited number of inside structures precisely devoted to the task. The conceiving of new articles is, and will continue to be, in the hands of those who make a worldwide name for themselves in creativity and design, and are at the same time capable of taking advantage of the huge opportunities opened up by new technologies: new materials, dyes, finishings, showing the way to innovative solutions to respond all the better to the consumers' demands; computer science and telecommunications, the intensive use of Internet, leading to a hitherto unknown flexibility and a drastic reduction of the "time to market". But the possibilities are even vaster, requiring dialogue between countless operators and the availibility of varied knowledge and skills. For instance it means guaranteeing the greatest "comfort" in clothes, which can be measured, at the same time as its physiological properties, by electronic instruments: thermal insulation, resistance to perspiration, its use in fabrics under normal conditions, but also in motion under unforseen increases of heat and humidity, or under sudden variations in outside temperatures, in order to guarantee an ideal microclimate by using the layers of air between skin and fabric, the cut of the clothing, the circulation of outside air. This means that it is becoming a must to develop an authentic "clothing science" to study, for instance, how to achieve with the materials and the way of assembling them the best-suited thermal insulation (knowledge of the behaviour of birds and other animals, for instance, can contribute to this end).

But the typical manner of proceeding of Italian culture is not just an attribute of the sectors most closely associated with fashion, even considering almost exclusively traditional sectors and not the most advanced ones. Just think about the concept of the scooter and its production, as illustrated in the essay "Behind the Myth of the Vespa" by Marino Livolsi in this same book: a means of transport that combined aesthetics, response to the market demands, practicality, and that adopted (and continues to do so) brilliant avant-garde technical solutions. Just think even about the idea of the "utilitaria" (the runabout) of the Topolino, equally discussed in this book by Omar Calabrese, a car that, although made by the most typical of the conventional Italian industrial firms (naturally without the slightest negative connotation in this term), for its design, materials, and needs of a market that is financially hard up, but culturally demanding, calls upon the typical way in which a product of the "Made in Italy" model is conceived. And again just think about the sector of small-steelworks, which made the foreign producers, failing to see how custom-made steel could be produced at such prices, lambast about "dumping". That sector aimed at technical solutions, like using scrap and flexible plants, was attentive to the diversified market and small niches, and built itself up—according to the typical conception of the Italian way of making industry—in concerns producing steel and its components and others producing plants for the steelworks. The latter soon gave up the preconceived approach and the entire execution of the steelworks, even those including the variants requested by the customer, and reversed their own way of operating: instead of producing to sell, they sold to produce, in other words they structured themselves to respond to the demands of the market with an "*ad hoc*" design for each individual case, and the execution and the assembling of the various components of the steelworks for a specific customer, only a small part of the components being made inside the concern, the others being ordered from outside concerns, connected in an integrated system from a certain angle not unlike that of the estates. Danieli of Udine is significative of this evolution; it is technically at the avant-garde, today seeking to extend its presence by taking over one of its major competitors, in a market where there is already a very small number of operators (five in Europe).

The number of medium and relatively large-sized Italian concerns (Danieli, for instance, has a turnover of approximately 2,000 billion Lire) operating in the most varied sectors with an approach typical of the Italian industrial model, is quite high and on the rise, a sign that such a model reflects the cultural features and the entrepreneurial vocation of the country and, at the same time, is clearly competitive on the international level. We should add that the large Italian firms themselves are reverting to approaches that greatly differ from those of the past regarding the small concerns, which used to be considered vassals and then useful collaborators, whereas today they increasingly represent a very lively market to be backed with new articles and specifically studied solutions. On this subject, it is worthwhile observing the unusual attention Montedison is paying to the system of estates and small and medium-sized Italian concerns, with which it is developing precious interactions offering reciprocal usefulness.

The Italian industrial model is an outstanding innovator, not only as regards fashion, aesthetics, market approach, but also on the level of technology, whether it be the small estate concerns or the more important ones, even if in general such concerns perform little research. We can recall, among the countless innovations carried out by these companies, the passage from double firing to single firing for earthenware tiles, the execution and production of the "Leonardo" loom, the fastest-working in the world, on behalf of Vamatex of Bergamo (remember that feats of this nature used to be typical of Swiss and German industries), the Parmalat UHT for milk conservation. An even more relevant aspect is the fact that conception, design and protoypes of the machines (and above all of the integrated systems of production using them) required by "Made in Italy" are usually entirely Italian, including the electronic components; only later important worldwide companies are requested to carry out the commercial development of the electronic components; nonetheless the final execution of the machines destined for the market, resorting to "personalised" electronic components, is performed by Italian concerns; among the significant innovations we can mention packing and wrapping machinery made by IMA, which creates tailor-made solutions for concerns all over the world. "Made in Italy" also features significant novelty products, such as: "light wool", commercial fresh pasta, tele-assistance for senior citizens, modern stoppers for liquor bottles, modern ski and mountain boots, modern bicycle seats. And last, "Made in Italy" has particular expertise in organisation and marketing innovations: franchising in clothing (Benetton and others); the creation of syndicates for logistics and services in the estates; agencies for the development of the estates; the new way of organising the estates as described in paragraph 3.

The dynamism and the success of "Made in Italy" innovations can be contrasted with a certain difficulty—which can be attributed to many different factors of a technical nature, but above all of organisation, of the capacity to understand the market, or social factors   that the conventional industrial system in Italy has in innovating, despite its clear success in research and developed technologies. We refer to the nuclear field, to electronics and computer sciences, and large chemical firms. The case of polypropylene is significant: an invention obviously not typical of "Made in Italy" nor of the "Italian industrial model", but certainly of great importance, the result of excellent scientific and technological research carried out in collaboration between Piero Giustiniani's Montecatini and the Milan Polytechnic with Giulio Natta who, in 1963, was awarded the Nobel Prize in Chemistry for that discovery. However, despite the fact that the Montecatini management was aware of the value of the discovery and determined to exploit it, insufficient knowledge of the market and of the international competitive system caused the advantages gained to be far less than what could have been expected.

To conclude this brief essay, we can say that our model presents, as regards the "industrial production" component associated with Italian style, certain weaknesses that give precarity to our position of leadership on the world markets, in sectors where other countries have at their disposal conditions that are far more favourable structure-wise, in terms of cost of labour and other factors of production. Obviously, there are fields of activity where Italy excels throughout the world, enjoying today a competitive advantage. But we must ask ourselves how long it will be able to keep up this position of strength, without an outstanding effort as regards professional training, higher education and scientific and technological research. A losing game would be a defensive strategy aiming at protecting the present-day typology of employment, also directed towards exporting low-medium level technology goods, and relying too much on the art of making do, this too being a typical Italian trait. The time has come to re-examine the Italian model in terms of strategy, and attempt to understand how to best place the manufacturing system in a global economy, the pace of which will be increasingly more ruled by the unceasing progress in science and technology.

G. Becattini, *Distretti industriali e Made in Italy*, Bollati Bolinghieri, Turin 1998.

G. Federico, G. Toniolo, *Italy*, in *Patterns of European Industrialization. The Nineteenth Century*, edited by R. Sylla and G. Toniolo, Routledge, London 1991.

G. Fuà, *Problemi dello sviluppo tardivo in Europa*, Il Mulino, Bologna 1980.

G. Fuà, G. and C. Zacchia, *Industrializzazione senza fratture*, Il Mulino, Bologna 1983.

L. Meldolesi, *Dalla parte del Sud*, Laterza, Roma-Bari 1998.

F. Momigliano, *L'innovazione industriale e la condizione dell'Italia: problemi di analisi delle determinanti ed effetti dell'innovazione e risultanze di ricerche empiriche*, Conferenza Nomisma, Milan, 2-3 December 1983, in G. Antonelli *Innovazioni tecnologiche e struttura produttiva: la posizione dell'Italia*, Il Mulino, Bologna 1984.

H.Ogawa, *Industrial Districts of Small and Medium Sized Manufacturing Enterprises in Italy*, JETRO Milan, 1997.

M.J. Piore C.F. Sabel, *Italian Small Business Development: Lessons for U.S. Policy*, In *American Industry in International Competition, Government Policies and Corporate Strategies*, edited by J. Zysman and L Tyson, Cornell University Press, Ithaca, 1983.

M.J. Piore and C.F. Sabel, *The Second Industrial Divide: Possibilities for Prosperity*, Basic Books Inc, New York 1984.

M.E. Porter, *The Competitive Advantage of Nations*, The Free Press, New York 1990.

R.D. Putnam, *Making Democracy Work, Civic Traditions in Modern Italy*, Princeton University Press, Princeton, N.J. 1992.

Behind the Myth of the Vespa

The Vespa scooter was the product that, more than any others, was the emblem of Italian industrial creativity immediately after the Second World War. It is a myth that is indeed still going strong today. Yet many other products—fridges, the Fiat 600, etc.—could also have been taken up as the symbols of a miracle which, in the space of just two decades, saw Italy rise from a state of destruction and destitution to one of good standards of living that were as widespread as they were perhaps unexpected: for families that had lived until only recently in the fear of a future that held the continual risk of stable employment, a situation developed whereby they could afford to give their children a proper education, buy their own house, and even afford holidays abroad.

The Vespa is the story of an invention, but of course it is also one of entrepreneurial genius. Piaggio was originally established as a company working in the aeronautical sector and some of its aircraft have indeed written pages in the history of Italian military aviation. At the end of the war, the company was practically in ruins, as had obviously been the goal of the Allies, and was at grips with the problem of its own conversion. At the time, it was unthinkable to carry on designing and building aeroplanes so the company

turned its attention to new products and markets.

One idea was saucepans, another was a project to design and manufacture dish-washers. But at Biella, where Piaggio had temporarily transferred its working operations, the company directors by chance came across a small motor-scooter that their host, Count Troissi, said he had found in an aeroplane or seen used by the German or allied parachutists. The mini scooter became the subject of a study while the war was in its final throes.

It was the first insight to mark the history of the Vespa: the creation of a product that had never previously existed a motor vehicle running on two wheels that was not strictly a motorcycle but which was cheaper and more functional. A prototype was started, called Paperino (Donald Duck) because of its almost cartoon-like appearance. But the idea was not convincing so Piaggio called in a brilliant aeronautical engineer who, among other things, had also designed a successful helicopter: D'Ascanio. Instead of developing the project in progress, he started practically from scratch, inventing a new and different product that would be more suited to the times. D'Ascanio's insight was to apply certain guiding principles to his creation: the scooter had to be practical and easy to drive; the rider had to be able to mount it easily like a women's bicycle and also it could not be too heavy; it had to be easy to handle (the gearshift mounted on the handlebar allowed for safer driving); it must not get the rider dirty in bad weather or when driving on uneven road surfaces (the front shield protected the rider from dirt and also the engine was covered); it needed a spare wheel that was easy to change and also solid (the mono-tube support originating from the aeronautical field was integral with the front wheel), etc.

All of these features were in effect cutting-edge solutions born from the practical, yet very important requirements of the potential buyer. This was a mark of the kind of attention towards customers' needs that was highly innovational for the times but which went on to characterise the new industry emerging in the post-war years. On the backdrop was a revolution: from poverty to the discovery that work allowed people to live a better lifestyle, one more in keeping with their needs and, for some, this also meant being able to realise their dreams.

An attractive, lightweight motor scooter was born, called Vespa or "the wasp". It was both functional and well-packed with technological innovation.

In more down to earth terms, this meant a product that was solid, safe and easy to handle. But more than anything else, the Vespa was attractive and had an enviable acceleration that made it the most ideal means for dodging amongst the urban traffic. It was also the "secret weapon" for the youngsters who later began to show off their prowess in the first wheelies. The advantages of this scooter didn't stop there: it was also highly economical to run, easy to park and also had a silent engine.

The success was immediate: in the first year, the first 2,000 scooters manufactured were sold out; in the second year, over 10,000 were made and sold. The manufacturing capacity, at least at the beginning, was unable to keep up with the demand—a result that was also fruit of a shrewd marketing strategy that was another great insight by the company. At the beginning, Piaggio considered the setting up of its own sales network a difficult and costly operation and instead sought—and struck up—an agreement with Lancia. Thus, the Vespa was put on display nationwide in the Lancia car dealers and beside a car which, even to a more modest degree, was also to leave its own mark on the history of Italian motoring: the Appia. Years afterwards, Piaggio went on to

make itself independent, but as an initial sales kick-start, the idea was a winner and allowed the Vespa to quickly become a family name around the country.

But the successful sales figures only told half of the story. The Vespa was such a hit with the people that it was clear a myth was in the making. The scooter appeared on the pages of the daily papers and was presented to the famous people of the times. It aroused huge interest and the public in general identified with the scooter in many of its more intrinsic and real needs. Above all, it was a means of transport that afforded great mobility, something that was not to be underestimated for the times. Cars were still very expensive and very few, while the cheaper motorcycles were inconvenient and did not enjoy a wide market acceptance. In the towns and countryside alike, the bicycle was still the main means of transport used by the people, especially those with more restricted budgets. But the bicycle only allowed short-distance travel—and of course it entailed fatigue. The Vespa came along as the ideal answer: literally overnight, people were suddenly able to travel tens if not hundreds of kilometres at a time, taking with them a passenger (or even two!) or their goods to trade.

A Vespa Club rally. Vespa Clubs were a spontaneous and self-organised response to the scooter's success. The clubs were an international, not just Italian phenomenon.

Vespa adopted by the Finnish army, 1950.

Acrobatic display group from Pontodora.

It was a new-found freedom the potential of which was of course explored as much for work as it was for leisure time. In towns and cities, people were now avoiding public transport and in the country saving huge amounts of time to get to work and back. And when the weekends came round, the roads beckoned them for trips and holidays farther afield, to the coast, countryside or mountains. In a sentence: for the people of the time, it opened a door to discovering the world.

Apart from the obvious geographical mobility it offered the people, the Vespa brought with it also a cultural one. It was about discovering a new way of life; it was about being able to do those simple but lovely things that only yesterday had seemed difficult or virtually impossible. Until yesterday, the train had been the only way to travel any kind of distance. Now everything was so much easier and freer. And it was a freedom that had a spicy tang of innocent transgression—it signified a kind of escape from social control, from the family most of all. Courting couples were thrilled to be able to get away and spend some time together. It was not about sexual freedom—most had very strong traditional teaching and fear of sinfulness—but more of an intimacy which had been dreamt of and which was so eloquently expressed in independence; a dream of possible escape. A picture by Guttuso shows a boy and girl on a Vespa as they ride towards a world of many meanings and illusions. For people of the time, it was the journey itself that meant the most; the escape from the here and now. Of course, the Vespa immediately became a status symbol too. Those who owned one were seen by peers and colleagues in a different light: they were perceived as being more modern, able to do more things, and perhaps as being more attractive to the opposite sex. The Vespa was a product which from the outset had a vast yet homogeneous target market in terms of desires and aspirations. First of all, the people who bought one where those who until only recently had been poor. These people knew the fascination of mobility, which consisted in having money that could be spent not on immediate subsistence or in other essentials, but on something that was nice to own. It was like matching the frugality with adventure, a match of great significance, at least for those times. The race was on for the modernisation of Italy and, in only a decade and a half, the country achieved a miracle that was not economic alone:

Advertisement photo for the Vespa in the '60s, the period when Piaggio began associating it with environmental friendliness.

Below: one of the many Vespa Club rallies.

Entertainment and sports celebrities astride Vespas. Actors were particularly favoured as endorsers. But then the film industry often included the Vespa as an actress: there are more than ninety films featuring the Vespa. *From top and from left to right*: Nino Benvenuti, William Holden, Manuel Fangio, Vittorio Gassman, James Stewart, Domenico Modugno, Jean-Paul Belmondo.

it withheld latent, and inextricable, social mobility—the aspiration of no longer being on the bread line—mixed of course with a geographical mobility that was not, this time, about emigration but about the day trips which soon became a fetish, a rite of "exorcising" economic hardship, and a symbol of the possible entry into a much wider world than that of Italy's towns and country hamlets.

And obviously, being a scooter, the Vespa lifestyle was taken up mainly by the generation of younger factory workers or students who together testified to the sign of the times. It was the modernity that they showed off to peers and colleagues outside their working environment or schools. A few years later, it would be the younger still who would be able to drive a vehicle (without number plates or driving licences). They were the precursors of a phenomenon that was to grow over the years, especially during the '60s: the generation of young people who discovered the desire for, and meaning of, being together; who wanted to be together because they felt different from their parents and the values they represented. A story characterised by an increasing detachment that began slowly as a progressive liberation from family and cultural control, and which went on to become an attempt for social or revolutionary change and later an independent sub-culture.

The Vespa was around at the beginning of all this, initially as the vehicle for its inception to later bequeath its place to heirs such as the Ciao, the Boxer and the Sì.

But there was another component of the target market that we cannot forget here: women. Initially they were the pinion passengers, sitting behind comfortably, not astride but with both legs on one side, underlining the functionality and convenience of the scooter. Then they became riders and customers. The emancipation of the woman, at least in this field, was synonymous with the Vespa, for the possibility it offered

of being a motorised means of transport that was easy and effortless to ride and didn't really require the rider to change clothes.

Today, the young women we see speeding past on fast motorbikes are unrecognisable as such, apart from perhaps the extra hair flowing from the back of their helmets. The memory of the genteel and smiling girls and ladies on their Vespas can seem insignificant and almost a sign of the past. But in those times it meant a break with tradition, small but significant, and yet another sign of the changing times. Also from these brief descriptions, it is clear that the Vespa has met with a very wide popularity. Its owners have identified themselves with the scooter and have understood and approved its spirit and advantages. And Piaggio has always been careful about understanding its customers' needs: we can simply mention its policy of support to the many "Vespa Clubs" which, with their rallies, have for many years represented a tangible, joyous expression of the Vespa "population" which has promoted exploits—in the form of trips and journeys—and shows, in all parts of the world.

This was a highly intelligent product strategy, even if it coincided with a highly favourable period. Perhaps it was an unrepeatable coincidence. Many years would have to pass before a similar product would experience such a phenomenal success as to become a symbol of its time. Today we could talk about mobile phones but in the first thirty years from the reconstruction to the threshold of consumerism, no other industrial product achieved such acclaim as the Vespa. At most, we could cite highly successful sectors as examples of Italian creativity among which plastics, home appliances, and run-around cars. For years Italy was synonymous worldwide with these objects, together with "design", the cinema and music. Later, Italian fashion began to make its mark (first with shoes, then with clothing), thus projecting further Italy's

Gregory Peck and Audrey Hepburn in *Roman Holiday*, 1952.

Opposite and page 22: two shots not used for the 1965 Piaggio calendar. Raquel Welch and Ursula Andress are only two among the many actresses whose images were used for the calendars, which became cult objects in their own right.

A drawing by Villemot for the 1954 French advertising campaign.

image around the world. But for many years the Vespa was synonymous with Italy, both as a vehicle and as an image of smiling celebrities astride it, or as an emblem exemplifying almost impossible enterprises.

The invention of a unique product for a new young consumer market nurturing aspirations of geographical and cultural mobility, matched with an efficient distribution strategy, certainly explain the Vespa's outstanding industrial success. Yet they are not enough in themselves to account for the myth which began at the very outset and which has continued to the present day—and all despite the radical transformations of the market. For the last twenty-thirty years, mobility has been practically saturated by the car and, more recently, the arrival on the scene of hundreds of other small motorcycles has caused the ruthless extinction of many brands and products, both Italian and non. Yet the Vespa is, still today, something more and different from all the other scooters around. Its trademark has a unique symbolic meaning born from being the most famous product to come forth from the genius and entrepreneurial wisdom of one company—among many—which built the Italian miracle, and which succeeded in transmitting Italian taste and style around the world. Today all this may seem to be taken for granted, but it's worth pausing to reflect on how the Vespa, only shortly after scenes of total destruction and poverty, projected out to the rest of the world an image of Italy made up of inventiveness and elegance. Even tradition—the pizza and mandolins—were regarded with a trifling superiority by the first armies of visitors to Italy a few years later.

In the history of the Vespa, and one of the factors that has certainly contributed to making it a myth, is the contribution of its promotional and publicity strategies.

Also from this perspective, Vespa is an exemplary case and it was the attention given to this aspect that constituted the third great intuition of Piaggio. Ever since the early '60s, when advertising in Italy was still in its infancy, Piaggio—or rather the Vespa—presented brand new solutions, some of which have written the annals of Italian advertising. Before looking at these, it is worth remembering first the very modern techniques used to launch the product. The Vespa was presented to the representative of the American military forces in Italy, the Pope, and to many politicians, as the best opportunity for being featured in the press or on the radio and of having the new product spoken about. These were all techniques that still "only went on in America". But a myth is born when, on a general scale, the functionality and technical specifications of a product are transcended. The Vespa was a great scooter, but it was also, as mentioned, the symbol of a mobility towards times and values which were new and better. It was as if, through the Vespa, Italy had gone from being a poor country as represented by jaded black-and-white photographs—to a worldly city teeming with new things and wonderful possibilities, rather like in the fairy tales of a colour movie.

It is by no coincidence that we were given an emblematic image, which was immediately translated in its meanings as a latter-day fairy tale, that everyone knows and which shows a beautiful, rich and enamoured princess (Audrey Hepburn) gracing the world she sees as beautiful escorted by a journalist (the modern profession of the future mass media) around the streets of Rome. And of course, what other steed could the princess and dashing journalist (Gregory Peck) be astride but a radiant Vespa?

But the myth was not built only upon the fairy tales of paper and celluloid but also, or rather mostly, on the true-life stories of millions of young Italians who, with the Vespa, succeeded for the first time in seeing places previously unknown to them. Whether these were new loves or trips, experimented in a different way from staying in a group, cruising around the streets and piazzas, showing their newly-acquired skills (wheelies in front of their schoolmates or work colleagues), or spending long, lazy hours lounging across their Vespas chatting in clustered groups. An era of great social and cultural changes in the passage from a traditional, rural society to one based on industrialism and innovation. It was a journey that many made on Vespas while others had to make it in envy of those who could brandish that status symbol of the "emancipation from poverty", of style, and of belonging to the new way of life that had begun to move ahead at a relentless pace.

A myth is not born of fortuitous circumstances alone. At its root at least two fundamental conditions must be fulfilled: the first, that the object takes on nonmaterial aspects that became the symbols of an era; it must take on aspirations and illusions which arise and gradually evolve during those years. Thus, especially when looking back, the object returns as one of the typical elements of that season, the memory-triggering key that most easily unlocks the string of associations with the people, situations, and events that constitute the single frames of a film that is its history.

The second is that the object must have, either when it first appears or during its lifetime, a sort of collective consecration or acknowledgement: the strong and shared admiration, the desire to possess it and to use it as unique and special. It must be seen as superior to its competitors, aside from mere functional specifications. Its real or imagined characteristics thus become further "nonmaterial" features of the way it is collectively used so that it is seen as the symbol of at least some of the aspirations of a social group—whether larger or smaller—for a certain period of time.

In the first case, we have seen how the Vespa "object" appeared as the vehicle of cultural mobility, the one used by the Italians to leave the old and to rush towards the new and different world that lay beckoning before them. It was what the beautiful and famous people of the times, not to mention the more enterprising younger generation, used to get around on. In fact practically no star—whether from the theatre or sport—went unphotographed on the seat of a Vespa. Although today using well-known personalities to promote products is normal—if not even overexploited—in those times it was a real novelty. And the way the Vespa used the technique from the beginning immediately succeeded in projecting the dream of modernity as a way to present the product.

And this being at the centre of the attention and desires of all Italians leads us to look at how the second condition came about for the Vespa to become a myth. Another great intuition of the company—perhaps one of the most effective—was that it consistently conveyed the Vespa message with great intelligence and in a way that was wholly different from the advertising of the times. In the '50s, without television and a poor distribution coverage of daily newspapers and magazines, only the radio and road-side advertising could be used as effective publicity instruments. Piaggio made an extensive use of placarding, hoardings and posters. The Vespa banners always made a big impact on the public, to the point that with the famous campaign summed up by the slogan ("if you *vespa*, you'll eat the apples"), they became a phenomenon of fashion and discussion like an important cultural event. From the beginning, the Vespa communication strategy was characterised by a great originality, first of all for its contents, which were always fresh and virtually unfettered by the technological and functional

characteristics of the scooter itself. The greatest invention was the one of "verbing" the trade name, thus allowing the first great message to be launched as early as in the '50s: "vespizzatevi" or "get *vespa*-ed" was an incitement that people should break down the barriers keeping them tied to places, and the conventions and obligations—that they should go out and discover the world. Although apparently authoritative—and perhaps also harking back to the recent wartime experience—the message was backed up graphically by drawings and colours to make it more evocative than imperative. So much so that it found easy echoes among those who received it and was immediately in tune with its "promise" all about moving, changing and exploring new avenues.

At the beginning, the new product was proposed in two ways: graphically, using famous artists like Savignac (the all-yellow poster of a jolly little man driving his Vespa into the sun), or Sozzi (the small comical elephant nonchalantly riding a Vespa) or, earlier still, with the somewhat stylised elegance of Longanesi's drawings.

Another approach was to move closer to reality, with many pictures showing the Vespa in all parts of the world, to underline that by now the Italian Vespa was a true citizen of the world. Still another idea was to show a young couple about to leave to go somewhere that held much promise for them. In one case, the message was even more explicit and was also used in France and Great Britain: it showed a young couple travelling, the boy driving with his hands on an imaginary handlebar while the girl, behind as a pinion passenger, tenderly hugging him—but the scooter itself was absent! The couple were suspended in the air. As accompanying comment to the picture was the slogan "To crown their joy, all they need is a Vespa".

The only concrete statements about the scooter itself concentrated on its advantages: easy to park, ideal for getting around in chaotic traffic, a quiet

engine, etc. These too were very modern statements in that they addressed the kind of issues—urban traffic, pollution, etc.—that were only to become real in the future. Thus, they were the forerunners to the ecology theme by at least two decades. Exemplary in this regard was the early '70s' campaign that defined cars as *sardomobili* to say drivers as being packed into a metal can like sardines.

Another modern attitude repeated in Piaggio's campaigns of the '60s and '70s was that of wit and irony. These were not uncommon aspects in the culture of the era, which was still suspended between the slightly curious seriousness of learned culture and the exaggerated tones of melodrama on one hand and the more modern Italian-style comedy in the cinema on the other.

But the forerunning modernity of Piaggio's communication initiatives reached its apex in 1969 with one of the most famous advertising campaigns ever staged in Italy. Again the brand name was "verbed" in the expression "chi vespa mangia le mele, chi non vespa no". Literally "if you *vespa*, you'll eat the apples, if you don't, you won't!" It was a sort of futuristic expression that equated *vespa*-ing with a world of freedom expressed through the action of eating apples. It humorously invoked an immediate participation in a lifestyle made up of non-explicit promises that everyone could realise according to their aspirations and reasoning, yet which come together in the invitation to transgress as one wants to—as is now possible in this time when everything seems possible. Elsewhere it was thought that imagination had attained power and that everyone ought to (not only can) ask for what they felt was right and whatever met their needs. Obviously in the Piaggio advertising the tone was very different: on one hand the playful provocation, on the other the invitation towards great, almost revolutionary, change, even if individual. But the spirit did, after all, have common ground: the freedom from conventions and the urge

A Vespa flies toward the sun in a drawing by Raymond Savignac, one of the most important poster artists of the century.

Gilbert Becaud as a testimonial figure in a Vespa advertising campaign in France.

Charlton Heston on the set of *Ben Hur*.

The Vespa 98 cc. pre-series prototype designed by Corradino D'Ascanio, 1945.

Two posters by Gilberto Filippetti for the famous "Chi Vespa... mangia le mele" advertising campaign.

"Vespizzatevi" ("Get *Vespa*-ed"): the advertisement peeks out along with Tina Pica in *Mia nonna poliziotto*.

Enrico Piaggio among the Vespas on the day the millionth scooter rolled off the production line, June 1956.

Below: the Vespa 125, 1948.

This page and opposite: Franco Mosca's drawings for the Piaggio calendars of the '50s and '60s, resembling American pin-up calendars.

to the travel that leads to the discovery of subjectivity. It also amounted to a foresight of the themes that were to become central in the culture of the ensuing years: the me-generation, narcissism, and so on.

There was a recurrent theme with the previous campaigns: the direct invitation (after "get *vespa*-ed", "if you *vespa*..."), the playful tone engendered by the colourful and innovative graphics, the explicit mentioning of the reference target (explicitly indicated by the images), which was young and modern, etc. But the provocation game lay completely within the metaphor of the apple: the fruit of both sin and desire. Everyone is free to give it the meaning they believe in or "feel"; the apple is a sort of projective test that invites us to think not only about possible transgression but also about our capacity to be different, to not have to give way to conventions and obligations. The thinly concealed meanings connected to the apple are obviously sin and sex, but they are also nature and life. It is the transgression associated to good as opposed to evil; it is the temptation, the

adventure of biting and savouring at all times; it is about breaking out from obligations and morals and the day-to-day routine that keep us tied to routes and habits that constrict our alternatives. The possible projections were open: everyone could invent the things to do for themselves, so they could either "get *vespa*-ed" or aspire to do so. Some recommendations were given though, even if expressed somewhat abstrusely. Thus the public were told to eat "the sprint apple while riding", "the heart apple with one's partner", "the daisy apple in the meadows", "the blue apple on the cliffs", "the star apple with your headlights on", "the bold apple with your head held high", "the green apple with your eyes well open", and so on. All the recommendations were given on as many glimpses of the imagination, or projections of desire, or the possible lives that everyone should subjectively create using places, people, situations, and feelings which have great meanings for all. Yet beyond the dream, the invitation was explicit: to take up the opportunities that come your way, to not give up your desires; to enjoy your freedom and fill it

to the brim; to race, on a Vespa of course, to reach the goals which your heart gives you—even if others want to stop you from reaching them.

This advertising campaign was a decisive turning point in the morals of the daily life of the times. The end of social control (of certain morals, the family and the other socialisation vehicles) and the opening towards an individual moral founded upon rights (on what desires make one believe something is good or possible) and not only on duties. It was a turning point that was more likely to lead to consumerism and hedonism than to a general process of social and cultural change. But that was another story and did not obviously depend on this campaign. The fact that it was part and parcel with the times is borne out by the quotations that may be ventured when analysing the campaign: from Marcuse to Pop Art, with echoes of the works by Rauschenberg and Lichtenstein.

But there is a stronger aspect which is tied less to the subjectivity of the onlooker. The themes evoked by the campaign are the ones that became central in the youth culture (or

contestation) of those years. It was by no coincidence that Piaggio was soon to employ a communication strategy for the heirs of the Vespa (the Ciao, Boxer, Sì, etc.) that focussed its attention directly on the youth market by suggesting to it that the moped was the sign of belonging to the group, that it meant being with others, and creating interests and specific values of a culture that had little in common with that of adults. The message was about spending time with one's peers, going around with one's friends without necessarily having anywhere special to go, and about not going to the places—or following the habits—that the culture of adult society was no longer capable of indicating. After all, the Vespa has always been "young", right from the Vespa 50—for which no number plate was necessary— which was the symbol of status and independence in the '60s and which later became a mass consumption commodity (in 1965 the Vespa was clear market leader), through to the advent of the Vespone, which, with its almost dream-like acceleration, speed and range, was envied by the many who

could not afford it. In the '70s, the original Vespa mixed with its more recent heirs like the Ciao and Boxer and lost some of the limelight.

But it has remained the myth that continues today. At the end of the millennium, it's featuring again on the cinema screens, taking a leading role in the journey full of uncertainties of the Hamlet-like actor-cum-film director Nanni Moretti, who asks of himself about himself, and about the world evolving around him.

The myth has made the Vespa into one of the world's best known products. We have all seen one and know its name. In every corner of the planet, thousands of Vespas are being ridden—in all types (including its humbler brother, the Ape), colours and states of repair. The Vespa is part of the fabric of a country and an era. It still maintains its symbolism as belonging to a philosophy of life held on dearly to by all who, in this age of traffic and pollution, feel they are free, that they enjoy the idea of moving and of being independent. It is the myth which transformed forever a scooter of the '50s into a symbol of mobility and freedom.

Giuseppe Furlanis

Furniture Design and Its Philosophies

Some rooms reflect the personality of their occupants so well that they could belong to no one else. "The home becomes a museum of the soul, an archive of its experiences", writes Praz in the introduction of his *Filosofia dell'arredamento*.

The home and its furnishings represent the truest expression of the man: *tel le logis, tel le maître!*, i.e. the way you live is who you are! As an expression of the ego, furniture design puts on the semblance of a cultural mirror, attesting to the evolution of customs and the unfolding of aesthetic languages. Such was Praz's conviction that he wrote: "Furniture goes even farther than painting, sculpture and even architecture in revealing the spirit of an era".

Gone is the age in which styles were a coherent indicator of a period of history, when a certain particular type of design identified the interior as a whole, and each and every detail within, to such a point that the styles of the furniture and clothes to be worn inside were adapted to fit in, giving an accurate sense of the taste of the era.

Contemporary furnishings deny classification according to a linear space-time construction process, and home surroundings are currently forged which are based on the juxtaposition of a profusion of diverse objects. This is exactly why, perhaps now more than ever, interiors mirror the culture of their inhabitants, of those who have chosen the actual objects with which they have fashioned their own living space.

This is a furnishing concept which has gradually caused the business of interior design to shift its focus from the room to the objects, cramming them full of symbolic values and expressive marks more than ever before. As a result, the vision so dear to Loos which married beauty and function (*ornement = verbrechen*, i.e. ornament is a crime), has been cast aside in favour of a more extensive semantic content for the forms. Although, by its very definition, interior design is divorced from the pervasive intrusiveness of public life, at times even in conflict with it, furniture is increasingly permeated by the character of the times, by the evolution of customs, by the advance of technology, by the seduction of the arts, and by the bombardment of models of daily life inculcated by mass-communication systems, TV, the press and cinema.

It is in the development of Italian design that this very particular condition has been most effectively expressed. Above all, from the '60s onwards, it has been more successful than its counterparts in interpreting the trends associated with the culture of living: not just limiting its action to pursuing change, but becoming an active part of the process,

Enzo Mari, Tappeto volante, Flou, 1988.
"Minimal" beds raised from the ground by simple cylindrical legs or set on mats clearly reminiscent of the Orient. The tapestries constitute an atmospheric setting and draw attention, in contrast with the "superficial" décor, work of elevated content.

Gio Ponti, house in Via Dezza, Milan, 1957.
Seen from the day area. Foreground: the Superleggera chair designed by Ponti for Cassina. The environment is characterised by a spatial continuity afforded by the folding walls.

in some cases even anticipating its effects.

This has enabled Italian design, precisely in the furniture sector, to enjoy considerable success on the international scene. A statement confirmed by its sales figures and the cultural approval with which it has been met: to such an extent in fact that, as happened in the fashion industry, Italian products are again shaping new trends in terms of taste and markets.

As far back as the years immediately following the First World War, Italian design has shown a tendency to couple the innovative tension of avant-garde art with the more reassuring models of

Franco Albini, the lounge of his apartment in Milan, 1938. Antique objects and modern furniture brought together to create a rich, refined furnishing. Among the furniture is the audacious Veliero bookcase and the radio with two crystal plates to make the inside visible.

tradition. The vital influence of the avant-garde trends, which received generous coverage on the pages of *Casabella*—with Pagano and Persico advocating functionality in furniture which was to take its inspiration from the new language of Rationalism—was countered by a popular conservative train of thought whose main mouthpiece was Ugo Ojetti. Using the magazine *Pegaso* as his soapbox, he headed a crusade in favour of reviving the styles of the past, becoming the

fanatic upholder of Italian style in furnishings. The spearheads of the crusade were the restoring of local traditions and the classicist language: a stylistic tendency whose greatest exemplification is to be found in the twentieth-century furniture designs like those of Paolo Buffa, Tommaso Buzzi, Emilio Lancia, Giovanni Muzio and Guglielmo Ulrich, and which took off in a cultural sense at the Monza Biennial exhibition in 1927.

Whereas Modernism and tradition represented the two extremes of that critical debate within which the furniture culture in Italy had developed, the exponent who expressed Italian design with his own autonomous language more than any other was, without a doubt, Gio Ponti—architect, artist and designer.

Ponti, heading the magazine *Domus*, which he founded in 1928, was actively involved in cultural promotion, and a relentless creator of forms, decorations and slogans. With a constant watchful eye on the abounding contribution made by Modernism, and nonetheless remaining open to the idea of reviving the tradition of the applied arts and to the contamination of the arts, he had determined a specific Italian line of furniture ever since the '30s.

This very Italian Rationalism—although geared towards the search for a new figurative language and an *ethic of aesthetics* within which design would become both the expression of technical development and the tool of social commitment—manifested a leaning towards the softening, in interior design, of that rigid formal dogmatism which was characteristic of international Rationalism.

Edoardo Persico, the most acute critic of the time, and sustainer of an uncompromising course to modernity, when presenting Luciano Baldessari's design "A Flat in Milan"), wrote in 1933 in *Casabella*: "A house is not, in fact, merely a 'machine à habiter', rather an aspect of the personality of the person who lives there". Again commenting on a design by Baldessari in the 7th issue of the *Colosseo* magazine in 1934, Raffaello Giolli pointed out, "how one might free oneself from the mould of Quaker Functionalism and consider architecture as an essentially creative work". These contributions are evidence of how a typically Italian road to Rationalism was paved, which was dealt with extensively on the pages of *Domus* and *Casabella*, and which was to see Franco Albini become its main exponent.

The interior design produced by Albini for his own home in 1938 can be considered as a veritable banner of this Italian concept of the rational home: figuratively rich and refined furnishings where antique pieces were set alongside their modern counterparts without a set, rigid layout. Large paintings decked the walls and traditional carpets the floors, whilst other pictures, held by uprights, served as dividing screens, and temporary partitions made using curtains enabled the space to be divided with a great deal of flexibility.

Albini's design featured a living room dominated by an innovative bookcase, emblematically called Veliero, or sailing ship. This audacious piece consisted in a stretched flexible structure with V-shaped uprights made from ash and safety glass shelves suspended on steel cables. The overall effect was to give the piece an air of strength, efficiency and, at the same time, extreme lightness.

The radio set, placed in the living room in front of the French windows, also had an incorporeal appearance. Here, the technical mechanisms were contained by two thick plates of glass, meaning its technological entrails were on full show. In the bedroom, the tradition of the religious presence was observed, and at the same time innovated by placing the portrayal of the Holy Family in the centre of the whole room on a high stand—as opposed to in its usual place above the headboard—as a symbolic and aesthetic fulcrum of the couple's intimate retreat.

However, more than the furnishings of the home, it was the exhibition displays and the fittings of the bars, shops and, even more emblematically, the displays presented at the Triennial Exhibitions, that spoke volumes for the formal credo of the Modernism. The Triennial Exhibition of 1933, and subsequent 1936 edition, were particularly significant, with the designs becoming paradigmatic of the type of dialectic relationship established between furniture and architecture, between fixed and movable elements, between indoor and outdoor spaces.

The furniture presented met the new demands for mass production and the flexibility of unit furniture both formally, aesthetically and constitutionally. Deliberately proposed in "poor" materials, they represented a palpable expression of the autarchic regime enforced in the country.

It was through the Triennial Exhibitions that the popularity of metal furniture spread, having crossed the domestic threshold partly as a result of the seductive powers of the cinematographic models—a particularly effective means of propaganda at the time which presented spectators of the '30s and '40s with numerous images office and home interiors populated with smooth tables, chairs, armchairs, bookcases and beds with tubular steel frames. Thus, the promotion of metal furniture as an essential and emblematic image of modern style was set under way. All the other new materials, partly in relation to the autarchic regime, were also subjected to extensive experimentation, with the result that furniture was steered towards the search for new product types: a search, however, which was abruptly cut short by the outbreak of the war.

The need for reconstruction which characterized the post-war years had a considerable impact both on the furniture production sector and on architecture. The design discipline was geared towards an undertaking which was first and foremost moral—the design aspect relegated to second place—aimed at defining the essential conditions for the comprehensive development of the nation in the democratic sense.

In this sense, a significant factor was the considerable commitment shown in favour of the requalification of popular furniture, both in terms of function and appearance. In fact, it became the central issue of much design research and various exhibitions, such as that organised by RIMA, the Italian bureau of furniture expositions. Strangely enough, despite these commendable intentions, the popular furniture in its current forms was deeply rooted in the interpretation of past styles, and was therefore substantially conceived on a *room* basis: a concept according to which every single distinct area of the home was considered a stylistically specific unit and belonging to a type consolidated over the years.

Despite the profound effect the renewed blossoming of the industrial world was to have on the lifestyles of the "poor but handsome" Italians so eloquently portrayed in the film *Poveri ma belli*—transforming them, in hardly any time at all, from the "bicycle thieves" of De Sica's world-famous *Ladri di biciclette* into the proud scooter knights of the new age—it seemed it was not going to manage to touch their homes, to influence living habits, renewing them. The reassuring revival of tradition even characterised the interiors belonging to the upper classes, which however featured individual pieces of extremely high quality in terms of form and manufacture, exemplifying a rich artisan mastery. In some cases, these items of furniture appeared to represent a taste for past tendencies reinterpreted with formal elegance and restrained decoration. This is the case of those produced by Azucena according to designs by Cacciadominioni, Gardella and Magistretti. These items of furniture were aimed at the educated middle classes, but were overtly marked by nostalgia for a bygone era.

The decisive driving force which would lead towards a true modernisation of the home was finally delivered in the '50s by the introduction and rapidly expanding success of the sectional kitchen model, and the large-scale adoption of electric household appliances.

The communicative and symbolic room represented by the traditional kitchen—the very heart of family life—was dismissed in favour of a functional space specifically designed for preparing meals, and isolated with respect to the other rooms of the house.

Marco Zanuso and Richard Sapper, 4999 little chair, Kartell, 1964.
Made of polyethylene and in various colours, it can be stacked and is made like a 3-D puzzle, for children's imagination to experiment with.

The furniture layout typical of the kitchen-cum-dining area, which had established itself a place in the home during the early years of the reconstruction—consisting in the dining table placed between a sideboard and its smaller counterpart on the other side—was replaced by the so-called "American kitchen". The latter was first characterised by a generously sized unit used to house the appliances, and subsequently by sectional elements which, apart from accommodating the electric appliances, also enabled the furniture to fit in with the varying shapes and sizes of the available spaces.

The sectional kitchen was a theme to which the leading Italian designers devoted much attention at that time, producing innovative solutions both in terms of the form of the appliances and of the compatibility and use of new materials.

Some of the first and most significant examples are to be found in the work of Augusto Magnaghi with his Saffa kitchen, and the Homelight kitchen by Marco Zanuso, both created in 1954. The Italian electric household appliance industry was to develop along these lines, establishing itself as a leading element in the sector. The formal quality of the products, coupled with their good technological level, took Italy to the heights of the electric household appliance production market in the space of just a few years, becoming Europe's leading manufacturer, and the world's no. 2.

Italy owed its achievement to the excellent entrepreneurial skills of a number of new enterprises such as Candy, Castor, Ignis, Merloni, Riber, Zanussi, and their collaboration with young designers such as Marco Zanuso, Richard Sapper, Gino Valle and Pierluigi Spadolini.

Whereas the "white goods" were responsible for radically altering the organisation and furniture of the kitchen and, at the same time, the rituals related to the purchase, preparation and consumption of foods, it was the impact of the "brown goods" which was destined to radically transform people's approach to the living room, and to influence its very layout.

Television made its début in the home in the early '50s, becoming the main attraction of the living room and establishing itself as a status symbol. Oddly enough, despite forever being accused of having a negative effect on interpersonal relations, during this initial phase of its rising popularity the TV represented a powerful instrument of socialisation. It became customary for a number of families to be invited round by their more fortunate neighbours who had a television set to watch the more popular programmes.

This socialising effect was above all, though, the direct result of the then-limited diffusion of the means. More to the point, through its broadcasting of films and hit programmes, the television immediately stood out as a unifier of cultural models. In particular, it affected the people's living habits and the development of the furniture, which even became the topic of a TV programme entitled "Il piacere della casa" (the joy of the home) hosted by Mario Tedeschi and Paolo Tilche. Whilst radio sets had, by then, shed their boxed-in shape in favour of a more specific form, the design of the early television sets was still largely conditioned by the need to fit in with the rest of the furniture, to adapt to the existing forms. This was partly due to the need to house the bulky picture

tube: the technical equipment was in fact contained in furniture units which took their figurative inspiration from the *preciousness* of the home's furnishings. The development of the shape of the sets and their reduction in size were to change as a result of the subsequent technical innovations. The first of these was the introduction of aluminised screens, followed by the important switch from tubes to transistors. As the role of television grew in importance both in functional and symbolic terms—a window onto a changing social scene—it also started to affect the layout of the furniture. The actual living room, which had normally been furnished with a couple of armchairs facing a generously sized three-seater sofa, was transformed into a *corner-type* room which allowed both for conversation and viewing.

During the '50s, electric appliances—

Afra and Tobia Scarpa, Coronado sofa, C&B, 1966. A reinterpretation of the traditional upholstered sofa using a lighter perspective and an industrialised component manufacture. The steel supporting structure is embedded in cold-foamed polyurethane.

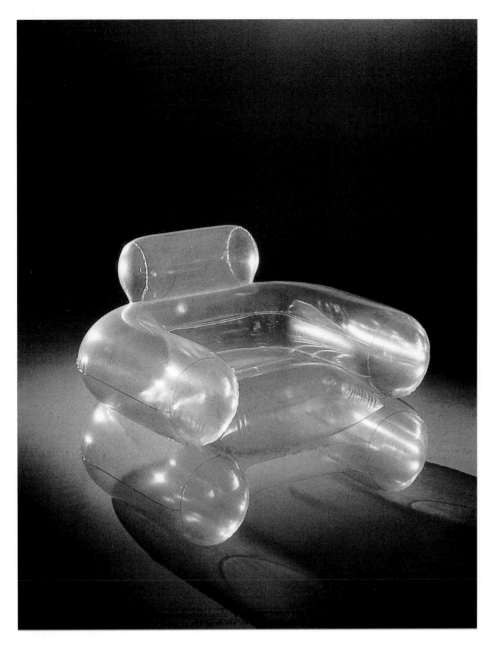

Jonathan De Pas, Donato
D'Urbino and Paolo Lomazzi:
Blow inflatable armchair,
Zanotta, 1967. Photo by
Ramazzotti and Stucchi.
The first Italian air-filled object
made of transparent PVC. Sold
in kit form, containing the
folded and uninflated armchair,
a pump and a puncture-repair kit.

place of privacy and the symbolic space of the couple: it was hardly surprising, in a Catholic society, that tastes mirrored a highly conservative tendency.

Increased wages were to lead, though, to a rapid increase in consumption, with a quite apparent impact on the furniture and on its formal qualities. Going from strength to strength, the furniture industry developed in well-defined geographical areas, giving rise to the so-called "industrial zones": production areas which all seemed to have been built with the same mould, characterised by the considerable presence of (mostly small-scale) enterprises. The result was a sort of factory territory where products were manufactured in phases, going from one workshop to another, thus passing through various skilled hands and being forged by differing technologies. This explains how a number of major furniture companies have not only managed to combine mass production with made-to-measure processes, but have also successfully reconciled technological innovation with the tradition of craftsmanship.

The organisational flexibility inherent in this type of production system encouraged the continuous processes of innovation in furnishings and, together, they gave rise to a constant renewal of the formal languages which adopted the designer as their main interpreter.

In fact, from the second half of the '50s onwards, the designer took on a strategic role for the development of the Italian economy: forced by the progressive increase in labour costs to change tactics, it replaced cost with product quality and aesthetic content as the main competitive factors.

Following in the wake of a series of previous collaborative arrangements, such as that between Cassina and Ponti and, earlier still, Ducrot and Basile, many young company owners in the furniture sector entered into a fruitful association with young designers. What followed was a decisive development towards formal innovation based on the definition of new types of furniture and

partly owing to their practical requisites, but above all having become palpable symbols of a certain level of well-being—thus became indispensable means for families to feel integrated in the modern industrial society.

Nonetheless, despite the modernisation of furnishings being encouraged by the widespread adoption of electric household appliances, there was still considerable reluctance to accept aesthetically innovative products in the home. This was particularly true for the bedrooms where period furniture was still a predominant presence alongside allusions to the tradition of classic furniture. After all, the bedroom is a

Achille and Pier Giacomo Castiglioni, Lounge-studio, presented at the exhibition *Colori e forme nella casa d'oggi*, Villa Olmo, Como, 1957. An eclectic mix of forms in which the specific quality of each produce guarantees the overall quality of the composition. Among the objects, Sella and mezzadro, later produced by Zanotta.

Opposite, G.P. Allevi and L. Parisi, Holiday home, presented at the exhibition *Colori e forme nella casa d'oggi*, Villa Olmo, Como, 1957. The architectural design was conceived as a composition of four hexagons; furnishing is minimal with innovative proposals such as the ceiling-hung wardrobe and the vertical piece supporting the TV.

Achille and Pier Giacomo Castiglioni, Lounge, presented at the exhibition *La casa abitata*, Florence, 1965. Furnishings made from items already on the market but redesigned – as in the case of the Thonet fold-away chair. On the wall is a composition of two objects expressing the passing of time: a large clock and the remains of a pole, and a ladder as an emblem of functional design.

on the reinterpretation of consolidated ones. A reinterpretation which, however, dared to employ new materials, as in the case of the armchair Lady made from sponge rubber and *nastrocord* produced by Arflex according to a design by Marco Zanuso. Alternatively, the evolution leaned towards the mechanisation of the product, as was the case with the reclining sofas which Osvaldo Borsani designed for Tecno. Yet another development was the revisiting of the archetype forms using new production techniques, as in the Leggera and Superleggera chairs produced by Cassina according to a design by Ponti: chairs where the traditional product type was revised via the adoption of the chaste expressivity of the Nordic production on the one hand, and the elegance and lightness of the traditional Chiavari chairs on the other.

In view of the decisive role taken on by design in the promotion of Italian furniture, numerous undertakings were gradually initiated with a view to making the formal innovation of the products increasingly popular.

A multitude of new magazines emerged, including *Interni, Stile Industria* (1954) and *Il Mobile Italiano* (1958), whilst in 1954 the Compasso d'Oro award was set up and in 1955 the first edition of the Selettiva del Mobile was inaugurated in Cantù, followed in 1958 by the Biennale dello Standard of Mariano Comense.

In 1961, the first edition of the Salone del Mobile finally opened, a furniture show destined to become the most important in the sector on an international level, both in terms of the quantity of exhibitors and visitors and of its intention to give exposure to the new market trends on the furniture scene.

In an attempt to determine new formal languages in furnishings, which were often excessively influenced by pre-established tendencies (Swedish style, abstract organicism, etc.), a number of architects tried out new directions in research. With a series of allusions and quotations, this research aimed to merge the formal rigour of Rationalism with various figurative references to past styles, determining a particular tendency which was most significantly represented in the *Nuovi disegni per il mobile italiano*

exhibition. The works presented, defined by the critics as *Neo-liberty*, gave rise to a lively debate which, to date, has still not been entirely assuaged. Among the items on show was an armchair of particular significance: Sanluca, designed by the Castiglioni brothers for Gavina. The piece was distinguished by a strong figurative expressiveness and by a dynamic decomposition which seemed to recall Boccioni's Futurist interpretations. The close relationships between art and design, which on occasion resulted in a genuine process of osmosis, came to represent another of the most distinguishing aspects of Italian furniture—perhaps even the most important, in a product culture for which, in its creative exploits, the language has always been its primary goal.

Achille and Pier Giacomo Castiglioni were again amongst the protagonists in the 1957 exhibition *Forme e colori della casa d'oggi*, set up in Villa Olmo in Como, presenting a living room which is destined to remain one of the most significant examples of Italian design. The interior proposed featured a collation of normal commercially available industrial products, objects of material culture, and other objects which had been specially designed for the show. The latter included Mezzadro and Sella, functional interpretations of the ready-made, and perhaps the most successful formal provocations of all Italian design.

The furnishing idea resulting from this experience was an eclectic collection of forms in which the specific quality of each product attested to the overall quality of the entire composition, demonstrating how it is possible to produce a collage of different languages. The highly evocative language of this show made clear reference to the fertile relationship between design and art. A relationship which was to become increasingly close over the following years and was to lead to a vision of design which transcended

interdisciplinary barriers. Evidence of this phenomenon is to be found in the fact that numerous artistic movements developed partly thanks to the contribution of designers, with the result that their influence was strongly felt by the design and furniture disciplines. This was the case for MAC (Movimento Arte Concreta), the concrete art movement founded by Bruno Munari and Gillo Dorfles amongst others, and later joined by Joe Colombo, a central figure in the Italian design of the '60s.

In the same year in which Neil Armstrong and Buzz Aldrin were taking their first steps for mankind, the prevailing climate of new and fervid technological flights of fantasy inspired Joe Colombo's "Habitat futuribile Visiona 1" designed for Bayer. Here, the traditional division of living and furniture spaces, and the rooms

themselves, were broken up and replaced by multifunctional blocks, vaunting the most recent technologies and positioned within the available space at will. Although seemingly inspired strictly by functional factors, in fact it was the linguistic aspect that took precedence in the designs. Futurist furnishings, with their smooth and enveloping forms, "spatial" forms like those of the "Djinn" furnishings of *2001: A Space Odyssey*. Furniture which seemed to reflect that climate of self-congratulating, optimistic faith in technology and scientific research which. Although this was an era shrouded by concern owing to the events surrounding the Cold War and by the ambiguous, fascinating and threatening power of nuclear development—it is characterised by the mood which led mankind to conquer space and challenge disease by transplanting organs in

Joe Colombo, "Habitat futuribile Visiona 1", Bayer, 1969. Experimental idea for the home of the future, where the traditional subdivision into zones is replaced by a system of environment blocks equipped with the latest technology.

Joe Colombo, *Total Furnishing Unit*, presented at the exhibition *Italy: the New Domestic Landscape*, Museum of Modern Art, New York, 1972. Designed as a "possible habitat", it is made up of four monoblocs equipped with the latest technology.

Mario Bellini, Le Bambole, B&B, 1972. Photo by Oliviero Toscani. Produced with expanded polyurethane in various colours. The famous Oliviero Toscani advertising campaign wherein the model Donna Jordan is depicted as a human doll rendered erotic by its postures and makeup.

human bodies for the very first time. As furnishings with enveloping lines were really catching on, together with rounded and seamless items of furniture and objects—deriving above all from the use of plastics which were making an increasingly strong statement in homes at the time, and for which Joe Colombo's designs provide the most significant examples—so was unit furniture production taking off in a big way. The unit furniture derived from the increasingly widespread use of panels obtained with wood particles, commonly known as "chipboard". The technically innovative qualities of the panels made them ideal partners for the concepts of mass production, modularity and composition flexibility so dear to the Modernism, enabling them to be applied on a production and industrial level without recalling their ideological contents.

The product which, in the '60s, became emblematic of this new tendency towards modularity was Cub 8, a partition produced in 1967 by Poltronova according to a design by Angelo Mangiarotti: a modular system of upgraded chipboard panels which could be used to form a range of compositions with the aid of PVC joints.

The concept of form as the result of the reiteration of a standard module reappeared in various types of products, from tables to lighting and seating systems, finally reaching the case of infinite furniture, as in the sofa design Lombrico by Marco Zanuso and Serpentone by Cini Boeri.

Although Fordism's hallmark in this tendency is unmistakable (i.e. mass production clearly inspired by economic and production criteria), its rigorous geometric figuration and the quality

of its composition generated by the module, used as the main formal element, and by the reticular grid used as the matrix on which the composition is based, recall that search for absolute rationalism in visual experiences typical of the contemporary Arte Programmata movement. This was particularly true of those designs with greater formal quality, such as those by Enzo Mari.

Thanks to the sectional structures, home furnishings were regarded as flexible systems which could be adapted to the particular living trends which, in the '60s, were witnessing radical transformations never before encountered. The first and foremost of these transformations was that of a less strict separation between the rooms of the house, in the living/kitchen area in particular.

The unit furniture also led to what might be defined as a figurative *neutralisation* of the living space: a reduction in expressivity which nonetheless found itself countered by that parallel explosion of marks, forms and colours with which homes were besieged though advertising, magazines and the small screen—the amplifiers of a seductive system created for the consumer culture, and of the global progressive aestheticisation of society.

Pop Art marked the introduction of the mass-communication languages and persuasive codes of advertising into the visual arts. With its overpowering forms, it sought a figurative renewal of furnishings in which the image of the product tended, with its strong symbolic values, to involve the user emotionally.

The new materials and, in particular, the plastics, enabled bold and brilliant colours to be incorporated in furniture, recalling those used in advertising or in Warhol's "icon" silk-screen printing, or Rosenquist's billboard-like paintings. Pliable forms, with their anthropomorphic inspiration, seductive to the touch, thus worked their way into homes as message-bearing objects, with a predominant semantic dimension.

In 1969, Gaetano Pesce designed a polyurethane armchair for C&B featuring rounded lines alluding to those of a mother to be which, vacuum packed in a PVC pouch, expanded automatically when it was pulled out as if by magic! The body of the armchair with its feminine forms was attached by a cord to a spherical pouffe—a kind of "ball and chain" arrangement—as both a conceptual and expressive metaphor of that exclusively female condition.

A decidedly ironic element, on the other hand, could be discerned in the pop interpretation in the furniture coming from the De Pas, D'Urbino, Lomazzi studio: in the transparent inflatable PVC armchair Blow for instance, designed in 1967 for Zanotta, or in the sofa Joe produced in 1970 by Poltronova—an enormous baseball glove made from polyurethane which alluded directly to the legendary American player, Joe Di Maggio.

These objects were the precursors of an emerging culture characterised by a distinctly youth-oriented element. In fact, it was the youth of the '60s that was to determine the acceleration of the home's transformation through a less

Gaetano Pesce, Donna armchair, from the "Up" line, C&B, 1969.
With unmistakable anthropomorphic references, the expanded polyurethane armchair was sold vacuum-packed as a thin mattress in a PVC envelope which, when opened, made the armchair self-expand into its final shape.

conventional approach towards one's living space, thus indirectly encouraging the production of more flexible, adaptable and socialising objects.

An emblematic product of this lifestyle culture is, without a doubt, the shapeless beanbag-like chair Sacco by Gatti, Paolini and Teodoro, produced by Aurelio Zanotta in 1968 who was rewarded for this courageous choice by an entirely unexpected commercial success.

The object consisted of a bag containing polystyrene balls, capable of adapting to the body's various postures. The use of the object, nonetheless, called for a rather casual attitude. Suitable for rough-and-ready, informal use, it was entirely unacceptable to the hapless "clerk Fracchia" (played by Paolo Villaggio)—the comic and pathetically grotesque face of Italy's oppressed and stubbornly conservative lower middle classes of the time.

Furniture in the houses of the younger generation of the period became part of a backdrop rich in colour; stylistically speaking, more closely resembling advertising images or the creativity of pop record sleeves than the traditional features. Walls, furniture and objects were personalised using unconventional paintings, posters were plastered on the walls, and seats improvised with a few cushions scattered on carpets. The stage was set, complemented by a score which had the physical room swaying to the sounds of the melodic Beatles, the subversive drive of the Rolling Stones, the corrosive pacifism of Bob Dylan, Leonard Cohen and Joan Baez, and the songs from the first Italian bands conducting their toned-down rebellion. The culture surrounding the youth's revolt—protesting against the prevailing consumerism, and therefore, in theory, also champions of new and different aesthetic languages—paradoxically became the source of a new reference market for industrial development. Initially, it was mainly targetted on the aspects of young people's clothing and

Jonathan De Pas, Donato D'Urbino and Paolo Lomazzi, Joe sofa, Poltronova, 1970. Clearly inspired by Pop, the Joe sofa is a huge baseball glove made of upholstered polyurethane, alluding to the legendary baseball player Joe Di Maggio.

Piero Gatti, Cesare Paolini and Franco Teodoro, Sacco armchair, Zanotta, 1968. Photo by Masera. Leather bag filled with expanded-polystyrene balls; adapts to the shape of the body. Extremely light in weight, it can be taken easily to different places around the home.

the record market, but as time went on, gradually extending massively to cover all types of users and all production sectors, furniture included.

That chaotic overlapping of economic and commercial opulence, aesthetic Pop Art influences, political student's revolts and the repudiation of old canons—with the sexual revolution leading the way—determined a new and extremely vast reference context for design. A context described visually and highly effectively by Antonioni in his great *Zabriskie Point* (1970).

Within this overall context, a number of students from the University of Florence, during the second half of the '60s, in a city still suffering the aftereffects of the flood of 1966, pioneered the "Radical Avant-garde" groups, Archizoom, Ufo, Superstudio—which, as the name might suggest, radically opposed the still-central role of Rationalism in the design discipline. In 1966, at the *Superarchitettura* exhibition in Pistoia, they presented their theoretic manifesto: "Super-architecture acknowledges the production and consumption logic and brings it back down to earth". The furniture-displays Afrotirolesi and Gazebi by the Archizoom members—with their ironic architecture aimed at inducing individual meditation and a non-

systematised way of life—introduced a note of sour provocation into the self-satisfied hedonism of Pop Art.

For the radical groups, the official consecration arrived with their participation in the exhibition *Italy: the New Domestic Landscape* organised by Emilio Ambasz at the Museum of Modern Art in New York.

The exhibition, which confirmed the success of Italian design and earned it international recognition, presented objects and rooms adhering to various different philosophies of design which appeared—as the catalogue pointed out—as astute indicators of possible new home and lifestyle models.

Some of the leading Italian designers were then asked to *materialise* their idea of the home of the future. Out of these,

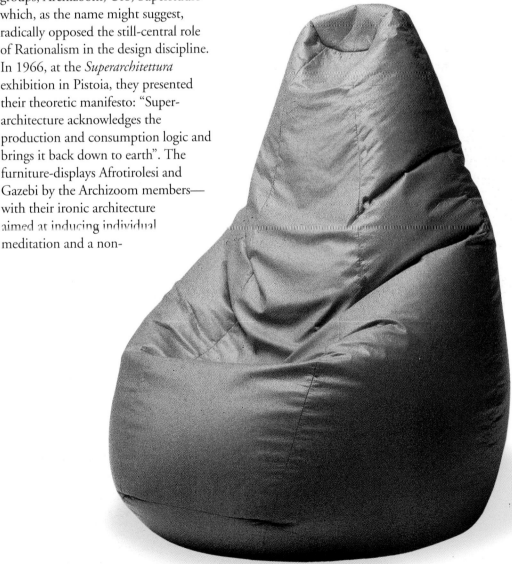

Alberto Rosselli, Marco Zanuso and Richard Sapper chose the theme of the mobile home. This theme was to be resumed and taken to its extremes, by Mario Bellini who proposed a "vehicle-passenger compartment". Vice versa, both Joe Colombo and Ettore Sottsass jr conceived the living space as a composition of ultra-accessorised polyfunctional blocks, albeit each adopting a different figurative language, with the first tending towards the functionalist mould whilst the second featured a more semantic content.
Gae Aulenti, in the wake of the Modernism tradition, came up with quite a different proposal: furniture-architecture with a markedly figurative inclination given by the pyramidal form of the containers, and an evidently symbolic content.
The Archizoom members' participation in the exhibition took the form of an empty room filled only with the voice of a little girl describing a peaceful domestic scene, full of light and colour, thus leaving visitors to imagine their *own* house of the future based on the emotions aroused by the child's narration.
Whilst Italian design, with its creativity and formal innovation, was making an increasingly significant statement on the international scene, Italy's furniture sector was witnessing the beginnings of a return to consolidated tendencies.
The '70s marked the twilight years of those utopias which had characterised the previous decade. The natural consequence was a progressive and relentless return to the private sphere.
The period was marked by the dramatic encounter with political terrorism and by the austerity imposed by the energy crisis resulting in a host of drastic consequences in an economy already debilitated by an economic crisis.
The sum of these factors caused the economic and political structures of the country to shake, along with the attendant idea of progress based on industrial development.
Ettore Sottsass jr interpreted those years

metaphorically with a design for Alchymia "Even Structures Tremble". Moreover, this was to become a cheeky provocation of the features of the Modernism.
The return to the idea of the home as a place of reassurance, and the rediscovery of the essential value of nature as opposed to the technology-based model, were reflected in furnishings in the form of a progressive rejection of those products which more manifestly denounced their technical mould. First against the wall were the plastic objects which, following their enormous success of the '60s, began a considerable decline

subsequent to accusations regarding their harmful and pollutant nature. However, as contradictory as it may seem, a tendency started to take shape whereby young people in particular started to give products made from steel or stamped plate, originally meant for the industrial sector, pride of place in the home. Motivated by the ideas which had conceived these products, in their unpretentious forms, as an aid to a more essential modernity without excessive formal stress, this tendency was also reflected in design with the designing of new high-tech products or the consolidation of the success of those already on sale created along similar lines. This was the case of the metal

Ettore Sottsass jr, Grey Room, Poltronova, 1969.
Photo by Aldo Ballo.
The various elements of the furniture, which create the supporting structure and the curtain walls, are replaced by an unbroken face.

Bruno Munari, polyfunctional structure Abitacolo, Robots, 1971.
A modular structure, plasticised with epoxy resins that provides various uses and becomes a genuine polyfunctional space for children's rooms.

bookcase Congresso CU25 by Lips Vago, or Abitacolo designed by Bruno Munari in 1970 for Robots, a minimal living space for children, made entirely from rod iron where they could study, work, play, sleep and receive their playmates.

Despite the increase in high-tech production, the trend which constituted the figurative epitome of the furniture of the '70s was the return to natural materials, above all wood—especially ash—but also untreated linen, wicker, leather, and in particular fabric. The latter, apart from its more conventional use, was also exploited for the figurative redefining of a number of items of furniture which, in some cases, became new product types, such as the armchair AEO that Paolo Deganello and the Archizoom members designed for Cassina in 1973.

AEO overturned the idea of comfort linked to the softly rounded lines of the foamed polyurethane units, instead promoting and exploiting the fabric's particular ability to adapt to the shape of the body. This approach also reappeared in other designs by Paolo Deganello and was to be given even more emphasis in the subsequent design by Gaetano Pesce, Feltri, a sort of armchair-cum-quilt. The armchair AEO, which is still produced today, is characterised by a high back in fabric supported by a steel frame finished with stoving enamel from which the seat juts out, planted in a durethan base.

Having made a big entrance, fabric continued to hog the limelight. Even bedroom interiors welcomed the development with open arms thanks to the Flou industry which produced a series of upholstered beds entirely covered with fabric and which were designed for use with covers and duvets in coordinating colours and patterns. Their astounding commercial success was translated into a new tendency of taste.

The upholstered Flou beds promoted the idea of the bed as an autonomous, separate item of furniture, stylistically independent from the rest of the bedroom's finishings. This notion went entirely against the stream, as the predominant concept of the bedroom at the time—a legacy of past traditions—was that of a self-contained room which was nonetheless attempting to bring itself up to date (employing methods of dubious merit) by adorning the beds with accessorised headboards built into superfluous frames.

The growing concern regarding the man-environment issue led to the development, towards the end of the '70s, of research into decorations, colours, and light within a new concept of the home as a multi-sensorial space. Andrea Branzi who, along with Massimo Morozzi and Clino Trini Castelli, was an active participant in various experiments (Colordinamo, Superficie attiva, Fisiolight), designed a display with Ettore Sottsass jr for the *Italian New-Renaissance* exhibition (Rotterdam, 1980), essentially consisting of the environmental sounds produced by Brian Eno and accompanied by a distinct smell of mint.

This research highlighted design's further shift towards the complexity of the object and space itself in terms of performance and communication.

The multi-sensorial factor has always been evoked in the furniture designed by Denis Santachiara, intended as theatrical scenes where the purpose of technology is to bring them magically to life and where the apparent simplicity of the forms often serves to underscore the high level of technological performance.

The dining room of the restaurant-bar Aquilone created by Santachiara in Reggio Emilia in 1984 was furnished with simple black tables on which blazing braziers recalled mysterious rituals. At the far end of the room, two French windows afforded a partial view onto an artificially created secret garden which, all of a sudden, was rocked by gusting winds and a deafening thunderstorm—again artificial of course, though the water was real, as were the electric discharges used to simulate the

Anna Castelli Ferrieri, Outline system, Kartelll, 1977.
Gae Aulenti, 4794 armchair, Kartell, 1972.
Outline is a modular system to make walls functional; inspiration was evidently taken from Shaker community decor. The 4794 armchair, made of polyurethane, was designed by Gae Aulenti as part of a general project of corporate images for the interiors of Fiat dealerships.

Vico Magistretti, Nathalie bed, Flou, 1972/1978.
Completely covered with fabric, it requires coordinated sheets and bedspread. It sets a warm atmosphere and reinforces the idea of the bed as a piece of furniture independent from the rest of the bedroom décor.

Archizoom - Paolo Deganello, AEO armchair, Cassina, 1973. Photo by Andrea Ferrari. The various structural components are resolved by different technologies. The high backrest can be covered with fabrics of many colours and designs. The base is made of durethan.

Gaetano Pesce, Feltri, Cassina, 1987. Photo by Bella and Ruggeri. Armchairs made with a felt structure covered by a quilt available in various colours. The felt is hardened in the lower part by impregnating it with polyester.

Opposite: Denis Santachiara, Aquilone Restaurant/Bar, Reggio Emilia, 1984. Photo by Mirco Zagnoli.
View of an area, open to an artificial garden, where a violent storm, with rain, wind and lightning bolts (real electrical discharges), alternates with clear skies and birdsong.

Achille Castiglioni (coll. Aoi Kono Huber), Dining room, presented at the *Design Furniture from Italy* exhibition, Tokyo, 1984.
The traditional table-and-chairs set is replaced by a set of individual-use functional units consisting of a small foldable Cumano table and a Primate seat.

lightning—alternated with the return to a peaceful, sunny scene punctuated with bird song.

Santachiara's interior design is devised to force the user, with the use of playful tricks, to interact with the space. His inventions go beyond the simple use of the room, instead determining a construction of events in which the user is both the actor and spectator.

The increasingly marked shift of focus, in furniture design, from practical functions to semantic content was to place increasing emphasis on the importance of the visual message, transforming the furniture into a *mythical entity*—a symbolic representation of reality which adopted the expressive language, chromatic strength and decoration as its main tools of communication.

Alessandro Mendini was to become the foremost theorist of this concept, with

relation to furniture design, and Ettore Sottsass jr his undisputed mentor. Distancing himself from the Alchymia experience, in 1981 Sottsass, together with a few friends, established the Memphis group, whose objects and furniture would charm the realms of international design. The group's designs were in fact met with a wave of imitations, and led to the birth of a genuine new style. The Memphis objects are distinguished by triumphant colour schemes, the symbolic revival of colour, and by playful compositions invariably open to osmotic processes with the world of art, fashion, and entertainment; in addition, lending themselves to contamination by other cultures and influences from the past.

In 1986, the exhibition *Il paesaggio domestico* featured at the Milan Triennial was based on the theme of furniture and the home, a theme which had already

been explored in the previous edition of 1983 with *Le case della Triennale*. At a time when the culture of living was undergoing a historical overhaul, the exhibition presented twenty furniture proposals whose contents alluded to the metaphorically interpreted values of domesticity.

Ettore Sottsass jr's proposal featured a room entitled "Beyond the Bed: Places and Machines for Sleep", where a four-poster, raised on a platform, was surrounded by objects symbolising a new culture of living: a totem pole made up of television sets, video recorders and hi-fi systems "letting it all hang out", wires and all, in a mass of cables on the floor. A bedroom which, in part, played the role of love nest and, in part, that of a living room ready to play host to its occupants for the best part of the day, a place to receive friends and send information with the aid of the increasingly sophisticated and efficient products of electronics. A design which, as Sottsass himself wrote, took its inspiration from the bedroom of his friend Johnny—from his habit of cramming the place full of electronic gadgets, as well as a potpourri of books, clothes and other objects: partly, a rather overt ploy to leave no room for any female visitors who happened through to sit other than on the bed.

Ettore Sottsass jr, Carlton and Casablanca furniture, Memphis, 1981.
They highlight the shift of furniture communication from practical to aesthetic functionality, assuming a strong expressive language and a triumphant chromaticism.

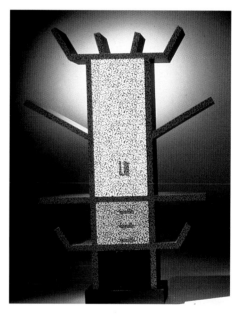

Ettore Sottsass jr, "Beyond the Bed: the Places and Machines for Sleep", room presented at the exhibition *Il paesaggio domestico*, Milan Triennial, 1986.

Once again, Sottsass acutely interpreted the evolution of the culture of living demonstrated in this display not so much in the design of the forms—which tended to reconfirm his own poetic language—as through the representation of a new vision of the house in which the identity of the rooms is modified owing to the development of electronics, thus implying new behavioural models and upsetting the codified functions of some of the places in the home.
A multitude of designers, in the '80s, concentrated their efforts on the theme of the telematic house. The resulting proposals more closely resembled imaginary technologies belonging to the world of sci-fi than reality itself, thus expressing their need to convey the idea of the house of the future, above all symbolically. To name but a few of the many proposals, the "Telemathic House" by Ugo La Pietra from 1983, the "Neo-spatial Kitchen" by Bruno Gregori for Alchymia from 1986, and the "House-Terminal" by Denis Santachiara, again from 1986.
As strong an influence as the electronics boom was, it did not bring about a decisive transformation in interior design like the one deriving from the shattering of the formal languages, which was also related to the segmentation of the market.

Gaetano Pesce, Tramonto a New York sofa, Cassina, 1980. This modular sofa made of polyurethane allows for positioning with striking effect.

Iosa Ghini, Disco Ring, set design for RAI 2, 1986. A mark of strong dynamism that goes back to the Futurist language and the streamline, reinterpreting it. A new figurative trend taken from the first Iosa Ghini projects takes shape, the *bolidismo*.

Antonio Citterio, Sity, C&B Italia, 1986. Seating system that consists of various elements with different forms that allow multiple configurations and various uses.

Opposite.
Paolo Deganello, Artifici tables, Cassina, 1985. Strongly shaped object, the double glass tabletop allows the user to choose and, if desired, modify the décor.

Paolo Deganello, Torso armchair, Cassina, 1982. Photo by Serge Libis. The armchair's shape is the result of various and possible "body prints" left by the users through their various postures (sitting, lying down). It expresses a new formal type for the armchair.

These were the years of hedonism, of unbridled mass consumption, where designer items acquired legendary value, and furniture design could do little to escape this tendency. On the furniture market, the segment and trend logic started to take shape, and consequently so did customised design.

The user became the key figure in a logic which leant towards participation in the design process rather than an increase in consumerism. Quite the opposite to Paolo Deganello's prediction for the future delivered with his "Communal House" project—the metaphor of a society characterised by a pluralism of languages and cultures which nonetheless assured the identity of the individual.

Furniture gradually transformed into an eclectic stage where the individual objects tended to emerge through an increasingly accentuated figurative connotation. It was at this point that several lines of research and the multi-faceted nature of the various tendencies began to overlap.

Stylistic references to past tendencies (Neo-eclecticism, Postmodern) rubbed shoulders with product innovation as the expression of new technologies; the growing expressiveness of the sign (Bolidisti, Philippe Starck) and its accentuated reduction (Minimalism); the revival of the nostalgic and traditional forms of the past (Aldo Rossi, Ugo La Pietra, Abitare il tempo); and reference to languages belonging to other cultures. Not even the anonymous "household goods" (coffee-pots, oil cruets, orange-squeezers, etc.) escaped the tendency to create objects with an increasingly figurative connotation, and therefore also took on highly ironic aspects, to such an extent that their true function was about as clear as mud: am I actually supposed to use this object or is it just for decoration?!

Enzo Mari, Tappeto volante,
Flou, 1988.

Kairos, decorating system, PAB,
1997.
Minimalist design.
The composition consists of
elementary forms and neutral
colours. The horizontal
development and perceptive
lightness are dominant.

Andrea Branzi, *Small tree*,
Design Gallery. Photo by Studio
Azzurro.
Visual poetry created by the
contrast between the minimal
structure and the "small tree";
between abstraction and
nature: forcefully expressive
minimalism.

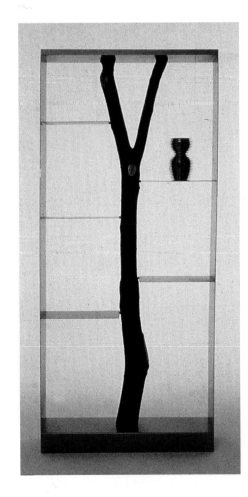

In a consumeristic whirlwind, the home began to become a place for new rituals linked to the cult of individuality and body consciousness. Hardly surprising, therefore, that the most radical transformation in the transition from the '80s to the '90s was in the bathroom: no longer characterised as the room hosting all that sanitary stuff, it became a haven of relaxation and a place for pampering the body. This new notion was reflected in both furnishings and accessories.

The '90s also commenced in a rush of consumeristic euphoria which, however, was a false front masking the underlying anguished cultural upheaval in progress at the time: having developed over the course of just a few years, it was now also managing to affect the world of design and the culture of the home. The demolition of the Berlin Wall and the rejection of certain ideologies failed to liberate Italian society from its uncertainties. On the contrary, what economical and social transformations were in store for the country in this post-industrial age fell within an increasingly grey area.

Progress is never just a source of well-being, but also one of degradation, the cause of social unbalance and of the destruction of natural resources. The complexity and urgency of the environmental issue became quite evident, not just with respect to the need to assure livable conditions for future generations of mankind, but also in relation to the need to respect the variety of the living species.

A series of factors are pushing us towards a new concept of consumption in line with the idea of *there is a limit*. This idea is starting to penetrate our homes—not just modifying purchase habits and the use of resources, but also the formal language of the space we live in.

Furniture is giving up that hypertrophy of sign-related communication which characterised the '80s, in favour of restoring an emotion which is not severed, this time, from the values of reason and the essentiality of things.

Whilst information technology has been left to bask in the limelight as a form of *sign*-free communication, a real, continuous and circular virtual flow of information and contacts, the furniture sector is experiencing a progressive formal reduction. This is a tendency which induces the standardisation of furniture production and which, in the more emblematic cases, seems to be taking the shape of a new *formalism*, not so much arising from the excess of signs as from their absence. A *minimalism* of a prevalently aesthetic nature, therefore, and a far cry from the content-rich essentiality which characterised the designs by Castiglioni, Magistretti or Mari.

Although furniture is still determined by a multiplicity of languages, it is nonetheless evident how the furniture development tendency is geared towards a progressive reduction of marks. The resulting formal modesty means furniture is no longer the absolute centrepiece of interior design, leaving more space for ourselves given that we are the ones who have to live in there, enabling us to put our own personal signature on it, fill it with atmosphere, populate it with objects which have accompanied our own real-life experiences.

An interior design with an increasingly *autobiographical* slant—increasingly a *mirror of the soul*.

Omar Calabrese

The Italian Utility Car

Foreword

One consumer product has certainly been a part of Italian life and customs for a long time: the small passenger car, an all-Italian legend that lasted without interruption for about forty years, from the first production of Fiat's Topolino (literally "little mouse" and also Italian for "Mickey Mouse") in 1936 until halfway through the '70s. Until, that is, the production of its legitimate heir, the Fiat 500 was finally stopped, to make way for another small car, the 126, which, however, no longer had the features of its ancestor, and for which the new reason for buying it was that urban households demanded a second car. It was no coincidence that this change was reflected by language. During the era of the Topolino, the term *utilitaria*—generally translated as "runabout" but literally an invented word deriving from the Italian *utile*, "useful"—was coined to define a dual model: one an object, the other consumption. With the advent of the Fiat 126, instead, the English term "city car" was adopted. This referred to the small cars used in towns and cities like the Mini Morris and—in the '90s— the small Japanese cars, to describe the two aspects of the small car's evolution: its functionality or its "secondary", almost luxury, use.

The word *utilitaria* was certainly highly appropriate, because it combined the object's meaning with the way it was used. The principle adopted by Fiat for building its small cars—and then all the others—was in fact one of economising. The overall small dimensions conferred a saving on raw materials and workmanship: from the car chassis to the engine components, and from the interiors to the bodywork finishings. In this way, Fiat succeeded in segmenting the market and in creating a new type of consumer: the Italian home consumer, who was sought among the social classes which, until only very recently and except for motorcycles, had been excluded from the market of individual transport. These were the office workers, employees, factory workers, small traders, and the young generation. Of course, the growth of mass motoring depended on the manufacture meeting certain consumer criteria. The Topolino, for example, was highly economical on petrol and its very simple engine did not need the high-octane "super" petrol but preferred to run on "regular"; its air-cooling system made maintenance easy for a population which was new to motoring and thus somewhat reticent to engage in such "complex" operations as changing the radiator water; the easy access to the rear engine meant lower repair costs; and, last but not least, the bantam engine capacity of 565 cc—very close to that of motorbikes—meant that

The Fiat 500 in a shot later used in advertising.

59

LA VETTURETTA DEL LAVORO E DEL RISPARMIO

Mario Sironi, Fiat 500 advertisement for posters and magazines, 1936. Sironi was one of the artists whose work was most used by Fiat, along with that of Felice Casorati and Giorgio de Chirico.

road tax and insurance were also kept to a minimum. The "usefulness" to which *utilitaria* referred was therefore twofold: the first was the concept of economising on the object itself, the second of economising on the object's use. Only much later, after mass diffusion had taken place, were other guiding concepts added, namely those of the small car's functionality in relation to urban space and traffic (to the ease of parking or its competitiveness with respect to public transport) and, lastly, that of the second car for driving-age children or ladies.

The Origins

Although all this typified Italian society after the Second World War, it is not all of Italian origin. On the contrary, from the viewpoint of a production "philosophy", we must look at two moments—each very different from the other—which created the model for Italy's *utilitaria*. The first dates back to the first decade of the century and the great transformation enacted by Henry Ford (1863-1947) in both the car industry and the world of business in general. As is known, it was as early as 1908 that Ford began to envisage the

creation of a car that not only the more well-to-do would be able to afford but also normal working people. The consumer taken as his model was precisely the car-factory worker who, he thought, must be able to afford to buy the car after it left the factory. Thus the idea was born of the Ford Model T, a relatively small car that reproduced a scaled-down version of most of the functions found in other cars. By boasting a competitive price-tag, it would thus be suited for the middle- to low-class American family. The concept certainly appeared economically viable and clear in its goals: in this way, not only would a new mass customer base be created to expand the market, but an entirely new consumer growth sector would also be built. The use of the car, indeed, meant a consumeristic appropriation of the whole sphere of employee leisure time since it would take families out of their homes and give them—with the short working week—a mobility that was previously inconceivable. And, as we know, compared to individual space, a collective space is a much more fertile one for consumption. Ford wrote in

M. Barbara, Fiat 500 magazine
advertisement, 1936.

Below: the Fiat 850.

1925 in his autobiography that not only should the worker's daily employment satisfy his primary need, it also should offer him a little comfort. It should allow him to pay for his childrens' education and to offer his wife some of life's pleasures.

But Ford's idea was also in need of a collateral theory, and the man to rise to the occasion was the American engineer, Frederick Winslow Taylor (1856-1915), who was the first to conceive and develop the idea of assembly-line production (scientific management and work efficiency) that would rationalise work processes, thereby reducing costs and prices. His system, which was based on the principle of corporate organisation, was given the name Taylorism. Ford, instead, was the first to apply it in the factory, and from then on the model was called Fordism. The new concept consisted of applying certain fundamental principles. First, if the car was to be sold to the masses, its price had to be reduced. But a price reduction could be achieved not only by saving on materials but most of all on labour costs. And this was a problem since, thought Ford, if a change in the customer's social class were to take place, these same customers also needed an increase in income. Thus, an increase was made necessary in the income of the factory workers themselves. But the solution was soon found: the transformation of the production method from the craftsman model—several workers working on one model—to the industrial one, whereby many workers worked on the same portion of the product, with an assembly phase to mount the various groups. The "assembly line" was born and with it the concept of the division of labour, which was put into practice in 1913. This was after, however, the world's first car for the masses had already been built in 1908— the already-mentioned Ford Model T. But the growing alienation from work, which was the first consequence of the assembly-line system, was also compensated in monetary terms, thus

creating a complete production and consumption cycle like the one mentioned in the Foreword. Indeed, Ford enacted a policy of increasing salaries—creating "company pride"— and put into practice an incentives scheme, which even provided for company profit-sharing for the workforce and, with it, a competitive atmosphere within the factory. Ford also reduced the working week—thus making more time for consumption— and, as mentioned, reduced the prices. The results certainly spoke for themselves: 15 million Ford Model Ts were sold from 1908 to 1926. Ford explained his philosophy when he said that he was going to produce an automobile for the masses, and this car was to be big enough to fit a family, yet small enough for one man to drive and be able to maintain in good condition. He explained that his automobile was to be made with the best materials, the greatest skills using the least complicated design that modern engineering could offer. Yet, its price was to be so low that every well-paid worker could afford one, for he and his family to enjoy the blessings of leisure time spent in God's great open spaces.

Mass Motorisation and Totalitarian Consent

There was, though, another very decisive moment for the future growth of the "runabout" and this was the period of the totalitarian regimes during the inter-war period. Under both the Fascist and Nazi states—and also partly with Stalinism—a very precise idea was formed about using free time as a means for organising popular opinion. It is no coincidence that the idea of the mass holiday was born in this period (summer camps for children) as was the notion of sport as a collective pastime. It was also in this period that the new concept was formed of motorised transport as a testimony of a good standard of living for the people. The emblem was probably the world-famous German car (which was basically state-run) called

Sketch of the Fiat 500 for magazine advertising. The car later became the Topolino.

Cesare Maggi, *The Fiat 600*,
oil on canvas, 1955.

Volkswagen—car of the people—with a fully evident propaganda and social content. But the Volkswagen was born only in 1937 under the management of Ferdinand Porsche, who had been appointed by the Nazis precisely to invent a prototype car that was economical and suited to the working class. This was after the same engineer had founded a car workshop of his own in 1934 where he had worked out the concept of the solid, indestructible and economical car. This was to become, of course, the unforgettable Beetle. The only democratic European country where the Fordist or Populist policy of mass motorisation was practised was France: by Citroën. But their approach was different. First, the Traction Avant (which was not a truly economy-based vehicle) and then the 2CV by Citroën were aimed rather for use in rural areas and the provinces. Another feature of

Citroën's invention was that its was not just "economy-orientated" but indeed almost grimly uncluttered and had a concept of indestructibility that was different to the German one. If the Volkswagen was rugged—"whoever bumped into it would come out the worse"—with the 2CV the idea was more one of it being "undying": "it might virtually fall to pieces but it would keep on going anyway".
But for once in Italy a similar product was around which had a certain head start on its foreign counterparts. In as early as 1930, Fiat built the 508, widely known as the Balilla, a car with a 965 cc engine, as an open tribute to the Fascist regime. Although really not a car for the masses—even if it cost 10,800 lire as opposed to 22,000 lire for the 514, which came out the same year—it was nevertheless affordable for a middle class which also included employees—and

with whom Fascism was attempting to strike up a dialogue at the time. Another economical car had also been the legendary 501, which went into production in 1928. Here Fiat copied the American experience of buying on instalments, which had proved a success. And then came the Topolino, Fiat's real stroke of genius, again, for those pioneering times.

But the Italian "utility car" was born from a concept which was different again from those of its foreign competitors: in the Italian model, the theme was one of "pocket-size".

Some History about the Italian Utility Car

The Topolino, which still today represents a milestone of good design, was designed by Dante Giacosa—from 1934—and went into production in 1936. Controversy has it, though, that the first idea was not an original one from the Fiat ranks, but that it was born in Lancia, and that it was if not exactly "copied", it had at least anticipated the former. With this model, Giacosa became the representative father of the whole range of Fiat's economy series and indeed remained as company chief of artistic management for many more years to come.

The Topolino, though, did not succeed in immediately penetrating the market, a fact which was largely predictable because the Fascist transport policy was not very orientated towards individual means, but rather towards collective ones, giving much attention to railways, buses and trams. Although many road improvements were carried out, these were done thinking more of goods transport than that of individual passengers. Also, in 1936, the *inique sanzioni* (or "unjust sanctions") greatly slowed down the diffusion of the car due to the fuel restrictions imposed on Italy following its invasion of Ethiopia. The car thus remained a vision and a dream of luxury, speed and power. Until the end of the Second World War, the car was an item reserved for "gentlemen",

The first Fiat 500 model.

a sporting object for racing drivers' entertainment, and an instrument for showing off one's social status.

The Utility Car and the Reconstruction
We can say that the Topolino was to some degree reinvented in 1946—as was appropriately mentioned in a song "Topolino amaranto" ("Amaranth Topolino"), dedicated to "her" by Paolo Conte—on the wave of post-war reconstruction, to which we will return in greater detail later in this chapter. The production of a mass-consumption item such as the car should indeed be traced back to the more general choice of Italy to take the plunge and transform itself into an industrial nation. And so the utility car could not be left out of the group of other items of the same type such as the washing machine and refrigerator, to which the nation had been abundantly introduced precisely by the victorious allies. The Italians did not know it, but the route to industrialisation took a path through the model of a new lifestyle: that of comfort. The fridge and washing machine represented a reduction in fatigue at home; the car and scooter characterised less fatigue outside of the home. They also

transferred certain social costs directly to private family budgets, and spending among families on electricity indeed increased, as did that on transport outside the home.

The utility car, however, was destined sooner or later to encounter a problem which lay lurking for all. A classic observation of sociology is the principle of "social differentiation", which explains how the growth of a given economically-defined class causes its consumption potential to gradually become fractured, with a resultant loss in its unity and an increase in its internal differences. These differences are expressed precisely in the markers of social identity, or in the objects of that class, which, by no coincidence, are called "status symbols". Put another way, all mass consumption products must sooner or later create various, slightly-altered alter egos so as not to remain entrenched in the image of excessive uniformity. This led to two phenomena which took place in the '50s and which were largely predictable:

the first was the growth of very strong competition in the same market segment, with the mushrooming of similar products competing mainly on a symbolic level; this gave rise to the idea of a small social surplus. The second event was that brands were padded out with variation models, which aimed at exploiting the full range of the merchandise segment that was identified by the product.

The "Boom" Years

The competition among brands is a story of a genuine battle for the launch of the utility car during the '50s. Fiat, as mentioned, starting from 1954, flanked the Topolino with a slightly more powerful car, the 600. And just two years afterwards, in view of the new competitive clashes in the offing, it launched a direct replacement: the 500. They were two cars built using the same principles as always but they were much lighter in terms of weight, the materials used and in the shape itself, which, by affording a full view of the rear engine's air-intake grill, gave the car a sort of sporty, aerodynamic look.

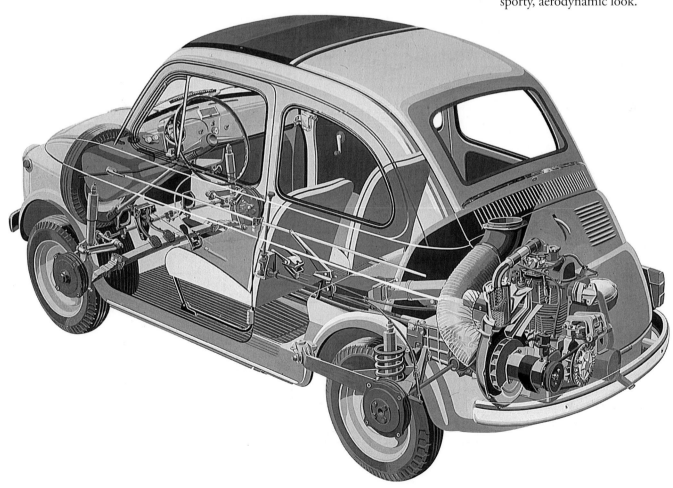

Nino Aimone, *The Fiat 500*, 1968.

Advertising poster for the
Fiat 500 B.

New colours were also added—as was happening more or less across the board in the industry: to the by now compulsory black were added white, cream and blue, and later a much broader range of colours, mainly of lighter shades. In concrete terms, the differences between the 600 and the 500 were marginal: 100 cc cylinder capacity, the fully synchronised gearbox of the 600 (the first gear of the 500 was not), and slight differences in space, performance and price-tag.

As mentioned, the mid-'50s however saw new contenders appear on the Italian market. The car which was without doubt the best competitor was the Bianchina by Autobianchi. Modelled exactly on the 500, it cost only a little more but was cleverly positioned as a more sporty alternative. While Fiat's utility cars had a linear and compact shape (a sort of giant tortoise shell) which contrasted with the classic car of the times (the overturned bathtub form), the Bianchina reproduced the classic form of the big, "real" car in a miniature version. Thus it gave the impression of offering better aerodynamics, greater

speed and more space. Moving in the opposite direction, instead, two unsuccessful attempts were made to market cars which were even smaller than the Fiat 500. In 1957, Piaggio, the extremely successful producer of the Vespa scooter, sales of which had already topped the million mark worldwide, tried its hand at entering the four-wheel vehicle market by launching the 400. In Italy the experiment flopped and it was re-routed to France, where it met with a similar dismal fate. Probably, engineer Romeo, who had previously designed an alike car—and who was anticipated by Piaggio—would have been relieved if he had still been alive.

Instead an engineer called Fanciullini, from Siena, designed a three-wheeler, which was typically urban and experimented a curious concept: called the Isetta, it had a very small engine, enough space for just two people and the door opened out in front of the driver. Initially produced privately by Fanciullini himself, the manufacturing licence was later sold to Messerschmitt, which launched it with limited success

G. Rossi, advertising for the
Fiat 500, 1936.

The 1960 advertisement for the
Fiat 500 estate car.

across Europe. In the meantime, after the unification of the European market in 1956, also the other European brands made their entry into Italy and some tried to launch utility cars to compete with the Italian ones. The best among these was the German NSU, which came up with a worthy competitor for the 600, the NSU Sprint, which was quite a good-looker and offered a performance and price that were indeed better than those of Fiat's little queen.

The New Consumers of the '60s
But in those years, Fiat was proving truly unbeatable. It began to differentiate its products. The 600 was used to spawn the Familiare, a car more for transporting numerous goods than a numerous family. Elegance was not its forte and it had a rear-end protrusion that was rather beetle-like. For the 500 instead, a different new idea was tried out: first the flip-back roof, and then the soft-top—a way of making the car more "summery", almost a sort of cabriolet. Instead the rival Bianchina pre-empted it by becoming a cabriolet in its own right: its dashing shape and soft top made of it a model which was decidedly mould-breaking.
For these models, the '60s was a decade of constant restyling, something which had indeed become necessary by the entry into the Italian market of highly successful European models such as Citroën's 2CV and its younger sister, the Dyane, or the Ami 6. But the most irresistible car of the times was the revolutionary Mini Morris, distributed by Innocenti. Revolutionary because, in its small dimensions, it succeeded in creating a truly sporting concept of motoring while offering cutting-edge comfort features on such a small vehicle. But the times were ripe, after all, for the utility car to begin a new era, one marked in the

short term by new expressions in quality. Indeed, the increase in wealth had made a large proportion of the previous car-driving population want a series of models which were superior to the existing ones, even if the change in segment was not yet feasible. This time, compared with their European counterparts, Fiat and the other Italian brands were slow to take the initiative, but a natural event was to act as the spark which rekindled the Italian industry's fervour. This event—or rather calamity—was the 1966 flood, which affected one-third of the country and which wreaked its most serious havoc in the art cities of Florence and Venice. The winter of 1966 still probably offers much scope for historical analysis for both the economic and social changes that took place. The damage caused by the torrential rainfall and unique wind and tidal conditions was extremely serious. Yet perhaps even more striking was the effect the disaster had at a symbolic level. Italian industry, indeed, responded to the challenge by working on a development model which, in shape and spirit, was much like that of the post-war reconstruction. And within the scope of the effort a primary place was taken up by the car manufacturers:

Advertising poster for the Fiat 500.

Advertising poster for the Fiat 600 Multipla, 1958.

Advertising poster for the Fiat 600 D, 1961.

Opposite, below: the Vespa 400, designed by Corradino D'Ascanio, manufactured in France and presented at Montecarlo in 1957. It is the true predecessor of the Fiat 500. Despite the name, it was a real car and not a scooter surrogate. Fiat's decision to manufacture utility cars convinced the Piaggio management to abandon the project.

Fiat, for example, calculated the sheer number of cars that had been lost due to the flood, and decided that the margins existed to enact a plan to change a mass motoring market which, although it was maturing, would have otherwise evolved over a much longer timescale. Thus, in the winter of 1966, Fiat radically changed all of its models in one swoop: the glorious 1100 was phased out and replaced by the 128; the 1300-1500 also retired, replaced by the 124; and also the 600 ended its days, replaced by a car with notably superior performance, the 850, which was one of the most important productions of all time by the Turin-based firm.

Thus the transformation in the utility car which required new expressions in quality was complete. Although initially a low-level transformation, it was to be increasingly aimed at the young-consumer market, which in the meantime had exploded in Italy as elsewhere in Europe. The 500 was renamed, somewhat stalely, as the Nuova 500, and was identical in substance to its predecessor, albeit enriched with some new optionals. The 600 cc capacity engine had become too small a step to create an upward differentiation and the

next car up in the scale was one that was faster—reaching speeds of around 140 kph—larger and more solid and comfortable. In other words, in Italy there was a demand for a utility car that was suited to whole families according to the new standards; after all, by then people were used to six years of *autostrade* (motorways) and the Autostrada del Sole, had been opened in 1960 and brought with it a huge change in national mobility habits.

The 850 was an enormous success, proved by the variations that rapidly ensued: a popular coupé, a miniature version of a fashion that had become established among the larger-engine cars; and an elegant spider, which was also built according to the same principles. A model was even brought out which harked back to the shapes of older times: the Siata with an 850 cc engine and a highly unusual form. Here too we encounter the same phenomenon as those already recorded: the transfer of all the existing fashions in the more up-market segments down to the utility car. In fact, for some time the in-vogue car was Britain's Morgan Spider, which returned to the origins with its prominent radiator, the elongated and

Advertising poster for the Fiat 600, 1957.

The Fiat 600 Multipla.

Advertising poster for the Fiat 600, 1957; *below:* the Fiat 600.

raised front-end, and spoked wheels. Again within the theme of "luxury for the poor", another successful cabriolet is worth mentioning: the Innocenti 850 Spider, which imitated another fashionable sports car of the day, the MG Roadster.

Market Crisis and Restructurisation
The '60s were the last years of a long period of rapid expansion in the car industry. It was the period that witnessed the fiercest competition in the industry of utility motoring, which had become a little more sophisticated with respect to the early post-war period. It was also during the '60s for that there was a growth of precisely those elements which made the great Italian motorisation possible: the first was undoubtedly the increase in individual, as opposed to collective, mobility, a phenomenon favoured by a national policy which was committed to developing the motorway network (to the detriment of the train) and this brought among other things an increase in goods transport. For the historic city centres, this put a severe strain on the road systems, where traffic became ungovernable and pollution increasingly heavy; as for the motorways,

these quickly became burdened with heavy goods vehicles. It was no coincidence, then, that the mid-'60s marked the beginning of a civil conscience with regard to traffic issues. In 1966 the historic centre of Siena was the first Italian city to be closed to traffic and the second in Europe, after Split, in former Yugoslavia.
The second element that favoured motorisation was the change in relative wealth levels and customs. The Italian working classes broke into the market with a force that was unknown in the rest of the world. And among the working classes, one social group in particular emerged in Italy which, precisely during the '60s, represented a big new consumption potential: the young generation.
In the '70s however, the market suffered a severe and sudden contraction, the main culprit being the OPEC oil crisis of 1972, which imposed serious limitations on individual transport. But the policies for environmental protection and for reducing urban traffic were also beginning to make their mark. As for the young consumers, they began to identify themselves with a new symbol of freedom, the motorcycle, thus

The Fiat 128 game.
Below: Pietro Annigoni, poster and magazine advertisement for the Fiat 850, 1970.

Opposite: advertisement for the Fiat 500, 1957.

reducing the demand for the economical "first car". The time was ripe for a new change in the concept of the utility car. The Fiat 850 was transformed into the 127, which vaunted a more modern design and better performance and without spider or coupé models to flank it, in keeping with the newly dampened-down spirit of the market. Shortly after, exactly twenty years from its appearance, the by now legendary Fiat 500 began to be taken off the market. It was replaced by a slightly enriched car which used the same engine: the 126. Unlike its predecessor, from the communicational viewpoint the 126 featured completely different characteristics. It was indeed more of a second car for the family rather than a first one. Its shape was more aesthetically pleasing, its colours preferably rather loud, and the driver's area more refined and comfortable. The unsynchronised first gearshift was finally eclipsed and there was even the semblance of a luggage space—under the bonnet. The 126 was definitely more of a middle class and female-orientated car. In the meantime, Fiat undertook a policy of expansion that, over the decade, was to lead it to take over all the competing Italian companies. The first step in this direction was the merger with Lancia (which does not come

within the scope of this article in that Lancia competed at the upper end of the market spectrum) and of Autobianchi. It was precisely with the Autobianchi brand name that a model made its appearance which was destined to vie with the highly successful Morris-Innocenti Mini Minor: the A 112, which mirrored the former's structural form and performance characteristics in terms of acceleration, road-holding, and a sporty handling with road-hugging effect. This was probably the winning model, even if the A 115 went on to achieve important, but not enormous, success. Indeed, in its traditional meaning, the utility car was by now disappearing and, in the tastes and demand of the public, a new concept of car was taking its place.

The Middle-Class Rebirth of the Car
The approximate date of this change was, in Italy at least, 1979, which marked the latest in a long line of strategic policy changes by Fiat. 1979 was the year when the Ritmo (marketed under the name Strada in the UK) went into production. With an engine capacity that started at 1200 cc, the Ritmo did not represent merely the entry of a new car into the so-called "C segment". Rather, it marked a change

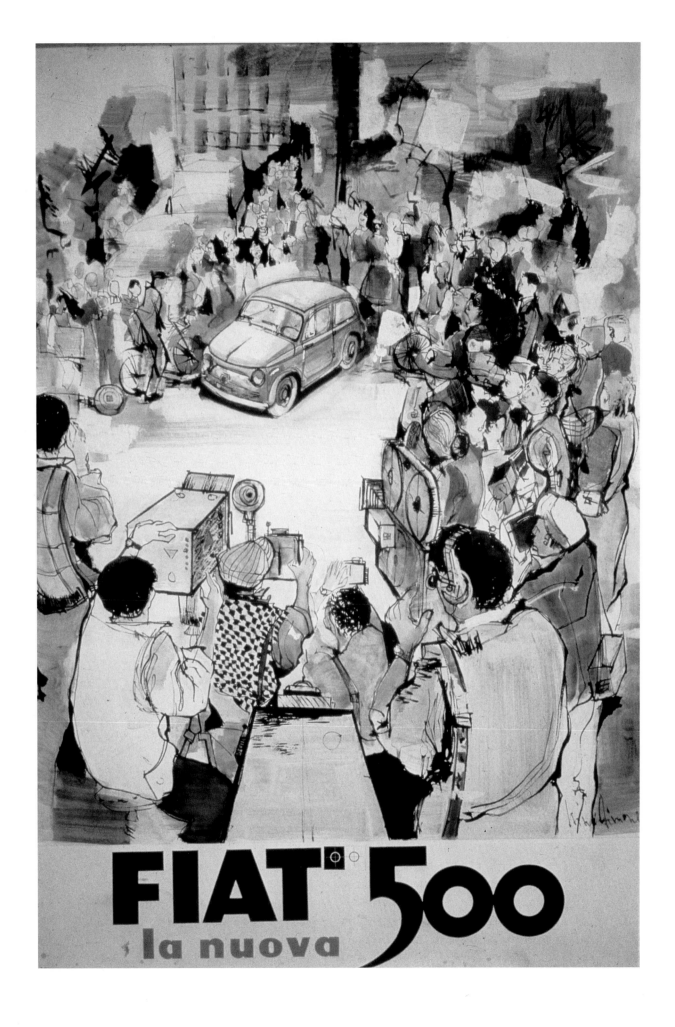

in direction for Fiat, starting from the name, which was no mere auxiliary fact, but a strongly symbolic choice. No other Fiat car had been given a name, except for the special case of the Balilla and this naming aimed at making the user's relationship with the car more friendly, since the car was by now a genuinely "family" object for Italian society—even in the emotional sense of the word. The "operation Ritmo" was therefore the first step in a change in the perception of vehicles that was completed immediately afterwards with the Panda—the new utility car in two versions: 700 and 900 cc. The Panda, as its name suggests, was simple, fun, young-spirited and uninhibited—and even slightly ecological (the panda is the symbol of the WWF, with which, incidentally, Fiat had to fight a small communications battle).

The size of the utility car was by now getting slightly bigger, and the car, which was still of reduced dimensions, had the dual function of offering relatively low fuel consumption matched with easy manoeuvring in the cities, but it also had to provide space and convenience for longer journeys or even holidays. It could be targeted to a market with a larger spending budget; in fact it was used very much as a second family car. And for families who could

not afford two cars, the Uno came to the rescue. The Uno also covered various engine sizes starting from 1000 cc. The working-class segment of the car market thus radically changed—and was further segmented. Production of the 128 was ended, its chassis recycled into the restyling plan of the unsuccessful Duna; and production also ceased of the 127. But this was not all: the number of optionals for the various models was now extremely high so as to meet the demand for differentiation mentioned earlier. The mass-consumption object thus multiplied into a whole series of personalised ones ready to bring out identities that would otherwise have been cancelled by the uniformity of industrial production.

Also with the parallel company Autobianchi, Fiat produced an extremely interesting small car: the Y 10, which replaced the A 112 filled the gap in the market left by the eclipse of the Mini, which Innocenti (bought by Alejandro De Tomaso together with Maserati) had first tried to replace with an all-Italian car, the Metro, and then with the Mini itself. This Mini was built completely in Italy (except for the bodywork which was on licence) and it had an engine reduced to three cylinders (both operations were however unsuccessful). The Y 10 was

instead an interesting test. In fact the car was presented as an advanced technological experiment: the engine was the newly conceived "fire" type, the car size curiously small compared to the acceleration and top speed, the futuristic form, the "miraculously" comfortable space inside. It was a car that interpreted certain social changes taking place in European society (it was by then unthinkable to separate the national car industry from the international one). The first was that this highly advanced car also had a female target (its advertising campaign was launched with the "female robot" of the post-modern Japanese architect, Isozaki). This meant that women who bought cars were beginning to express very personal tastes which had little to do with the lampooned "lady at the wheel" stereotype. The second was that a utility car had by then been born which was truly different from its predecessors. The "utility" of this car no longer lay in its purely cost-cutting features; rather it was above all a symbolic utility: urban functionality, ease in parking, elegance and the car's driving personality. These were the characteristics of the utility cars of the '80s and '90s.

The Y 10 on one hand and the Panda (with the Uno) on the other found

Fiat 127: 1967 car of the year;
below: Fiat Panda.

themselves combating on an international market which was by then increasingly liberalised. The competitors were initially only European, but there were certainly enough of them to contend with. France had modernised its successful car of the '70s, the Renault 5, which represented the normalisation of the rather too basic Renault 4. But the real phenomenon was the Peugeot 205, heir of the small Peugeot-Talbot, which had also begun in the '60s. Aesthetically very innovative, the 205 achieved huge success also thanks to its zippy performance. The 205 acted as the flywheel to a new emphasis on improving the utility car: that of its bodywork, which from then on would be created by the best designers in just the same way as for luxury- and special-edition models. Having retired its Dyane, Citroën moved on to propose the Ax, which, while maintaining a cost-saving approach, was made more middle class in its lines. In the same way as Fiat had done with its Uno, the French manufacturers joined the bandwagon too, and flanked some slightly superior models to their smallest-cylinder cars: Renault thus invented the Clio and Peugeot the 206. Ford UK launched the Fiesta instead, another model which would soon become universal. As for the German companies, Opel (UK Vauxhall) brought out the Corsa as heir of the Kadett and perhaps more interestingly—at least at the time—was

Volkswagen's Polo, which was interpreted as a miniature of the emerging success of the family estate car, which on continental Europe is still called "station wagon". There was even a "Spanish" competitor (Spanish between inverted commas because Seat was initially owned by Fiat, and copied its models, and only later was bought out by Volkswagen): the version of the Panda from the Iberian Peninsula was called the Marbella.

The Japanisation of the Utility Car
This then was the scenario at the threshold of the '90s, when the utility car accentuated the features described in the previous section. First was its aesthetic character, the prevailing of "good design" also for the cheapest models, was called by someone "Japanisation" because it probably contained an impulse from the marketing strategy of the Japanese manufacturers. The protectionism which continues today towards the imports from the Far East (Japan and, more recently, South Korea) forced companies like Suzuki, Toyota and Mazda to justify a higher sale price with the added value of beauty. It had been a phenomenon marked by Peugeot in France but in this period it became the real novelty of the car market. Nearly all industrial production of this *fin de siècle* aimed at delivering mass aesthetic enhancement. Alongside the values of functionality and cost saving was added

FIAT PANDA.

FIAT

Advertisement for the Fiat Panda and Fiat Uno.

beauty, even if its expression came packaged within the constraint of standardisation. The Japanese, who were the newest arrivals on the European market, launched a series of models that almost seemed taken from comic books or cartoons: the Micra, by Nissan, the 121 by Mazda, the Maruti by Suzuki (made in India and the cheapest car of all). The generic name finally given to them was "city car", to reflect—also in the name—the change in use of the small-sized car.

The response from the European

manufacturers was vehement. Most launched themselves headlong into revamping their design according to the Far Eastern model. The Opel Corsa, for example, is one such successful case of a futuristic design. It was followed in 1992 by the Renault Twingo, which introduced (in tune as always with the phenomenon of miniaturisation) a small single-volume car that flaunted a lively image and colours. The by now classic Fiesta and Polo were also worked on further, while, to contrast the "estate lookalike" model, Innocenti brought out the Elba, which was a real estate car with a very low sale price—even if the car was not really very new since it reused the chassis and engine of the Duna (what a life cycle for the old 128!). Even Rover, Britain's somewhat sedate manufacturer, had a stab at the city market with its 111, which did not however meet with

much popularity. As for Fiat, the company sensed that there was something "legendary" about the new wave of city cars; that a sort of "return" to the original spirit of the utility car was in the air. Its response was thus a new, super-compact car—the smallest available today together with the Maruti—with a classic name: the Cinquecento ("Five Hundred"), written this time in letters not numbers to give it a proper name since the model of nearly forty years earlier had, for its owners, become more than just a number.

We are near the conclusion: the utility car seems once again to be taking on its former dimensions and engine capacity; yet it has radically changed in the eyes of the public. By now it has more to do with luxury and comfort in the face of urban congestion and much less to do with overall cost saving, which, in developed countries, is no longer necessary. And above all it must be pretty, or trendy—an exercise in aesthetic delight.

Some Sociological Notes

Having considered the long and adventurous history of Italy's *utilitaria*, it is perhaps worth taking time out to take a closer look at what it has represented for Italy's culture. First, with the invention of the Topolino, the phenomenon created something that was very original in the international industrial system. Although the prehistory of the utility car belongs to the United States, we can say that, after all, Ford succeeded in giving life (even if it was no small achievement) to what was only an economic and production revolution. His vision remained anchored to a conception of the private vehicle in which the concept of comfort remained of paramount importance. Instead, with the Topolino, Ford's system was completely translated into the framework of a less affluent economy at the time, thus allowing Italy to take a long cultural step forward. Here indeed, the utility car fully transferred a whole society from a rural to an urban one, from a society founded on family-based relations to one guided by outside-based ones, a society that had moved from local customs to at least regional ones, from archaism to modernisation. The car fostered interpersonal contact: it got people moving about not just for work but also for travel and enjoyment; circulation increased and with it came enhanced awareness and national cohesion; by favouring the pleasure and interest in technology, new industrial ideas sprung to the fore and a transition was brought about from consumption according to needs to one based on wants, thus providing a new impetus to building a different public perspective. At the same time, this transformation in popular customs, albeit in a key of consent, can also be noted in other manifestations of the Fascist period: for example, the advent of mass holidays, first on the Tuscany Riviera (which had already been launched in this direction) and then on that of Rome-Pontina and then on the Emilia Romagna Riviera of the north-east coast; or the diffusion of the radio and the cinema as ways of spending leisure time for all. The dates were again those from 1927 to 1936, the period leading up to the imperialistic delirium and sense of omnipotence which swept the country and led to the tragic consequences we all know about. The same character accompanied the first relaunch of the utility car, the one which occurred during the Reconstruction and economic boom. Gone was the aspect of Populism, of the creation of a mass consent for the totalitarian regime. There was, however, the same spirit of relaunching the lower-middle classes that had been largely decimated during the war; the broad social class, that is, which was the only one that could afford to lead a large domestic market. In the post-war years and in the period of economic growth, we can at the same time see all this again in certain parallel phenomena, such as the race for home appliances, the

fascination with lotteries, the birth of television and the passion for light music.

The main characteristic of the indissoluble bond between the small middle class and the advent of the domestic market can be represented, as the philosophy of objects, in that which we have several times called "miniaturisation". The utility car, indeed, was rarely an independent item; rather, it presented itself as a solution to a desire that was too big to be realised: it reduced the demands of unreachable dreams, while keeping them all intact. The Topolino, like today's Cinquecento, was built to carry four people, never two (except in the case of the Isetta—or bubble car—which however was never considered a

Fiat Cinquecento and its section.

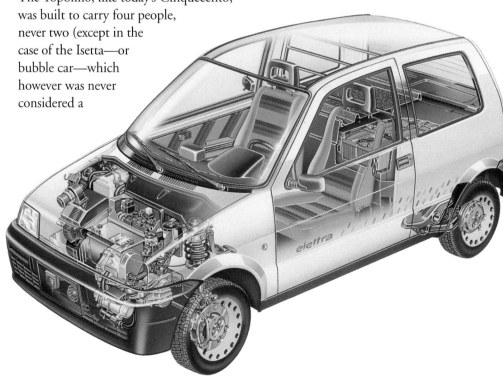

Autobianchi Y 10 and Fiat Uno.

real car but more of a covered motorbike). The top speeds are never very low; on the contrary, sports models were sometimes developed especially for tackling uneven or mountainous roads. The models succeeded in covering all the varieties of the car's range, including the luxury ones like the cabriolet, the coupé the off-road and even the estate. In the more recent versions, air-conditioning systems have also been added. Certainly a study of the different types of models offered in this process of miniaturisation in the various eras can allow us to register the signs of changing customs: the flip-back roof reminds us of the first holiday use; the reclinable seats at the end of the '60s have a lot to say about the sexual revolution taking place in those years; the short gear-stick, the sporty steering wheel, the lowering of the chassis tell us about the passion for sports driving which began at around the end of the '60s and continued throughout the '70s; the bright, not to say loud, colours tell a story of the desire for aesthetics during the '80s; the proliferation of optionals testify to the irresistible drive towards product differentiation, the authentic reflection of the fragmentation of a lower-middle class, which had instead previously been more stereotyped and united and which presented itself in a new and more individualistic way at the threshold of the '80s; and the increased aesthetic emphasis given in the '90s, to cite one more example, speaks of the need for elegance even spreading to the lowest-priced models.

So, to some extent, we could revise our judgement of the utility car given at the beginning of this chapter which talked of Italy from the '30s to the '50s. That judgement placed emphasis on the original functionality of the utility car (its "usefulness" in the strict sense of the term) and saw, in the changes taking place afterwards, alterations to the use of that object. Variations in use did undoubtedly take place but, from our closer study, it appears clear that the "usefulness" of the utility car was above all a symbolic one. In Italian society, the utility car performed the task of allowing whole social classes—the working classes first, but also the lower-middle class—to dream of the real possibility of being comfortably off. It brought a dream within reach and, indeed, immediately realisable.

The utility car therefore succeeded in "picking the lock" that was holding back Italian society from embracing a metropolitan mentality. As a symbol, it was much more effective than others, like the house was for example, among the British and Americans; or the garden for many European countries; or the abundance in food and eating, which still works in several Mediterranean cultures and, to some degree, in Italy as well. These are the reasons why, for better or for worse, the Italians owe much to the utility car. And certainly the Italians have given much back in return: they are by far the most fanatical nation in the world when it comes to cars and car racing; they transformed a working-class vehicle into a legend—the enthusiast clubs of the Topolino, Bianchina and 500 in their multifarious versions, are still very much alive today. In later times, the utility car has even experienced the most classic of

Taxi for New York City, Alfa Romeo, Italdesign project.

Opposite and below.
Ligier 162 GL and Ligier Ambra. The Ambra, manufactured in France by Ligier according to the style of the so-called "voiturette", was acknowledged by European directives in 1997 and is distributed in Europe by Piaggio.

paradoxes: a change in class, as has happened for some time in the field of gastronomy when a staple dish (like *polenta* flour for example) is raised from neglect and humbleness to be included among *chic* recipes. Indeed, a new model of the utility car is increasingly visible which is really the back-up car for the middle classes—and sold at prices much more in keeping with this luxury end-use.

But if this is true, does the utility car—or its latter-day cousins, the runabout, city car or small family car—still have a future? Or has its symbolic and economic function by now dwindled to the point of extinction? In the case of Italy, things appear to be in a phase whereby the market is largely saturated and no exciting developments seem to be in the making. We can only speculate as to the fact that, with the increase in the levels of urban traffic and pollution, the motor manufacturers will sooner or later have to devise different propulsion systems and therefore create "clean" cars like the electric car, which has been on drawing boards around the world for decades now.

A different marketing approach instead is the idea of exporting the utility car to developing countries. By the end of the millennium Fiat, for example, is planning to launch its so-called world car, which will be built in countries that

have no car-making tradition and which will be priced to meet the spending capacities of the various target nations. The Japanese and Koreans are perhaps already at an advanced stage of this strategy and the Suzuki Maruti, mentioned earlier—built in India and originally destined for sale in that country—is another clear signal of a move in this direction.

Within the scope of Italian inventiveness, then, the phenomenon of the utility car has been the expression of a special originality. An originality that was of course industrial but which was also social—to the extent that it became one of the most typical markers of Italian ingenuity and style together with the *espresso* or *cappuccino*, the *canzonetta*, the opera, fashion, and furniture. An originality that is moving on, its sights apparently set on becoming a social system for worldwide export.

Alberto Abruzzese

Man and Machines

In this chapter, I hope to avoid repeating the historic and venerating style common to many of the texts about the fascination with Ferrari, its inventor and public. I will also try to keep true to my aim and investigate the style of a national product which, within the process of Italian industrialisation, has become both motor and form, a device of technological development and a consumer product which is *famous* throughout the world: an automobile that has become a driving force of the myth of modern beauty.

Even with the use of a monographic summary, I would be unable to express what has already been said in the numerous interviews granted by Enzo Ferrari; those keen journalists, who, like Enzo Biagi, have identified themselves in the prestige of the character and the proud moments of unrepeatable experience (a dialect which has now become a universal language); all those who have been witness to, or have worked in this sector, have been deeply moved—in the same way as if they were gazing at a famous monument—by unforgettable meetings, magical lessons and recognition; the numerous articles, documentaries and books, are all great works which celebrate the Ferrari saga. The Ferrari site in Internet is accessible to anybody who wants an overall view of its past and present history, a history which is in a certain way fixed in a synthesis of these two moments having reached world-wide recognition as being the most *famous*. Much as I would like to avoid calling upon the richness of this source, it will obviously be necessary to do so, at least mentally, because, as is the case with epic poems, the literature on Ferrari always tells the same story, in the manner of a progressive choral union of different sounds and rhythms.

Even the most technical pages dedicated to the Ferrari engine or its bodywork seem to assume the same role as Homer's descriptions of Achilles' shield, in the same way that the sports reporters, when talking about the success of the Maranello racing car, transform the news into a description of duels and battles which will never be forgotten; in the same way that the sentiments of the heroes—both on-and off-stage as protagonists, families, protective divinities and the people themselves—are transformed as if they belonged to an eighteenth-century novel, period dramas, spectacular films or television serials.

This chorus about Enzo Ferrari is so intense (the protagonists: the *men*), so intimately meaningful in what Ferrari

The Ferrari F50 Barchetta.

(the means, the *machines*) has been and continues to be, as to impose the same structure of references and indicators on anybody whose approach to the theme resists the aspect of fame, and instead tries to read the single notes and movements of this irresistible chant.

When Ferrari died in 1989, he not only left the roar of thousands of sporting victories and dozens of world titles, but also the sound of a century, the landscape of an entire age—a hundred years of industrial progress, all the contradictory experience of the twentieth century. A life like his—born in 1898, when both the car and the cinema were created *together*— developed along with two distinctive periods of late, modern times, its two main motors: speed and communication. Ferrari managed to be involved in both the *civilisation of the machine* and *of the image*, in fact he managed to belong to their meeting point: *modern* experience at its utmost. Individual and collective history, in which personality and modern fate merge. This is why, when having to choose an epigraph with which to begin my speech, I have no hesitation in repeating the phrases with which Enzo Ferrari explained the secret of the Rearing Horse. A secret in which—as happened in the film by Orson Welles to the enigmatic crystal ball of Citizen Kane—the whole life of a great man unwinds, the history of his work, and the key to its interpretation.

The story of the Ferrari, as told by Enzo, is seemingly simple and fascinating: "The horse was painted on the nacelle of Francesco Baracca's fighter, who was the heroic aviator shot down over Montello; he was the ace of the aces of the First World War. [...] When we won the first Savio circuit in 1923, which was held at Ravenna, I met Count Enrico Baracca, father of the hero; this meeting led to another with his mother, Countess Paolina. It was she who told me one day: 'Ferrari, paint my son's rearing horse on your

cars: it'll bring you luck'. I still have the photographs of Baracca, with the dedication by his parents, in which they entrust me with the emblem. The horse was black then and has remained so ever since; I added the canary yellow background as it is the colour of Modena".

The new Ferrari wind tunnel was designed by Renzo Piano. The project by this famous architect, who was attracted, like so many other protagonists of the Italian style, to the orbit of the Ferrari myth, was finished in 1997. It can be seen on www.ferrari.it., a site where, more than anywhere else, we can recognise the sophisticated nature of a wind tunnel, where the materiality of the track is transformed into digital and analogical data, in pure simulation, in numeric coherence.

When facing this technological investment, the distance from the *human dimension* of the first sporting events when Ferrari came into the world, is evident from the numerous phases of its national and international success, from the progressive planning and organisation. The Fiorano track, built over twenty-five years ago near the Maranello site—where an explicit compatibility still reigns between technology and landscape, development and roots, organisation and personality—only reveals the intermediate point between the past of a man in flesh and blood, Enzo Ferrari, and the dematerialised, but solid, present of the wind gallery. In the vortex of the gallery it is still not possible to free the Ferrari idea—its consistency of object—from the personal happenings of its creator: once again the relation between man and machine.

There is a similarly intense conjunction between product, sporting heroics, enterprise and collective memories when you visit the Ferrari Gallery (over 100,000 visitors each year). It was inaugurated in 1990 in the Civic Centre by the Maranello

Enzo Ferrari in 1977 at the Fiorano track.

The Ferrari 250 GTO, 1964.

Council, thus reconfirming the popular and local sentiment which was already explicit in the choice of the Rearing Horse as the Ferrari emblem, a choice which can be traced back to various reasons: the relationship between the people and the aristocracy, individual heroism, the spirit of a betraying war, the dynamic forms of the aeroplane, the speed cult (in the Futuristic manner, in the same way that the colours black, red and yellow are Futuristic, which, even though they are a sign of emblems and banners of ancient civilisation, coincide with the base colours used for the publicity campaigns).

The Ferrari Gallery is a place where the cars and relics which are exhibited reach levels of real fetishism: from the highly selective space dedicated to the modern objects, that most challenge the perfection of classical proportion, to the collections for sports enthusiasts who are not just the drivers themselves, but also various levels of the public: *amateurs* in speed, *clients* of its beauty, *spectators* of the show.

The whole, vast repertory of non-fiction and journalistic literature—even that which concentrates on the technology of high-speed cars, or the competitive quality of the drivers, or the marketing of touring cars—does not escape, as we have already said, the explicit or implicit narration of a product which is inseparable from the personality who desired it at all costs, perfected it, drove it and managed it.

Ferrari as inspector, racing driver (for the first time in 1919, taking part in the Parma-Berceto race and the Targa Florio race), marketing consultant and manager of the racing department of Alfa, founder in 1929 of the Ferrari sporting company and trainer of the drivers, finally became *entrepreneur* and *director* of the talents that he knew how to gather around him, both for their technical and expressive innovation, and the vocation and attitudes of the drivers.

At the end of his training programme, Ferrari was able to do just about everything that he in turn expected from his colleagues and employees: a very special quality, tied in part to the person and in part to that typically Italian trait which runs through the

Enzo Ferrari's debut as a driver, on CMN, October 5, 1919, in the Parma-Poggio di Berceto uphill race. He came in fourth. Photo by Franco Zagari.

One of the Ferrari 158's first F1 races at the Monaco Grand Prix on May 10, 1964. The driver, John Surtees, was forced to retire from the race. Photo by Julius Weitmann.

small- and medium-sized industry of Emilia. It was a doubly local dimension, at once pre- and post-aristocracy, a type of enterprise in which the creative gesture is concentrated—as in an artist's shop—on the figure of the master-owner, in the manner of a Cellini who has come into possession of the market resources.

The fact that such an important figure, so full of small and great myth, has been so lovingly investigated by journalists and not, or rather not to the same extent, by members of the art world is a prime indicator of the heights reached by Italian style time after time, while without ever being absorbed by the tradition of the national system. The numerous acknowledgement awarded him, even early on in his career, announced his success as well as his singularity and his diversity.

It is not an isolated case: although Ferrari achieved extraordinary results throughout the world, various other firms like it were left to live in the creative intensity of their localism rather than serve as models—either general or shared—of an Italian style of doing business and designing. Ferrari was way ahead in this.

Each of these affirmations of creative diversity has created a singular adventure, which forged its own system of belonging well beyond its own environment: it has experienced the privilege of a dialogue between the great and with the great of social hierarchy, but not of belonging to a strategically agreed, unequivocal process. The Ferrari case is emblematic in this. Thanks to an eccentric rootedness in a spirit of enterprise, only this technician from Modena, with his exaggerated individualism, his expressive will, could invent strategies that were to fall among that small group of events that drive history.

For this, Ferrari—as Biagi noted in his interviews—was never a lover of politics. Whenever the conversation

veered toward politics or ideals, he changed the subject. He preferred to speak of human passion, of interior quality and commercial reality. The type of provincial culture that often comes out in Ferrari's words, as someone isolated and diffident, has something that reminds us of certain traits of the entrepreneurial style of today, even though it is within the "heroic" context of his time. It reflects a mental outlook that while open to the familiar dimension of affection, is closed, if not toward society, then toward government; it belongs to self-made men proud of their achievements, so proud that they will hide the difficulties encountered and resentments experienced in a private philosophy about the laws of men and nature, in a cluster of ethics, both small and infinite, local and global. Many vital worlds were opened up by the Ferrari experience, some of which are vast (for example, in *quantity*, like mass heroism, which, thanks to the media, has certainly been an historic flywheel), and others profound (for example, in *quality*, as in the investments in mechanical innovations and form). These worlds often came into conflict with one another, but it is just this conflict that contradicts itself to make the Ferrari one of the most universally recognised and appreciated products, in as much as it is a synthesis of the different worlds.

It is a synthesis in which each element is pushed to the furthest limits of possibility, beyond which the authority of form and the form of authority lose importance; they take on ironic tones and become subject to other needs. This was made clear when Ferrari's rival Lamborghini, trying to outdo the Ferrari model in that typically Italian, parochial-minded form of competition, entered the pretentious sphere of kitsch in the same way that the pop cars of American comic strips entered the superman—and thus superhuman—sphere of trash.

Right from the beginning, by

identifying a linguistic—and not just mechanical—engine, the car Ferrari designed was realised in systematic exaltation of the complex, while still carrying out a process of simplification: a global sequence of emotive icons all boldly identified by the red colour and rearing horse immediately left their mark on history: a vast score for various performances, each one different, but orchestrally harmonious together.

We will not be able to grasp the many facets of the Ferrari idea, and even less so the form it took, if we look at just the map of actions instead of the figures and territories of the imagination; if we just concentrate on the direct relationships between the public and the Ferrari phenomenon; or if we do not seek to detect how many things come together and regroup thanks to immaterial suggestions, subliminal areas and paths, peripheral causes and effects, multiple narrative frameworks, multicoloured friends and enemies.

In this respect, the Ferrari is an *extreme case*.

Staying within the Italian territory, it is an object of desire which—given the production and consumer strategies, the marketing network and the quality of its élite market—is situated at a completely different level with respect to that of the more popular Vespa scooter or Cinquecento small car, the huge successes of Piaggio and Fiat, which were reference points for Italy's nascent mass production.

Even so, these differences were interlaced during the disorganised years of the '50s and '60s, and they could not be considered as distinctive traits of different social strata if not on the basis of the analogies underlying them: the inclusion among emotional impulses which, when expressed, cancel differences in identity, roots and roles. The advent of the Ferrari marked the meeting point between the expressive tradition which moved from the top downwards and an assembly-line dimension with an increasing tendency to move from the bottom upwards.

The exclusive form of the Ferrari line, and the work involved, seemed not to belong to the national-popular proposals of the reconstruction period. Is that why it became a myth? As an affront to poverty, while also compensating for it, thanks to the same mechanism—superman of the masses—which Gramsci identified in the serial stories? Searching for the Hollywood dream instead of the Neo-Realist idea of resisting industrial speed in favour of nature and the emancipation of the poor classes? As

The Ferrari 365 GTB 4, better known as the Daytona, 1968.

reference to the centrality of the rich and powerful instead of the values of solidarity? As investment in the privileges of private property instead of in the culture of public services? We could sustain this idea by reading only one of the possible keys of interpretation. That the Ferrari idea would by necessity have opted for the most advantageous choice, being a company which was not yet structurally and culturally adapted to mass production, and which could therefore only target a small sector of the public, as has always been the case with high quality craftsmanship (right back to the value of the court artist, and

The Ferrari 250 Testarossa, 1959.

the social quality of the Renaissance artist).

The famous car brands of the time already had their own collective tradition, a modern style, cars designed for faithful customers, their own stories and myths, products sold to various social levels. A new car—sold at a price which its handmade production tended to raise all the time—would have needed a great deal of prestige and a very rich and motivated public; it was necessary to attract new customers from outside Italy as well.

The competitive spirit of the Ferrari men and machines gave the name the

advertising spending. Even though investments in car production were enormous, Ferrari exploited to the utmost the fantasies created not by the car user but by those who consumed the image of the name, its narration, its story.

For Ferrari, the entrance into the car market meant being paid for a cult object, a real and proper noble title, an implement of power. It meant finding clients in a very restricted and exclusive public by exploiting the communicative richness of a broader public, which was very emotively charged; reproducing and reselling the high visibility of the image in each of

prestige which—for the time spent in reaching such a high national and international position—would have been unreachable otherwise. What is more, it was a promotion of the brand carried out within the masses and with the spectacular logic of its general consumption: with a startling revelation—Ferrari did not produce images to sell objects and events, but produced innovation and competition to sell images.

Investment in production and quality was done therefore with a complex strategic policy that overturned the usual equation for consumer products of low production costs and high

those areas and sectors which—from the quality of the product to the quality of use—serve to *appear* strong in the market; finally transforming celebrities and Ferrari's powerful behind-the-scenes network into Ferrari testimonial-offering clients.

The material occasion to sell a new idea of a car to anybody who had or could accumulate riches was offered by those who were gaining the maximum advantage and profit, from the passage from the phase of primary consumption to progressive, large waves of products more suited to the pockets of the middle classes: refrigerators and washing machines, mopeds and family cars, cinema and television, meant to fill the spaces within the house, the physical territory and the image. Ferrari was at the top of the spiral during this phase, which saw the development of Italy's creativity. In it —with varying levels of waste between need and desire, necessity and superfluous—we find the soft aerodynamics of the Vespa line, the practical graciousness of the 500, the TV theatres and shows of *Carosello*. The same story of ownership of the Italian car companies is emblematic of a development logic in which Ferrari had a flywheel role, not only for the technological innovation and the turn to serial production, but more, perhaps, for the socialisation of consumption, for the modern project of beautifying daily life.

At the beginning it is significant that Ferrari—at the conclusion of an era and of an Italian style, of products and mass culture like that of the '30s—was born (1940-47) of an offshoot from Alfa Romeo. After this it is equally significant that the national generalisation of Fiat, at the reopening of a new consumer cycle, took over the Ferrari resources in 1969, thus filling a gap in their own global strategy which none of the prestigious car names could have guaranteed with the same success. The mass factory took over the Ferrari nobility.

From the Second World War till our times, each wage bracket of consumers has had its relationship with the market supply in the same form of emotional tension, of sublime condition, which the beauty of the Ferrari product automatically offers to any car user, lavishing the desire of the values held within the Ferrari idea, in its experience, on objects which in some way showed the challenge of the project and the semantic richness, but at more reasonable costs, *almost* within reach. The role, certainly not innocent yet socially rich, of the design masters is fundamental in this project, as we will see.

To own a Ferrari became one of the most certain signs of prestige and wealth—but not just in purely economic terms. It was more on the practical and functional level, and also a spiritual and ideological one. It was the spectacular and narrative education of a world undergoing drastic transformation, towards a consumer system in which more traditions, places, sensibility, expectations met— thus opening seemingly unlimited spaces.

It meant entering that bright aura of a Mediterranean product rather than a Northern one, famous and therefore universally recognised as a cultural emblem and not just technical power, speed on the road, guarantee of efficiency against time and space. It was the symbol of a real renewal of modernity. To succeed in the operation it had to stay at the top, highly visible to everybody, supreme.

A luxury item, ostentatious, but— contrary to the taste for the monument or for internal comfort—slim, functional, economical in its form, almost discrete, or at least essential, considering the engine inside. A Gothic and communal basis for a humanistic project gauged on the compatibility between individualism and collectivity. Unlike the imperialism of the noble and classic English cars, of the economic, well-equipped stateliness of the American and German cars, of the centralness of the Fiat, the turn towards the exclusive cost of the Ferrari was more amphibious, both below and above the nationalistic style of the competition.

Dressing and driving Ferrari, we wear a mask with the quality of a sporting choice, entering the heroic, vital, young hemisphere, which is often needed to compensate or complete the age of the person who is driving. The use of a Ferrari can openly demonstrate a real and authentic passion for the car: to exercise courage and modernity, to possess decisional qualities, to calculate the unknown,

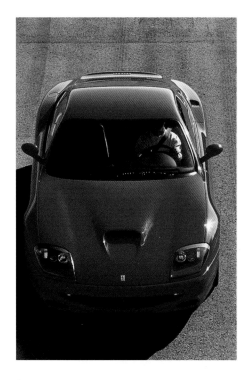

The Ferrari 550 Maranello.

The Ferrari 550 Maranello in action and view of the driver's compartment.

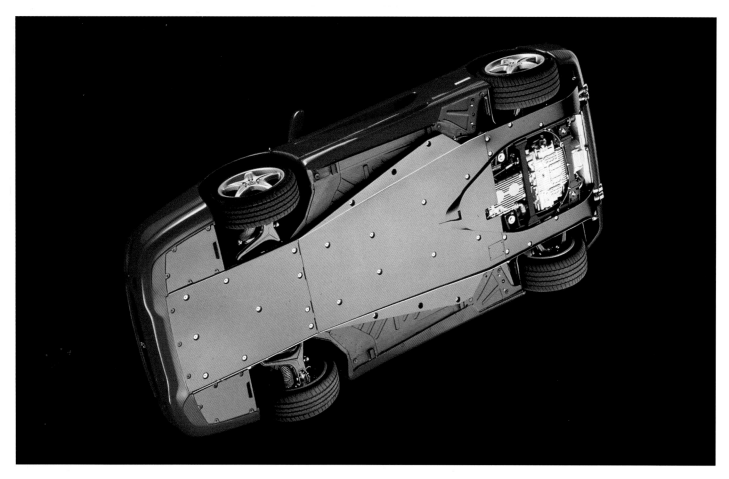

to have a competitive spirit.
However, it can also be a sign of irony,
of nostalgia, of acting, of having
reached a balance in self-ostentation,
of being carefree. Or it can be simple
exhibitionism, a semiotic confidence
trick, a look without style, social
egoism. And each of these
interpretations can conceal the others.
Is it therefore just the price—that
terrible abstraction of money—which
plays the leading role in recent modern
taste—so un-Calvinistic—for disguise?
We are trying to find an answer to this
question.
A Latin product—*Catholic*—like the
Ferrari finds its clients in the most
selective range of extraordinary
consumption, situated only in areas of
very high standards of living, or strong
social differentiation: a real *mass* for a
down- at-heel public, liturgies in
which the spirit becomes a golden
object. An exotic world, even more so
for those who do not belong to its
same roots; and Italy since the Grand

Tour onwards has been this. These are
its works of art.
The main Ferrari markets are the USA,
Germany, Great Britain, Italy, the
Pacific and Switzerland, with a
production of 3500 cars divided
between nine different models and
versions. But the map of the sales does
not make sense if we want to find the
real measure of all the apparatus and
the different areas which have
contributed both in the past and the
present to the success of the Ferrari
idea.
Anyone who has worked or still works
in production or sales has a baggage of
memories which goes beyond the
workshops, into the families and the
spaces in which clerks, technicians and
labourers have been involved. Modena,
among the most historic towns from
before the union of Italy, and among
the most political in the Republic,
makes the Ferrari pride its own, along
with its owner and its employees.
Circular sequences: the factory creates

Under-body of Ferrari's F355,
Berlinetta, GTS and Spider.

The Ferrari F355 Berlinetta.

a taste for production focused on quality, quality is dressed as human adventure in the races, the races gather groups of clients dedicated to racing. To sustain this expansive circularity, the Ferrari strategy has always been careful to guarantee different forms of enthusiasts' associations, all suited to support the product, its celebrities and its public.

If we continue to give a sociological space to this compact, visible and mechanical quality of the Ferrari—which has been described as *sculpture in movement*—it is because this *unique* quality has developed thanks to the composite quality of its creators. They—on entering the Ferrari project and work—discovered within their own personal field (for example the great designer Pininfarina) the various cultural and emotive areas, various memories and expectations which are involved, intertwining on the different levels, throughout the productive process.

These capabilities—this creative model common to both the technical-scientific and the humanistic sphere—

were able to satisfy the needs (sensed by Enzo Ferrari as producer) of the whole life cycle of a product, of the worlds and figures which are all part of it; even the worlds and the figures of those who buy and those who sit back and watch, that is, of those who are *bought* as a mass testimonial.

All this helps to give sense to the quality of the product, even the *distance* between the élite group of purchasers and the mass of spectators: spectators of a very privileged group, of something so impossible and beyond compare that it takes on a sacred aura, paganly religious, divine: no simple mortal is able to buy it, but only those who stand out as a hero; a man like the others, but who, for vocation, has courage and fortune in common with the Divine.

A vocation that needs a gift. As happens in fairy stories, the gods give a beautiful magical horse to the hero in trouble, and he uses it to overcome his impotency in front of the common danger, obtaining a victory which also represents the salvation of his people, as they all identify themselves with

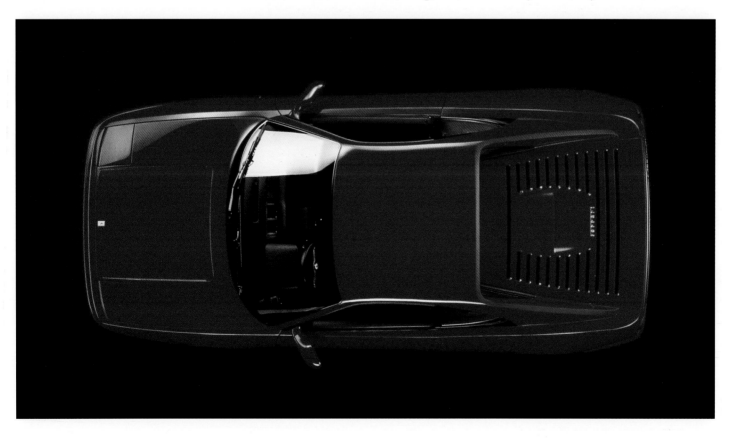

him—in his battle against the enemy. Even the hidden structure of popular fairy tales—all their prototypes, beliefs, unconscious designs, the way in which they are retold within the time and space of the socialisation processes—is inscribed in the Ferrari *mechanics*. Materials, gears, power, form and agents of a sporting and touring industry correspond to the primitive substance of natural and divine mysteries, of the sacred and of authority, of fear and hope, of beauty and force, of reward and celebration. This deep embedding of Ferrari in the structure of Western imagination was both spontaneous and planned. Initially it happened automatically— the only way myths are formed—but it only happened when the car from Maranello managed to gain access to the ingredients required for making a similar, short circuit between origins and the present. Ferrari reached this threshold when he strategically conquered and made his own the icons of power, victory, beauty and the sacred.

To break down the barrier that divides the earthly phenomenon of consumption from the heavenly sphere of the great works of the spirit— intuition is required to do the right thing at the right time: this is valid for an innovation to the engine or any other mechanical component, for the choice of a good driver, for the creation of different bodywork, for a decision regarding a sales strategy or a publicity campaign or a testimonial. When all this is achieved in full, overcoming the competition of all other consumer products, then the barrier shatters as if by a charm, and each of the qualities which has been reached recognises its link with the others, thus setting off the automatic device of an enormous semantic implosion. It invades every space of human experience thanks to an unstoppable, multiplying effect, which—as in all energetic condensations—crushes every historic

and territorial interval, whether individual or collective. This is the land of Fame.

Included in this picture are also the specific aspects of the strategies stemming from the creative work of Ferrari, widely covered by company historians and commentators: the provocative and personal style of Ferrari, craftsman and at the same time entrepreneur; his instinct for valid men who can work equally well alone or in teams; the idea of transforming a racing car (a symbol of war, a charger, a weapon) into a luxury sporting car (a symbol of riches, a carriage, a coat of arms), thus passing from the original sacredness of the races, of the great tournaments, to the worldly sacredness of fashion; the interactive relationship between the local scene of sporting competitions and the collective scene of national and international mass media; the attention paid to the creative element of design; finally, as we have already said, the choice of amphibious figures between clients and satisfied customers offering testimonials from the sectarian worlds of small and large hero worship.

Ferrari mechanics—in the strict sense of the word but also figuratively speaking in reference to strategic planning, progressive evolution of the logic and behaviour of its working— has thus reached the quality of a real stylistic manner, of industrial action which includes every material and immaterial mechanism.

The product is made for two levels of consumer, those who buy the article and those who buy the symbolic values. On one hand élite customers in line with the richness of the product, personally identified, virtually present at production (Ferrari produces custom-made cars). On the other hand, the consumer scene, the theatre of desires, the symbolic exchange of signs, the dynamics of identification. The fittings, the reinvention, which these two consumer forms bring to the product, are reflected at the beginning

The Ferrari F355, Berlinetta and, *below*, Spider.

of the production process: not just the design and the mechanics, the planning and the marketing, the image and the market, customer service and publicity, but also each of the memories dormant in the network which upholds these procedures. Even before it leaves the assembly shop, all this goes to furnish the aura of this precious, semantically rich object: a museum piece (the most prestigious models are exhibited at the Museum of Modern Art, New York) or a collector's item (including the widespread phenomenon of the model cars, giftware and gadgets).

But there is also the extreme challenge to meet—always at the limit of the impossible—of maintaining the myth which has been formed. On the track, the Ferrari cars primarily race against each other, trying to overcome the sacred image which at a certain point has become an irreplaceable expression. When Ferrari loses, the antagonist takes first place, but is never included in the same icon as Ferrari. They may win but they stay in their own place.

The technicians or drivers who are called upon to work with the Ferrari staff now belong to that same quality of specialists and resources—either Italian or foreign, it matters only as a slightly worrying sign of a lack of highly qualified personnel in Italy— which is also needed to maintain our most famous historic and artistic wealth. It is a richness whose fame cannot grow, only wither, but one that needs the specific techniques of survival to sustain the weight of its fame in the intense rhythm of daily life. The Ferrari myth, to continue living, cannot be hidden in a museum. According to the Zingarelli dictionary, style is "that special form in which literary and artistic expression is given life, and that belongs to an author, an era, a species"(here the term refers to the stylistic compatibility between author, public and era), "a normal way of being, of behaving, of expressing

oneself"(from which we can presume that the attribution of style tends to define social forms and manners referred to in everyday life); tendentially synonymous with "elegance, good breeding, distinction" (this tells us that the social use of the term has penalised anybody whose style does not conform with the rules of the upper classes); finally "a fashion, a performance technique in theatrical, musical and sporting circles" thus showing the existence of singular stylistic forms which are at the same time collective, and which correspond to the variety of techniques used, thanks to the universality of the single system of values.

Now let's look at design, which Zingarelli refers directly to. "Industrial design: product planning, for industrial production, which combines technical and functional needs with aesthetic features." We are well aware that behind this definition endless discussions are hidden in which theorists and operators of design—from Gillo Dorfles to Fulvio Carmagnola, from Thomás Maldonado to Vittorio Gregotti, from Ezio Manzini to Aldo Colonetti—are divided in their interpretation of creative work applied to an industrial product.

The Ferrari, both as a product and as a symbol of Italian style, is a good example of design values in that it combines strategies applied to an extreme object, both regarding its functions and its pretence (including money), but one that at the same time is socially legitimate in the name of entrepreneurial, media and creative barons: Pininfarina refers to Enzo Ferrari, Ferrari refers to Fangio, Fangio refers to the public, the public refers to the press, the press refers to the dominant values of taste, the mass culture to the power devices which control subjects, needs and dynamics, and the circle is finally completed when everything refers back to the creativity of Pininfarina.

Pininfarina—among the most interesting of those artistic figures, craftsmen of bodywork, who in the '50s passed to mass production—is a significant link in this chain of references, because in a certain way he is the figure who, with others of equal prestige, gave the car a body covered with a divine skin. It is the passage from the Lambretta of Pier Luigi Torre to the Vespa. From the utility car to the dynamic body of a car. Machines similar to men and animals.

Objects like the Ferrari are items of extreme pretence. In other design products this pretence can be masked in the free logic of form, in poetic

Cylinder head and engine
of the Ferrari F355.

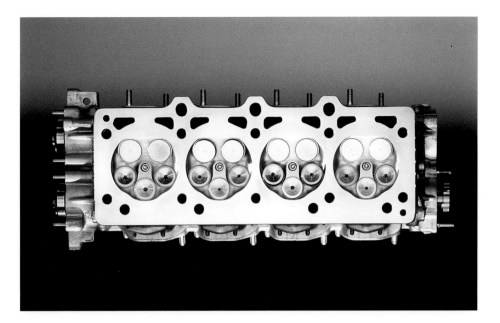

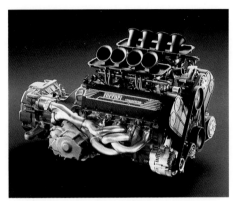

licence of the artist, in the ethics of modern planning, but in the Ferrari it is naked.

It shows its greatness and, of course, its deep-set roots: which do not refer to the bond between form and objects, that critical theories would like to divide giving an advantage either to the ethics or the aesthetics of social forms; rather, they refer to the historic contents of modern art and its effect on the mass society.

Once again the trait emerges (from behind industrial seriality which has nothing to do with wasteful and sublime models of development like the Ferrari), of a continued existence—which is clearly visible here—between the humanist splendour of the Renaissance and all the aesthetics of the industrial society, which either belong to the affirmative front of creative authenticity or to the negative one of modern planning, in any case, to design.

When talking of style or design we are talking of things which are similar, but at the same time different. Similar, even if the former has a wider range of experience with respect to the specifics of the latter, being directly connected with a precise manner of creative and professional work. Different, even if both have the same conscious, strategic determination needed for a formal

choice, in which production and consumption meet and are recognised, being entwined with each other. Style alludes not so much to production—the author and the works—as to the consumer, to his *way of life*. It therefore indicates a stylistic communion between the quality of the design and the quality of the market, between the subject and the object, and is therefore linked to the eighteenth-century roots of a conscious transformation of expressive structures aimed at interpreting the general quality of the public.

The twentieth century has been dedicated to progressive research into the aesthetics of the objects of daily life, beginning with Art Nouveau right through to Trash. During its course design has thrived as the analysis of the relationship between function and quality, fusing the tradition of decoration with that of industrial design.

Design is the result of modern planning, an extreme attempt to bring order to aesthetically divergent styles of life. The Ferrari has enjoyed constant recognition of its artistic qualities, beyond the tumult of those cultural and social styles with which it is connected. The Ferrari, perhaps better than anything else, can explain the modern sense of a work of art, the power of symbolically shared forms. A rare example of continuous formal redefinition—a job that places all car design in the forefront, similar to the trailblazing role of mass audio-visual production—Ferrari's proposal is based on the immediate recognition of the model, of its authority. A real coincidence between classic and modern occurs.

Some critical research could be done on the rhetoric used to make the expressive values of the Ferrari bodywork—the identity between function and fantasy—so supremely dominant. Ferrari displays, thanks to the semantics we have already mentioned, the forms of a universal aesthetic, seductively imposed and emotively mutual, giving a version of a perfect balance between style and design.

But the strength of the Ferrari beauty is distinctly removed from that style which wanted to be closer to the anti-aesthetic experience of its subjects, directing all its attention on the control devices of the design, so close to the formalisation of original life models.

According to this interpretation of the Ferrari phenomenon, we can attribute to its success the role of consolidation of the automobile culture—not only, but also every other dynamic form—set on a modern predestined flight path, high not only because it is semantically rich but also because it is vertical, and therefore with a polyvalence of a monocultural type. Always tied to the myths of modernity, however, in as much as they are specific devices of beauty, of the real and of taste, Ferrari sublimates these values retreating to the vector of its own formal success.

The refusal of some modern, urban and architectural planners to grant any expressive stature to the chaos of spontaneous forms in industrial and postindustrial landscapes represents a similar problem. Such landscapes sprang up in open contradiction

of the planner's need to formalise the relationship between the subject and the environment through aesthetically representative objects.

In Ferrari we can see the basic contradiction, but also the utmost control of the gap between the turbulent area of style and the Apollonian area of design (and even more so of the critical apparatus which sustains the work). It succeeds, having tested the local and global character of the Ferrari product for such a long time.

Local, in the style it gives to single national contexts, being rewarded by the affectionate, collective participation of the group. Global, in the quality of a design—like speed, like the great immaterial and collective abstractions, such as money—which goes beyond the territories of each lifestyle to be recomposed in a perfect model, which, with respect to contemporaneity, always comes forward like an alien apparition even when it is known and is unreachable even when it has been reached. Precisely in that exquisite quality of modern times.

At this point in our discussion, reference to *The Easy Life* is de rigueur, however obvious it seems. This is the only great Italian film which managed to tell the story in which the automobile worked as a narrative device, but which was also critic and catalyst of the dramatic action and the key to interpreting the text; a consumer item which is on the screen to interact with the spectator, at the end a real *deus ex machina,* sign of a fatal coincidence between destiny and the spirit of time, perfect coincidence between friendly object and enemy, between comedy and tragedy. Style— at the same time exalting and frustrating—was, the mainstay of the *Commedia all'italiana* in its golden moment, the Italian film industry in its single moment of a mature, cultural system, socially and economically founded, a period destined to end.

Berlinetta and Barchetta versions of the Ferrari F50 introduced in 1995. Production was limited to 349 cars and was concluded in 1997.

Analysing the meanings which are given form in Risi's film, we find a series of indicators—behind the apparent simplicity and frivolity of the story, of the text—which may offer a clue to many of the reasons why Ferrari cars are myths at the same time near and far from Italian style, with roots that probably could not have grown elsewhere, but with an abstract, sublimated dimension of its productivity which can only belong to the imperialism of the modern spirit. To an absent beauty, uprooted.

In the moment of Sunday boredom in Rome—in 1962—when Bruno, interpreted by Vittorio Gassman, asks the young, shy Roberto, interpreted by the French actor Trintignant, to go for a ride in his Lancia Aurelia Sport Pininfarina, we have the dynamics of a journey and a story which have their origins in the semantic richness of the automobile as part of the Italian system.

It is in fact a totally Italian story, which unfolds over the years of the economic boom, when the symbolic—and strategic—function is the distance between the mass consumer public and the élite public which exhibits its status. In the screenplay and the direction, the luxury car, elegant and fast, is entrusted to a personality who makes up for a lack of economic wherewithal with an immoderate capacity for prevarication, a way of making shift that is thoroughly theatrical, thoroughly Italian, where the sublime is obliged to become a grotesque form of happiness or tragedy. Only a foreign actor, a figure removed from those manners of fallen nobility, could have acted alongside those weak, yet functioning, forms, in which Gassman's (and Cinecittà's) histrionics are supreme.

Why, if the real rich they meet drive a Riva motorboat (something similar to the Ferrari miracle in boating circles), couldn't our two heroes drive a Ferrari? Because these two measures of European culture—these two spirits of the middle classes, perfectly integrated on the black and white celluloid, and therefore seen through a filter that had

The Ferrari F50 Barchetta.

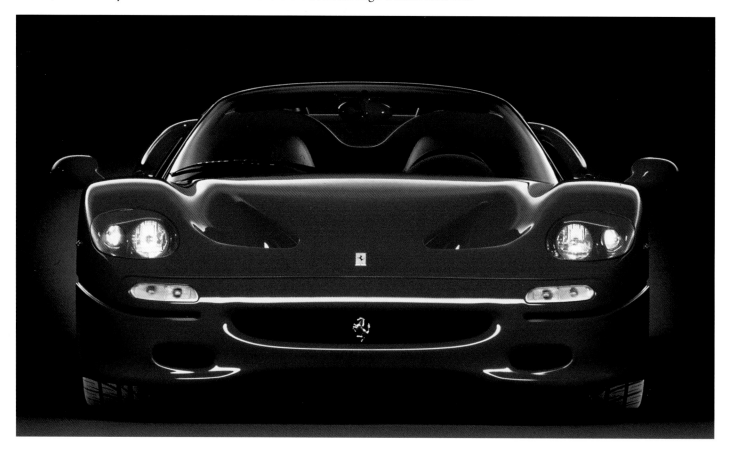

Detail of the driver's compartment of the Ferrari F50.

not yet been saturated by the colours of popular consumer items—could not have supported the symbolic force of Ferrari, its clamour.

The fire-red, dazzling, unequivocal colour, had the same ecstatic quality of a Hollywood film, typically bound to the great archetypes of heroism, of desire and challenge, like *Pandora and the Flying Dutchman*, not by chance interpreted by James Mason in the part of the Flying Dutchman and Ava Gardner, in the part of the femme fatale, the same type of star who—in high society—was living the privileges of Italian style (and it is, once again, not by chance, Roberto Rossellini who married Ingrid Bergman and who had a private passion for Ferrari).

In Alberto Lewin's film the mythical car which appeared was a red sports car, shown against a background of natural landscapes and great passions, as dictated by high-class tourism and car publicity. But if, in this case, the only reference to the fire-red colour seems forced to indicate the elective affinities between Hollywood and Ferrari, it is however quite obvious in *On the Beach* by Stanley Kramer, in which one of the characters—facing the results of the atomic catastrophe, the end of the world—awaits death by driving his Ferrari for the last time, which up till then had been religiously kept in the garage, within his heart. The interpreter of such a definitive desire, of such an intimate and universal relationship between man and machine, was Fred Astair: it was precisely the Ferrari which was entrusted to the culture of his dancer's body to run the last moment before nothingness. This actor was in fact the symbol—or such was his use in catastrophic cinema—of the roots of Hollywood civilisation, the type of consumer humanism (man through car-object) created and elaborated in the period of integration between Central European traditions and American mass society in the '20s and '30s.

On the contrary, the Italy of *The Easy Life*, even though referring to both the Italian spectator and the new rich classes, has nothing to do with the symbolic boundary-beating of the Ferrari, with its non-position. Instead, it is shown as a geo-political map of a socialisation process under way, as unequivocal as it is internally contradictory.

The Ferrari tells a different story from *The Easy Life*. The film does not talk of unrealised myths, but of strong endemic limits of Italian society and conversely of its vocation for grotesque comedy, of a *humble* national style. These styles bespeak an open wound after the catastrophe of the many pre-industrial traditions, of their more antique systems of belonging, of the economic-political structures of their towns and seignories, of their strong localism, of places in which art and people are mirrored in an orderly set of strategies.

The Ferrari tells of the margin of initiative, which only a few Italians had managed to gain, between the '40s and '50s, using the same gap between development and backwardness, not working on the more humble substance of things and passions, but, with a different talent; working instead on transforming the point of view, the decision to transform the gap into a step forward, an aesthetic adventure, a project.

In this sense the same direction is taken as that of the Italian Futurists, lit up by idolatry of the modern in a country tied to the past, by fast cars in a rural countryside, by individual gestures in a culture based on the masses. At this point, the aerodynamic relationships are now obvious—luxurious and winning—that the Italian design of the '30s and '40s (with the exemplary reference to the Cisitalia Berlinetta with Pininfarina bodywork and the ETR 300 electric train called the *Settebello*, designed by Giulio Minoletti) is reinforced and sustained in the Ferrari design, like many other items on a smaller and more functional scale, domestic even, like the espresso coffee maker designed by Giovanni Ponti for La Pavoni, the Olivetti Lexicon 80 typewriter designed by Marcello Nizzoli, and the Necchi sewing machines.

This experimental vocation will not be a winner. Just as in the film that here serves as our sociological backdrop, not even in the decadent and fast context, trivial and hero-comical, of the mass culture of the '60s, the flow of tourists, the crowded beaches, the bodies and the voices of the pop songs, is it possible to reach a conclusion, to overcome the insuperable barrier of Italian comedy.

The ending is tragic, not to punish Bruno for his frivolity but to confirm it, to make it coincide with destiny, to throw it back into the daily life to which it belongs, to its clamour, its absence of myth. Thus—in the accident caused by speed and competition which had enraptured the protagonists—the nature of being *different, foreign, a person* is sacrificed, as is the travelling companion, Roberto, a youth given up to his forbears' culture, to their incapacity to be heroes.

The Ferrari, however, does not belong to this destiny and does not live in that evil obscurity which undermines the model of the Italian comedy film, just as the social figures to which it refers within a few years will no longer be represented in a collective form.

An understanding of the reasons for the failure of the forms of this experiment—pursued on an arts level, by a type of well refined Expressionist writing by Gianfranco Contini, and on a company level by the experience of Adriano Olivetti—can be culled from an extraordinary letter which Carlo Emilio Gadda sent to Leonardo Sinisgalli, when the latter became director of the review *Civiltà delle Macchine*.

In those pages, written in 1953, Gadda concentrated on two points of great

historic importance for an understanding of the contents and forms of the Ferrari, its style: the aesthetics of the "design engineer" as a strategist of "mechanical truth", like a sensitive interpreter of a "sublimated quality"; and the anthropological nature of the machine as a modern *truing of* the nature of man himself, "an extension of human working", a form of thought which "in reality only belongs to man, who designed and created it".

Gadda shows an awareness here that later faded, or was too isolated, to allow him to become the leader of a national project. This would just follow the normal paths of the same middle-class realism of a narrator and intellectual like Alberto Moravia, who was strategically far removed from experimentalism.

Moravia, in 1953, once again in a letter to Sinisgalli of *Civiltà delle Macchine*, ended up interpreting the relationship between men and machines in terms which correspond to the image proposed by large factories like Fiat.

Moravia showed an enlightened point of view as he described an objective process: "really perfect machines, able to do by themselves the work which today is done by man, finally allowing man to live a human life, free and complete, in touch with nature and its limits. All this could seem Utopia, but I cannot see any alternative: either the machines are abolished and we go back

Engine and cylinder head
of the Ferrari F50.

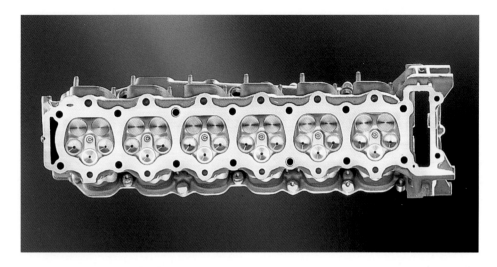

to handcrafts (which is neither possible nor desirable) or we free man from the machines through the use of the machine itself".

This stance, which was blatantly betrayed and offended, refers to Moravia, many years later, who was shocked and angry about the death of Pier Paolo Pasolini—suicide/murder. It is precisely the car that is both the symbolic and real means of execution, acting on the body of an artist who was, at least in appearance, anti-technology (besides the car, is not cinema technology as well?), however it is a Gadda-type example of a subjective and experimental approach to modernity. This move in the discussion about Ferrari towards the vaster question of the sense of relationships between men and machines is necessary, because it is this which it chiefly represents, but at the same time hides. Objecting to the sort of debate which in Italy has demonstrated all its endemic incapacity for bearing the comparison with the forms that modern design, pushed to the extreme, would have required; the Ferrari was instead the essence of a different response, where, as Gadda wrote, "man's control becomes design". The Ferrari is a symbol of an object that does not renounce its aristocratic roots in beauty, though it still makes use of—indeed, because it makes use of—the democratic vitality of goods to propagate itself as a value. It is the full, and not just symbolic, equivalent of

the "Renaissance city as time machine" (Paolucci, 1993), as a space-time construction which pushes itself into the world of television: the beauty of Ferrari lives "within the walls of the small community" (Carmagnola, 1992), which is still subject to a superior cosmic order, perfectly integrated in an unchangeable society, but all the same it glows in the presence of the market as universality of the senses and sentiments, as a symbolic value available to everybody, a technological *gift*.

We have tried to grasp at least some of the *passages* that Ferrari has made to become an aesthetic project to the umpteenth power, in the sense that the materials and the engine, like the public and the client, are dematerialised in the form of a single simulacrum. To do this, we have followed the same track indicated by Carmagnola in his fundamental essay *Luoghi della qualità*, in which everything that is described as initiative or fortune of Ferrari, is already deeply-rooted in modern development, anticipated in the relationships between production and consumption, and in any case implicit in the changes of technology in the communicative universe of goods.

It is not true that the history of contemporary art, its critical ideology, can dig up or discern (Dorfles, 1962) between those who are moved by the seduction of ostentatious consumption and publicity, and those who would always manage to revive the autonomous power of artistic expression. The difference is not between a design which is consciously art and a design which merely follows the trends, but rather between those works of art—no matter what content and or function they may have—that are more or less capable of affirming the traditional values of aesthetics and works that try to escape.

The complexity to which we allude today, looking at the scenarios of crisis and sensory saturation (Manzini, 1990; Carmagnola, 1998), shows that each attempt at un-defining art contains the contradiction of believing in its original models, of not being able to deny them. In this sense—showy as the red colour in which it is dressed and the classes it serves—the Ferrari represents and spreads the most explicit mass version of the dictates of modern authority, of its beautiful forms.

According to Carmagnola's accurate description (1994), the map of modern objects may be divided into two great historic extensions that are dialectic with each other, and a third movement, entirely immersed in the Postmodern sensibility of the *consumption producer*. The modern technological object has moved away from the utility regime to the beauty regime, according to the process that philosophy and sociology have defined as beautifying daily life; the object of art, however, has moved away from the regime of formal beauty to the restless and enlarged, expansive and deformed regime of "aesthetic indifference (an-aesthetics)".

And therefore—directing our attention to the revolution in knowledge of the third movement, which hoped to unmask the correspondence between technological objects and objects of art—what does the consumer of the Ferrari image produce, here and now? I believe that the Ferrari—its taut and shiny body—just like its engine, at

Suspension set and back brake disk of the Ferrari F50.

each new race, is living in the inter-zone of collective myths (Abruzzese, 1998). It does not prove just its overtaking, but, thanks to its emblematic capacity, also the set of modern factors which it has given form to and which the integrally anaesthetic horizon of a non-modern culture, really contemporary, should overshadow.

A final sovereign beauty reigns in this Ferrari Form which always skims along the line between itself and the negation of itself, launched in the expectation that the modern project is openly declared as the empty scene of a wonderful yet terrible battlefield. The quality of Italian style which we have attributed, in a special way, to the Ferrari, is flanked by many signs like organic and inorganic parasites—*cyber space and crash*—of an anti-modern dissipation (see for example Giacomo Marramao and Paolo Desideri, in *Gomorra*, 1998), which our country has experienced as much as the other countries of the world where the Maranello car still speeds through, like a symbol of power or a cult object.

Pedal set of the F50.

Bibliographic References

A. Abruzzese, *La bellezza per te e per me*, Bompiani, Milan 1998.

F. Carmagnola, *Luoghi della qualità. Estetica e tecnologia nel postindustriale,* Domus Academy, Milan 1991.

F. Carmagnola, *Dall'impero trasparente. Otto dialoghi sulla tradizione,* Guerini e Associati, Milan 1992.

F. Carmagnola, *Della mente e dei sensi. Oggetti dell'arte e oggetti del design nella cultura contemporanea,* Anabasi, Milan 1994.

F. Carmagnola, *Parentesi perdute. Crisi della forma e ricerca del senso nell'arte contemporanea,* Guerini e Associati, Milan 1998.

V. Castronuovo, "Premesse e attuazione del miracolo", in *Italia moderna. Immagini e storia di un'identità nazionale,* vol. III, Electa, Milan 1983.

A. Colonetti, *I segni delle cose. Grafica, design, comunicazione,* la casa Usher, Florence 1990.

P. Desideri, "I laboratori della paralisi", in *Gomorra,* no. 1, 1998.

G. Dorfles, *Simbolo, comunicazione, consumo,* Einaudi, Turin 1962.

C. Emilio Gadda, "Lettera", in *"La Civiltà delle Macchine". Antologia di una rivista 1953-1957,* Libri Scheiwiller, Milan 1989.

V. Gregotti, *Il disegno del prodotto industriale. Italia 1860-1980* , Electa, Milan 1982.

E. Manzini, *Artefatti. Verso una nuova ecologia dell'ambiente artificiale,* Domus Academy, Milan 1990.

G. Marramao, "Confini della identità e della differenza", in *Gomorra,* no. 1, 1998.

A. Moravia, *"Lettera",* in *"La Civiltà delle Macchine". Antologia di una rivista 1953-1957.*

G. Paolucci, "La città rinascimentale come macchina del tempo e Leon Battista Alberti", in *Le ideologie della città europea dall'umanesimo al romanticismo,* edited by Vittorio Conti, Olschki, Florence 1993.

R. Pierantoni, "Un feticcio contadino", in *Verità a bassissima definizione,* Einaudi, Turin 1998, which contains: "Enzo Ferrari's rural dream is a farmer's fetish, it is a dream of transparency, lightness, speed and escape, born in the emptiness of the open countryside, deserted by cars".

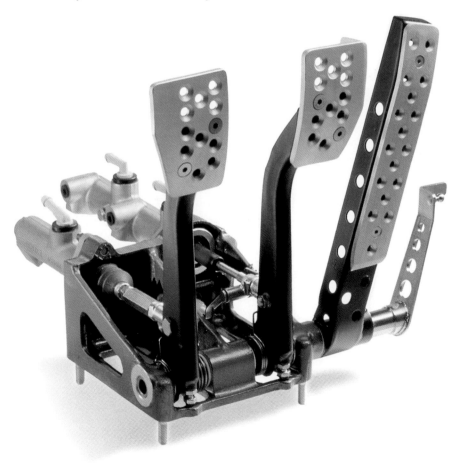

Andrea Rauch

Import-Export Graphics

From Livorno to Paris

When Leonetto Cappiello moved to Paris from his native Livorno in 1897, the world of "sign-making", as it was called then, was still heavily dominated by the leading Belle-Epoque graphic designers Jules Chéret and Henri de Toulouse-Lautrec. However, Chéret and Toulouse-Lautrec had experienced the age of Impressionism to varying degrees, and were an important part of the life and culture of the *tabarin*. Cappiello, with little more to recommend him than his youth (he was born in 1875), fell immediately and effortlessly into step with the dominant trends and tastes; his first works as a poster designer, or *affichiste*, were quite close to Chéret's "manner", employing the usual turn-of-the-century armament of leggy dancers and sharp-cornered singers. A skilled caricaturist (he worked with a number of Paris newspapers during his early years in France), Cappiello obviously paid close attention to the lessons of the great masters. Posters such as those for Odette Dulac, or for the Folies-Bergère, immediately recalled the many Moulin-Rouge works by Toulouse-Lautrec, but the melancholy cheer of the latter turned to calm cordiality with Cappiello; even if Odette Dulac, like Yvette Guilbert and Jane Avril, did adopt the languorous mood of her times, there's no hint of it

in the likeness smiling at us from the poster.

The decisive turning point for Cappiello came in 1904, when he fully achieved not only his own drawing "style", but a true "ideology" of graphic art. Indeed, Cappiello gradually but decisively distanced himself from every model of reference, however illustrious, to develop his own "mythology" that eventually became his signature and the key to his portentous international success. Life—real or idealised—tended to leave his works, making room instead for a highly personal world of elves, masks, and demons. Far from attempting an improbable escape to a sort of "poster Arcadia", Cappiello tried to reconstruct every product image in a symbolic-emblematic fashion, using a full-fledged meta-language to which the product could refer, far beyond any realistic definition. The drawn image stood out sharply from every coloured background, almost as though cut out and laid there, preserving its own important central perspective (with his characteristic upward viewpoint), and it always managed to remain in one's mind as an icon (quite a Renaissance undertaking) in place of the merchandise. "In my view," stated the artist in 1939, "a poster must be first and foremost a graphic experience, an act of authority over the passer-by. A

Max Huber, advertisement for Studio Boggeri, 1940.

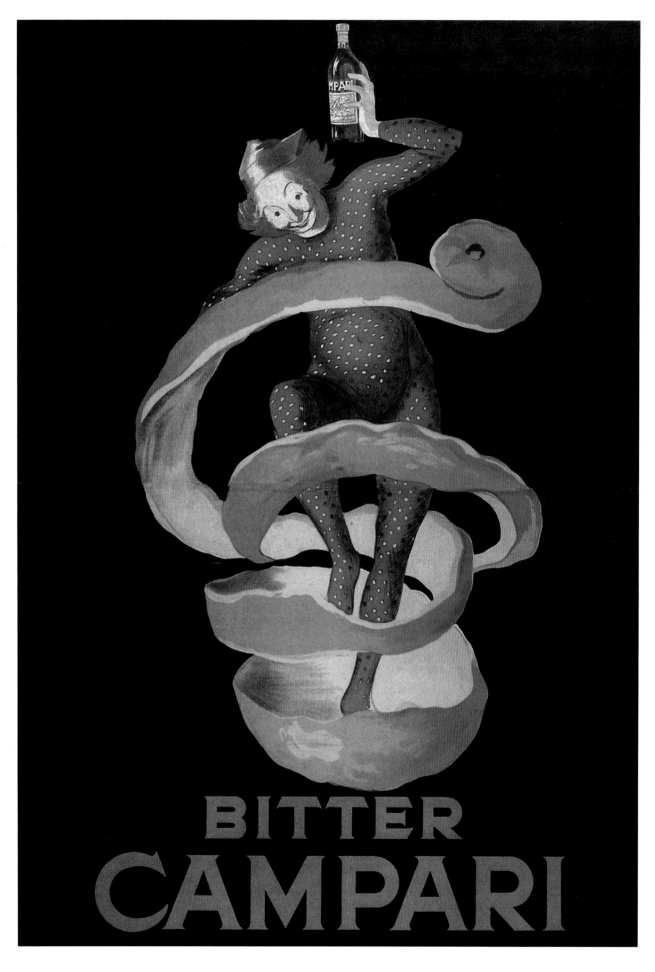

Leonetto Cappiello, poster for Bitter Campari, 1921.

Leonetto Cappiello, poster for OXO Liebig, 1911.

well-thought-out, well-executed poster can make a product famous in a short time, or give new strength to an old, forgotten one."[1] And: "You may never recall a single poster that became famous for how it depicted the product. All the posters you remember have stuck in your memory because of the image invented by the artist, which becomes indivisible from the product and its name".[2]

In terms of stimulating recall, Cappiello probably has no equal in the history of graphic art: just think of his famous posters for Campari, Thermogène, OXO Liebig, Bouillon Kub. The importance of the latter two images goes well beyond their formal value—however great—and is also exceptionally significant from a... how should we put it? conceptual standpoint in defining the philosophy of modern graphic art. Since it's true that there tend to be two distinct, coexisting fields in a poster—the typographic field, explicating the verbal message of the ad, and the image, which highlights its narrative and/or suggestive message—it is consequently obvious that a good poster is one in which both fields are perfectly integrated, with neither prevailing over the other, without any grating contrast. In Cappiello's posters for OXO and Kub, the short, essential lettering not only blends perfectly with the image, but becomes an illustration in and of itself, in essence creating a single, powerful field of suggestion and communication, highlighting the typographical and illustrative content as the two cease to exist on separate planes.

Cappiello's work was impressive in terms of quality, quantity and influence. In 1928 a group of young French graphic artists working in advertising, including Cassandre, Paul Colin and Jean Carlu, wrote in *Vendre*, "to us, you have been the proof that one could do real artistic work, without diminishing its value, while replacing the walls of official galleries with advertising posts".[3]

Yet Cassandre, the most illustrious signatory of the elegy, soon left the path broken by his mentor to turn his attention to the new experiences of volumetric and constructivist graphics. More obvious traces of Cappiello's influence can instead be found in all works by the last great French *affichiste*, Raymond Savignac, who personally made extraordinary use of an aspect present—though not central—in Cappiello's work: irony. But Cappiello's lesson can be most clearly felt in the fusion of text and image (remember OXO and Kub). In Savignac's work, the brilliant intuition of first overcoming and then creating a sort of osmosis between the fields of typography and art is pursued with such meticulousness and care that it becomes style. Images such as those for Monsavon, Maggi and Vespa integrate the lettering so thoroughly into the drawing that they have become examples of effective advertising and clear communication. Cappiello was obviously a reference point for several generations of graphic artists and sign-makers. In some ways, his lesson was carried to high levels. We have already mentioned Cassandre and Savignac, Paul Colin and Jean Carlu. We find a few of the most important syntactic expedients of Cappiello's work (the centrally-placed figure isolated from a monochrome background, separating it from the surrounding messages, for instance) in posters by Armando Testa, Celestino Piatti, Herbert Leupin. And we find much of his "mythology" in the work of the American artist Milton Glaser (here we could open a long parenthetical remark emphasising the graphic debts that even the founder of Push Pin Studios had with Italy, since right after the Second World War he came to complete his artistic training in Bologna, at the Academy of Art, under Giorgio Morandi).

... and from Bologna!
But the true heir to Cappiello's experience was another Italian, from

Bologna: Severo Pozzati (Sepo), who in some ways was his opposite and in others his superior.

While Cappiello had attempted throughout his work to remove the product's true physiognomy to re-create an icon, with semantic features and a life of its own, in Sepo's long career as an *affichiste* (he was also in Paris between 1920 and 1958) he always began with the real, tangible object, using graphic transposition to emphasise its essential communicative features. Sepo's posters are thus not populated by sprites and rural divinities, but by more prosaic starched collars and slices of cake, coloured ribbons and oil-packed sardines. Emphasising the novelty of Sepo's conceptual and artistic framework, Primrose Leigh wrote in 1931, "It takes a great deal of talent to forcefully, gracefully render collars, sardines and spools of thread. There is no great aesthetic appeal in a sardine. Even a magnificently painted still life of a sardine would have trouble being highly inspirational. A Picasso or a Matisse wouldn't dare challenge a sardine on canvas, especially if dead, and canned to boot".[4]

At first glance, the difference between Sepo and Cappiello appears to be significant from a conceptual standpoint, although their technical procedure is the same: an element, the product or its anthropomorphic metaphor, becomes fully central to communication for Sepo, and stands isolated and distant on the poster, far from the other images surrounding it on the same street, the same wall. Where Cappiello's self-referential procedure had attempted to grab the spectator's eye using colour, invention, imagination, Sepo always kept in close contact with his referent, offering a version that may not be authentic, but is at least plausible.

Sepo was affected by the changing artistic climate, as was Cassandre in the same period; the Art Nouveau world that rose to the fore before Cappiello's time had given way to the *vulgata* of Futurism and Cubism. Sepo constantly referred to the latter in his more mature and best-known works, with their figures dissected and rearranged in design and colour, and geometrically squared lettering. Famous posters such as the one for Van Houten Cocoa or Noveltex certainly cannot be extrapolated from the artistic climate in Paris at the time they were drawn, nor can they fail to reflect the care, as we mentioned, that the artist dedicated to trying to highlight the product and "make it talk".

Cappiello and Sepo are perfect specimens of the export half of the import-export equation we rhetorically used to describe graphic arts in Italy. They represent it because, in both cases, their original culture served as a launching pad for a highly diverse and autonomous experience, and not an inhibiting shackle. The Italian-ness of the two artists, their roots, were never questioned, but rather exalted and specified in the "other" culture they found themselves working in. On the other hand, there was no lack of contact with the most attentive portion of Italian industry, from Cinzano to Motta, Campari to Borletti. Cappiello and Sepo were in the ideal position to revitalise their two reference cultures—original and adopted—because they became an active part of them, and because to a large degree both were able and obliged to move on to critical evaluation. Thus, by initially sacrificing Italian-style graphic narration (aimed at melodramatic, theatrical action and realistic representation: think of Metlicovitz, Hohenstein, Dudovich, and how they were influenced by the lessons of Mucha), but also that sketchy sentimentalism always lurking in French art (and to which even the aforementioned great artists Chéret and Toulouse-Lautrec were not entirely immune), Cappiello and Sepo were at an ideal crossroads, where many of the new paths in graphic arts intersected and led.

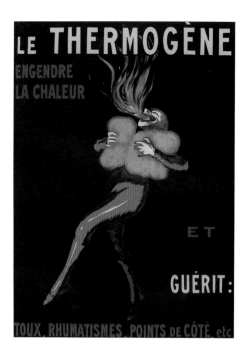

Leonetto Cappiello, poster for Thermogène, 1909.

Antonio Boggeri and the Spider Web

"Perfection was not good enough for him. One day, crouching down to compact his one-metre-eighty-five frame and raising his long, slender hands, he confided his spider web theory to me: like a spider web, Swiss graphic art was perfect, but often of a useless perfection. The spider web would become useful only when a fly dashed its meticulous structure."[5]

This is how Bruno Monguzzi recalls Antonio Boggeri thirty years later, offering in just a few lines a physical, professional and moral portrait of the man.

The figure of Antonio Boggeri is central to any contemplation of graphic art in this century. Not only because, like a lightning rod, he attracted all the moods that passed through European graphic design from the '30s to the '70s, but because he was always able to coagulate those moods around a precise, clear cultural design.

The opening of Studio Boggeri (Milan, 1933) is a date that marks what can be described, without fear of exaggeration, as an epochal upheaval in Italy in terms of how the potential and processes of graphic design were conceived. Several decades ahead of his time, Boggeri organised his studio based on the assumption that the graphic designer plays a central role, between the client and the printer, in correctly and completely overseeing every step of the communication process. And that's not all: the Studio was not limited to producing individual projects, but also offered to develop complex image "systems"; it did not stop at design, but took part in every stage of the project, from printing to layout, from illustration to photography. "Graphics," Antonio Boggeri said many years later, "to me represented acquiring a language that was more than different, that was opposite the repertory accumulated on the untouchable ruins of classic typography. It had to deal with new needs for communicating with images, whose visual impact went beyond the secular framework of reading."[6]

Boggeri immediately realised that a complex, ambitious plan like his needed contributions from many sources, and could not be identified or held back by the exclusive creativity of a single artist, no matter how brilliant. This realisation laid the foundation for the modern concept of the graphic team that has developed in recent years. Thus the Studio opened its doors (for more than forty years) to diverse experiences, which he was capable of reducing to a standard language while still respecting and highlighting the peculiarities of each. His list of associates was impressive in terms of both quality and quantity. To name just a few, and omitting a great many deserving names, we might recall Kathe Bernhardt and Imre Reiner (the first to arrive at the Studio after the 1933 Triennial Exhibition), Xanty Schawinsky and Max Huber, Albe Steiner and Walter Ballmer, Carlo Vivarelli and Aldo Calabresi, Bob Noorda and Erberto Carboni, Franco Grignani and Giancarlo Iliprandi, Enzo Mari and Bruno Munari, Remo Muratore and Marcello Nizzoli, Roberto Sambonet and Heinz Waibl. And, of course, Bruno Monguzzi as we mentioned earlier. It was essentially an Olympus of European graphic design.

What remains to be seen is the "give-and-take" within the import-export logic we have imposed on these notes: how much innovation was *imported* into Milan from design experiences throughout Europe, and how much each of the designers *exported* from their background as they continued their profession beyond and outside the Studio. Certainly the contribution of artistically complex personalities with well-defined professional experience, masters at the uses of illustration as well as photography and typography (Schawinsky foremost) helped the young designers at the Studio by acting as an example and inspiration. "In this case we can see, in the history of Studio Boggeri, a sort of field school that filled

Leonetto Cappiello, poster for Bouillon Kub, 1931.

the gap in Italy, which had no specific schools like those in Germany, Switzerland and England aimed at training professionals capable of preparing projects that combined design, typography and photography into coherent units of expression".[7]

Of course it would be near-sighted to assign Antonio Boggeri the role of a kind of talent scout, or team manager for the Studio.

Since the mid-'20s (thus before his professional epiphany) Boggeri clearly imagined the communicative potential of photography, at that time almost entirely neglected by graphic designers in Italy, relegated to purely illustrating events or, even worse, as unfinished backgrounds for the artist. He was instinctively drawn to the new areas emerging in this field in Europe; he reflected on the Bauhaus experiences of Moholy-Nagy and experiments by Rodchenko and Lissitzky. Closing his preface to the photographic yearbook *Luci e Ombre* in 1929, he wrote: "When advertising photography tends to detach itself from easy, figurative *Verismo* and draw upon the results of a less obvious form of communication, it takes advantage of the results of experimental research that have meanwhile come to light—such as the individual exposure—to enrich its visual language".

Photography always had a role in Boggeri's personal work, and served as the main means of expression by which he always tried to achieve the values of graphic "seduction" and spectacular communication that would serve to dash the spider web of cold, formal rigour, as Bruno Monguzzi recalled.

Across the Ocean

In Milan in the '30s, in the Galleria, Antonio Boggeri surely came across a pair of foreign youths who, with a bit of luck, could be seen taking part in serious billiard games in the cafés of Città Studi. Leo Lionni and Saul Steinberg (the latter even worked with the Studio, though only by accident) represent a strange *imported* figure that becomes an *export*, but later returns in a mature form to become a significant *import* item. Of Dutch birth the former, son of a diamond cutter and a Mozartian singer, Romanian the latter, architectural student at the Polytechnic, both were wandering around during those years in search of an artistic and professional dimension. Lionni had already experienced a slice of that "wandering Jew" life that always characterised him, and had already been through Brussels, Philadelphia, Genoa, and Zurich; he had already exhibited with the latest Futurists, and Marinetti

Sepo (Severo Pozzati), poster
for Motta, 1934.

Sepo (Severo Pozzati), poster
for Van Houten Cocoa, 1926.

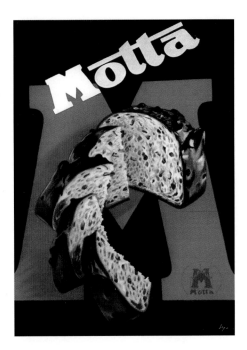

Sepo (Severo Pozzati), poster
for Motta, 1934.

Sepo (Severo Pozzati), poster
for Van Houten Cocoa, 1926.

had enthusiastically labelled him an
"aeropainter".

"I had never been in an aeroplane,"
he later recalled, "and it sounded rather
ridiculous to me. I didn't care for this
rhetoric about the world seen from
above."[8]

In Milan Lionni worked with the Motta
graphics department (Dino Villani) and
Persico and Pagano's *Casabella* before
trying his hand at freelancing; the latter
was abruptly interrupted by the
enactment of racial discrimination laws
(1938), and thus he returned for the
second time to the United States.
"Alone, with just a few dollars in my
pocket, I landed in New York. Luckily
my father had worked with a big
company in Philadelphia, and there, at
the advertising agency Ayer and Son,
I had the opportunity to meet first
Charles Coiner, then Leon Karp, whose
assistant I became… My first projects
were ads for American Steel Mills and a
few layouts for the magazine *Coffins and
Sunnyside*. From Italy I had brought
with me an imagination and creativity
that perhaps were rare in America, but
they had an extraordinary degree of
professionalism. I remember that once
I said I considered myself to be a
hundred per cent Italian and a hundred
per cent American; maybe I was
referring to these two components: the

creativity I had learned in Italy, and the
solid professionalism I had learned in
the United States."[9]

First in Philadelphia, then in New York,
Lionni came up against not only that
American professional situation, but
also that part of European Rationalism
("the Bauhaus Diaspora", as Giovanni
Anceschi called it) that had sought
refuge from Nazi persecution on the
new continent. He taught at Black
Mountains College under the guidance
of Joseph Albers, alongside Matter and
Bayer. As a consultant for Olivetti of
America, the New York Museum of
Modern Art, the Metropolitan
Museum, UNESCO, and especially as
art director for *Fortune*, he made a
decisive contribution to defining a new
American graphic style, strongly
mediated by the design and
methodological approach of European
Rationalism. In this, Lionni—along
with Paul Rand, Saul Bass and a few
others—was truly a founding father of
US graphic design, because his work
managed to be as "refined" as a
European and as "immediate" as an
American, all with the utmost
naturalness and depth. His designs from
those years, from the cover of the photo
volume *The Family of Man* posters for
the MOMA, to the "arch-graphic"
design for the USA pavilion

"The Unfinished Business" at the 1958 Brussels World Fair (dedicated to the civilised topics of racism, the home, and water, and decorated inside with drawings by none other than Saul Steinberg), are always strongly affected by this ideal framework. A sort of "salad" of colour that slowly but surely unwinds from the chaotic to the rational, from the indeterminate to the definite: "creativity" adapting to the "design".

Lionni returned to Italy in the late '50s, bringing with him the trends and experience of American editorial graphics. He directed the first series of Mondadori's *Panorama*, a publication with a broad cadence and scope, and especially dedicated himself to sculpting, drawing and illustrating children's books. Lionni's influence and lessons in the latter were truly unique, since he always managed to blend his experience— including moral experience—as a designer and cultured man with the more mundane requirements of the market (see his extraordinary *Little Blue and Little Yellow*).

Saul Steinberg also had to leave Italy due to the racial laws in 1940, after a brief but intense period of collaboration with Giovanni Mosca's *Bertoldo*. In New York he began working with the *New Yorker*, which—then and for nearly sixty years—was his professional *raison d'être* and primary laboratory for artistic experiment. Today, Steinberg is considered one of the most important visual artists of our times; his work always revealed a glimpse of his European training, but also the "openness" of the American frontier. The vastness and solitude of space, the gigantic size of the architecture and nature of that new continent, find an ideal counterpoint in the almost maniacal minutiae of Steinberg's pen strokes, that constant densification and dispersion of lines, the continuous upward motion of his markings. Steinberg's "American diaries" (but, earlier still, his extraordinary illustrated reportages from Italy, North Africa, China, and India, following the Allied troops) are sharp notes of reality, with a significant and unhidden charge of social and political criticism, together with a disillusioned, bitter resignation. "In America, one has no illusions that life is a romantic thing, something one can dictate according to one's whims. Here life is really that painful thing we have to put up with. This is a stoic country, that reveals at all times our shared fate of having to put up with life. This, in short, is a land where one lives without illusions."[10]

But Steinberg's work also contains that

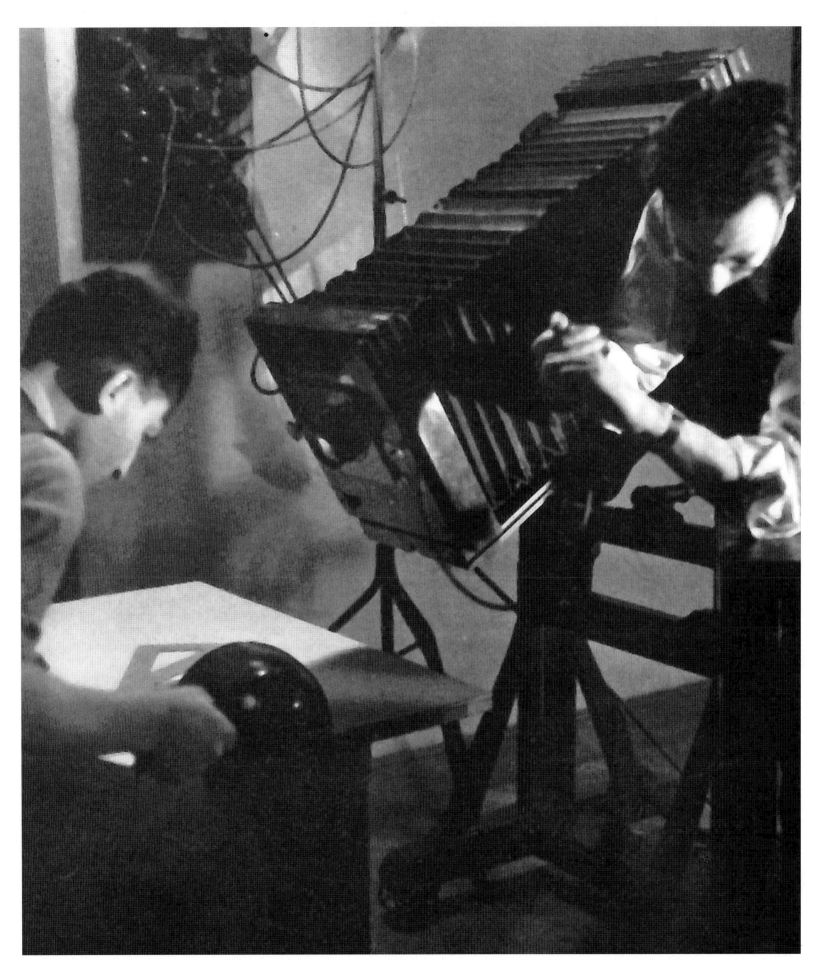

continuous, self-referential account of graphic design that celebrates itself, the line that draws its own tale, the paper that generates other images of paper from its folds or graphs.

The Utopia of Olivetti
"In order for a true logotype to exist and work, it is not enough for there to be a close association between the meaning of the graphic design and the meaning of the word: it takes perseverance, repetition of that nexus and its isolation from all other written discourse. In the case of Olivetti, the reader must simultaneously grasp the message contained in the name of the company (with all its aspects of technical quality, international character with Italian roots, research in all fields of information and communication) and the graphic message, consisting of solidity, cordiality, immediacy, duration. Now it should be said that this type of association has been made possible in our century, paradoxically, by the cultural diffusion of an inverse, opposite procedure: that which separates sign and meaning, which for a fraction of time steals the function of supporting a verbal value from typographic characters and leaves it to graphics alone. In other words, it is the multiplication of the written word in the modern city that makes it possible to separate words from writing… We experience it every day, walking alongside enormous elements of the alphabet, between advertising and signs. Constant separating and re-combining, without going beyond that, is inherent in symbolic thought, and today it is what we live in."[11]
Thus wrote Franco Fortini in his notes on the redesign of the Olivetti trademark (Walter Ballmer, 1971). Notes that bear witness to the attention to theory and cultural depth that the Ivrea company constantly used to assess itself in the general topics of communication and design.
Just as we saw, in the "Boggeri case", the will of a designer rise to become arbiter

and mediator between the demands of the client and those of the printer (obviously without ever losing sight of the spectator's interests), in the "Olivetti case" the company itself becomes the mediator between its, shall we say, commercial needs and its cultural desires, bringing the most strongly felt aspects of the "project culture" to interact at the theoretical and operative levels.
It was the generous utopia of Adriano Olivetti that, from the '30s on, conceived the grandiose project of integrating strictly corporate needs with those of design and industrial architecture, graphics, advertising, communication. Olivetti called upon architects such as Pollini and Figini, Peressutti, Belgiojoso and Nathan Rogers, graphic artists such as Munari, Carboni and Veronesi, designers such as Nizzoli. Plus, in no particular order, Zanuso and Bellini, Scarpa and Gardella, Schawinsky and Nivola, down to its prestigious international collaboration with Paul Rand and Cassandre, Savignac and Bayer, right up to nearer our own time with the lovely posters by Milton Glaser and the poetic images of Jean Michel Folon.
However, while it is true that Olivetti's overall image derives from a sort of continuous synergy between the client and the work of individual designers, it is also true that certain episodes of this collaboration certainly weigh more heavily on the scale of the company's image. Here we are referring to the long, fundamental total art direction run by Giovanni Pintori from 1950 to 1968, and the work of Marcello Nizzoli, parallel to Pintori's but aimed at defining product design.
Giovanni Pintori produced hundreds of ads, brochures, and posters for Olivetti; he designed booths for trade shows and exhibitions. He based his work on graphic research contemporary to European Rationalism, and exerted his influence on designers such as Leo Lionni (who, along with Costantino Nivola, will later oversee publicising

The Family of Man

Leo Lionni, cover for the catalogue *The Family of Man*, photographic exhibition at the Museum of Modern Art, New York, 1955.

Leo Lionni, USA Pavilion *The Unfinished Business,* Brussels World Fair, 1958.

Leo Lionni, *Portrait of Saul Steinberg*, 1937.

Below and opposite: Saul Steinberg, *Italy*, in *All in Line*, Duell, Sloan & Pearce, New York 1945.

Olivetti's image in America) and Paul Rand (who paid him public homage on more than one occasion). The poetics Pintori applied for Olivetti tried to veer away from easily identifiable styles or stereotypes, skilfully using both the rhetorical devices of metaphor and the more usual, "flat" expedients of product photography and illustration. Graphic art may thus be brought to the forefront as a sole metaphorical device for communication, or settle in the background and soberly contribute to the whole message, as a texture. In any case, the personality of Pintori "the graphic designer" was not at all negatively affected by this voluntary voiding within the company's overall image. This lack of a jealous search for his own stylistic cipher became, at the same time, the overall graphic style of Olivetti, and through the widespread international diffusion of its industrial communication programme, it also became the style by which Italy was recognised and admired from outside for many years.

The Soul of Post-Modern Design
Among the many designers who crossed paths in the Olivetti project, a significant role was certainly played by Ettore Sottsass who, in the late '60s, designed the Valentine portable typewriter, and also conceived its

graphic and advertising campaign, later defined by Roberto Pieraccini and Egidio Bonfante. The Valentine project was brand-new for the Ivrea-based company: an attempt to contact a new market segment, young people, that was about to become key. At the time, Ettore Sottsass had just returned from a long stay in the United States, where he had more than casual contact with the beat culture of Allen Ginsberg and Gregory Corso. His Valentine project cannot be fully comprehended without taking into account those years, those contacts, and the youth movements that were just beginning; behind it we can glimpse the hippie lifestyle, pages from *Pianeta fresco*, and surrogate psychedelic graphics.

However, to circumscribe an analysis of Ettore Sottsass' work to within an examination of his role and influence on international graphic art means placing a number of restrictions and limitations. Indeed, it is difficult to categorise and summarise the work of Sottsass, which was all aimed at defining an exclusive, complete relationship between the designer and reality. We must therefore refer simultaneously to Sottsass as architect and designer, decorator and craftsman. His experience with Memphis (1981-1985), in any case, was the one that best lends itself to our analysis because it falls within a context—generically described as Post-Modern—of world-wide impact, and with at least external direct references to much of contemporary graphic design. As in every other stage of his career, in Memphis Sottsass tended "to highlight that symbolic, not simply rational depth inherent in every object designed by man; an attitude that is not immediately functional, but which holds the keys needed to build a meaning, and guide the user to a level of

Milton Glaser, poster for
Valentine Olivetti, 1969.

Xanti Schawinsky, Olivetti
calendar, 1934.

'sympathy' with the object, through decorative and symbolic elements".[12] However, with the generalised and often poorly-received influence of Memphis and the "popular" international success of his proposal, that constant reflection which is the mainstay of Sottsass' design career, his thoughts on the connection between man, object and environment, became a largely exterior and superficial apparatus. Where the visual experimentation of the artist was a continuous blend of verbal, pictorial, photographic signs, always seeking out new formal balances, his influence too often—especially in a number of American experiences (remember how furiously they were opposed by Paul Rand!)—became a pretext for vacuously decorative swirls, rhetorical exercises of "marks" and "colours".

This obviously does not in any way detract from the designer, nor from the provocative strength of his work. Children often resemble their parents only fleetingly and superficially. The latter, we believe, is an export that Sottsass himself would have gladly avoided.

Underground Signs
Starting out in Amsterdam and Trieste, the paths of Bob Noorda and Massimo Vignelli crossed in Milan where, in 1965, they founded Unimark International, perhaps the most important Italian graphic design studio of the post-war era, not only in terms of the quality of their work or their sumptuous client portfolio, but also because of its instinctive openness to the international market, and the cosmopolitan scope of design that led its founders to face other cultures without fear or hesitation.
Massimo Vignelli, who soon left Unimark to establish his own studio in New York, was well known for his many idiosyncrasies, artfully disseminated to create a sort of austere, intolerant legend around him; he was known for his exclusive predilection for

red and black ("strong, lasting colours…"), his constant use of just a few, well-designed printing fonts (Bodoni, Times, Garamond, Century, Helvetica and Futura), layouts always in horizontal strips. He held a famous antipathy against new printing methods and Post-Modern graphics (but then we later find him arm-in-arm with David Carson in a souvenir photo from the Fabrica-Benetton seminars).
Right from the early days of his Unimark experience, Massimo Vignelli handled the studio's New York office (which over the years also set up branches in Chicago, where for example Heinz Waibl worked, and in Cape Town); great international notoriety soon arrived, with graphic design and sign projects for the subways of New York, Washington and São Paulo, which also allowed for field testing of that tendency toward systematic design that Vignelli drew from his experiences with Milanese graphics, and which in practice was always mitigated and made—as Boggeri would have said— "spectacular" by the brilliance of its design.
Yet, while on the one hand this insistence on an austere organisation, as Stephen Heller emphasises,[13] is one of the keys to understanding the success and international influence of Vignelli's style, on the other we certainly cannot forget the wealth of ideas and invention which always formed the foundation of his work, and which—within the most rigorous, systematic project—allowed so many exceptions to the rule that in themselves became the rule.
The letterhead to be read back-lit against the posters printed on crumpled paper-fabric; the image for Naples 99 ("Vedi Napoli e poi muori", with a good-luck charm *cornetto* as an enclosed gadget) to the signs for the exhibition *The Italian Metamorphosis* engraved on the road signs in front of the Guggenheim Museum, and fully visible only from the windows of the museum itself, everything in Vignelli's graphics seemed to refuse the label of slightly

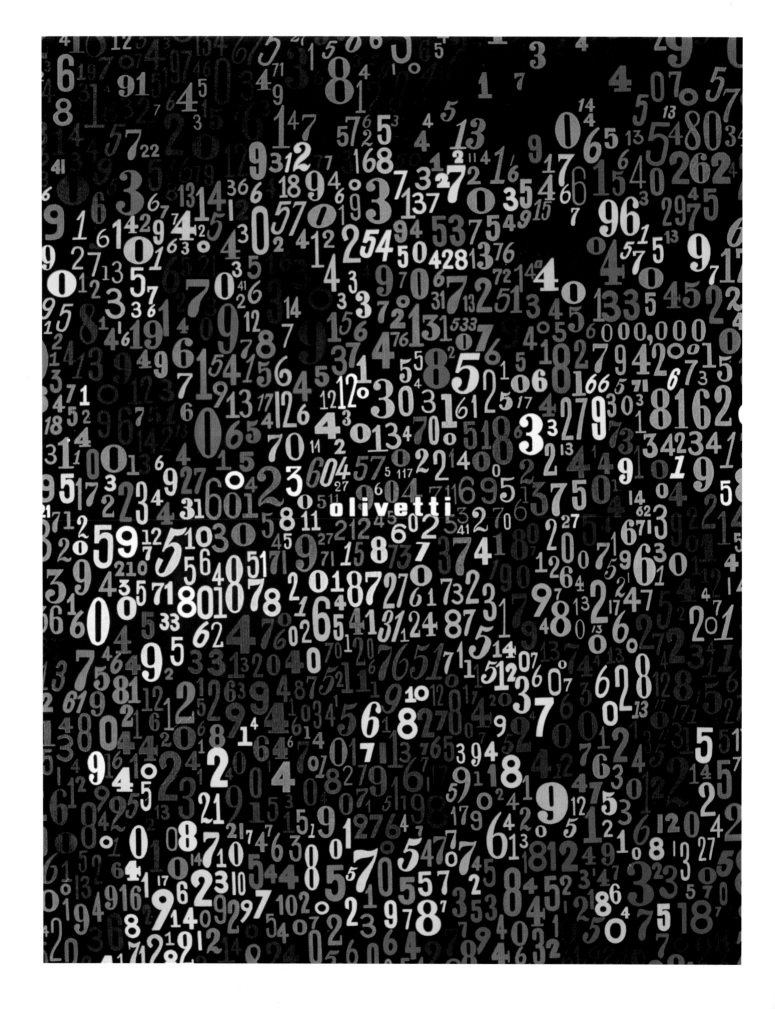

Giovanni Pintori, poster
for Olivetti, 1949.

Ettore Sottsass jr, poster
for Valentine Olivetti, 1969.

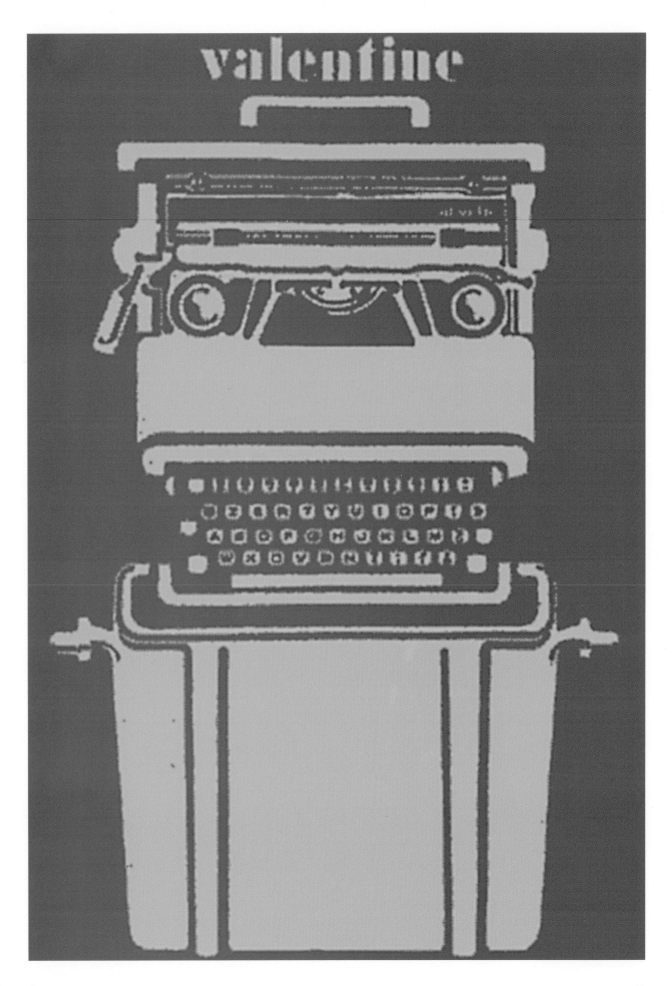

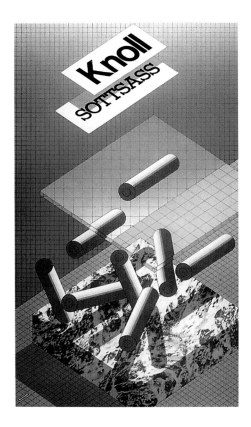

Milton Glaser, poster Sottsass,
Knoll, 1985.

glum and disagreeable pedantry that one is tempted to use on him, and instead sparkled with unexpected intelligence and wit.

The work that best incorporated the "wit-rigour" of Massimo Vignelli with the "rigour-rigour" of Bob Noorda, however, was the overall sign system and map of the New York subway. Here the graphics had to deal heavily with the most complex humus imaginable, from a complex of historical, environmental, and sociological standpoints. The system of signs showing the urban traveller where to go cannot, underground, reveal any uncertainty or ambiguity. The indifference of the architecture, the monotony and interchangeability of the horizons leave no room for mistakes, redundancy or missing indications. Thus we have the complexly essential nature of the map, that stood out quite sharply from what had been previously attempted in that field (remember the legendary map of the London transportation system) to become a pure diagram, refusing any representation of the path that was not the subway line, and with no

temptation nor justification to be representative, since any real reference points were invisible from underground.

"The map," Renato Giovannoli and Isabella Pezzini later stated, "is more like a formal (topological) structure than a view of the territory. Consisting only of dots and lines, it uses no criteria of measurement, requires no adherence to scale… The directions are reduced to a primitive weather vane: two pairs of overlapping perpendicular lines, creating 45° angles. This system no longer needs any abstract toponomastics for its points or a distinctive colour scheme for its lines."[14]

It is rather disconcerting to note, as Giovannoli and Pezzini do, that the map was replaced in 1980 with a more traditional format, closer to the city layout and road system of the overlying city. "The map that replaced Vignelli's overlays the design with a traditional physical map, it does not eliminate the curves of the lines, it restores the usual look of the city… Anyone who has seen the movie *Warriors* can get at least a narrative idea of the autonomy achieved

Alberto Olivetti, Commemorative stamp for Antonio Gramsci, 1997.

Ettore Sottsass jr, *Preliminary project for microenvironment*, drawing for the exhibition *Italy: the New Domestic Landscape*, Museum of Modern Art, New York, 1972.

by the underground city. With the new map, the subway is restored to its function for the surface, denying that autonomy. The non-humanist display of logical form is a scandal to be erased."[15]

Conclusions?

The work of Noorda and Vignelli, coming as it did at the end of that ideal "Milanese" path begun by Antonio Boggeri, in any case showed the full potential of systematic graphics to influence and contaminate every context, be it because of its endemic international vocation, its obvious cosmopolitan origins, or the relative ease with which any project can be relocated anywhere, released as it is from any vernacular culture. Thus, in our import-export project we can

include the many designers who have worked in far-off lands, starting from the Milanese school (we have already mentioned Heinz Waibl, and we might add Armando Milani, another of Vignelli's associates in New York, who later worked in the same city under his own name) or others who, although they arrived from different countries, so absorbed the rules of the "system" that they were able to export them again (in addition to Bob Noorda, consider the aforementioned Bruno Monguzzi, of Swiss origin, fully trained at Studio Boggeri and then transplanted back to Ticino).

But the overall influence of the Milanese school certainly does not stop at a mechanical, physical and professional emigration from one continent to another. The events that

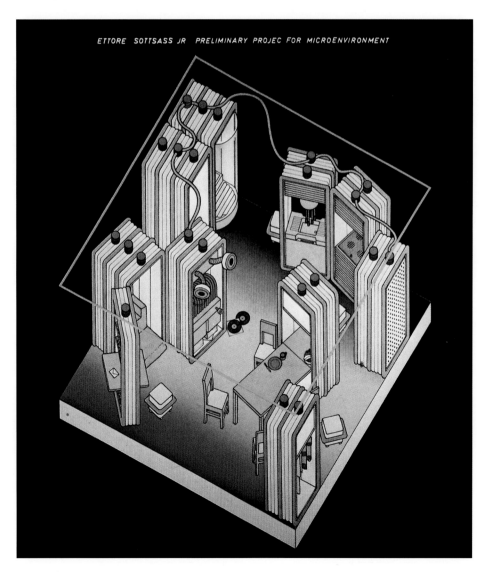

arose and took form in the post-war period are the core of that history of modern Italian graphic arts with its protagonists who, unfortunately, appear only as co-stars in this topical narration. The experiences of Bruno Munari and Franco Grignani, Max Huber and Albe Steiner, for example, or those of Giulio Confalonieri, Ilio Negri, Remo Muratore, Silvio Coppola, Pino Tovaglia, Roberto Sambonet, Giancarlo Iliprandi, maybe even down to the last Milanese Salvatore Gregorietti, Pierluigi Cerri and Italo Lupi, deserve a broader, more attentive narration than space and topic allow us here. Just as many of the new experiences of graphic design that stand between "systematic graphics" and that of "public utility" deserve a mention, which in recent years have

proven that they can play a role that is neither secondary nor irrelevant within the Italian context and in relation to Europe and the world. And also, why not delve into that frontier territory that is illustration, and which includes more than a few players of great international importance (for instance Roberto Innocenti, who has a whole collection of Golden Apples from the Bratislava Illustration Biennial, or Lorenzo Mattotti, who bounces from the cover of the *New Yorker* to that of *Le Monde*, or Paolo Guidotti, who displays his ready-made in New York along with Seymour Chwast)? Our unfulfilled curiosities are many, as there are many questions we have not been able to answer. We hope we can include it all in a future episode.

Massimo Vignelli, *USA Bicentennial poster*, 1976.

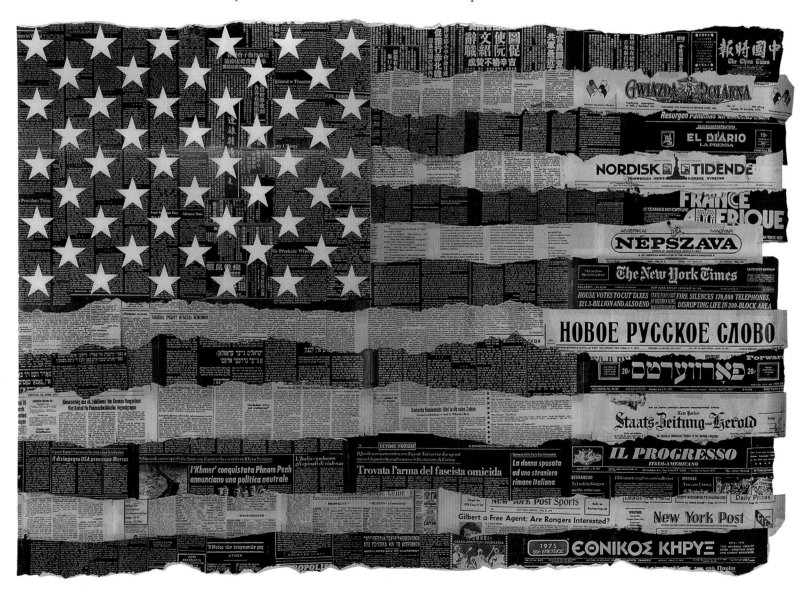

Massimo Vignelli and Bob
Noorda, sign system and map
for the New York subway, 1970.

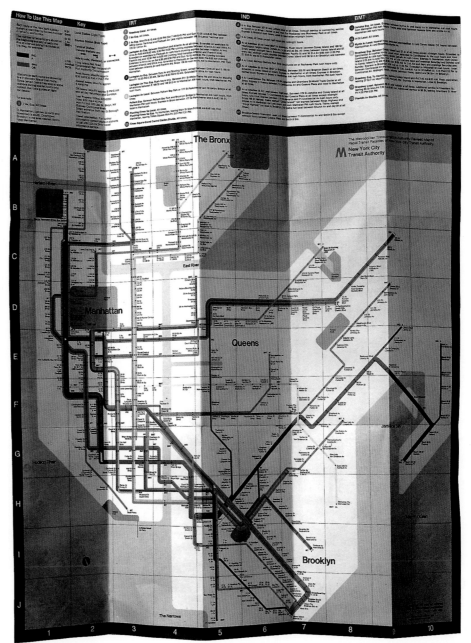

[1] "1939: un'intervista di Cappiello alla radio francese", in *Leonetto Cappiello, dalla pittura alla grafica*, Artificio, Florence 1985, p. 104.

[2] E. Matucci, "Fra Belle Époque e comunicazione di massa", in *Leonetto Cappiello*, pp. 18-19.

[3] *Ibidem*, p. 20.

[4] P. Leigh, "The French School of Poster Art", in *World Press News Advertising*, July 9th, 1931.

[5] B. Monguzzi, "La mosca e la ragnatela ovvero l'Italia e la Svizzera", in *Grafici italiani*, edited by G. Camuffo, Canal & Stamperia Editrice, Venice 1997, p. 31.

[6] "Una B rossa tra due punti. Colloquio con Antonio Boggeri", in *Rassegna*, 1981, no. 6, *Il campo della grafica italiana*, p. 20.

[7] "Lo Studio Boggeri", in *La grafica in Italia*, edited by G. Fioravanti, L. Passarelli and S. Sfligiotti, Leonardo, Milan 1998, p. 77.

[8] *Leo Lionni. Art as a Celebration*, edited by P. Vassalli and A. Rauch, Alsaba, Siena 1997, p. 107.

[9] "Alle origini della grafica italiana", conversation between Leo Lionni and Andrea Rauch, in *Grafici italiani*, p. 33.

[10] F. Cavallone, "Il filosofo mascherato", in *Linus*, no. 65, August 1970.

[11] F. Fortini, "Il logotipo, una parola-persona", in *Rassegna*, 1981, no. 6, *Il campo della grafica italiana*, p. 38.

[12] "Ettore Sottsass", in *La grafica in Italia*, p. 154.

[13] S. Heller, "Oltre l'Oceano", in *Grafici italiani*, p. 19.

[14] R. Giovannoli, I. Pezzini, "La rete profonda", in *Rassegna*, 1981, no. 6, *Il campo della grafica italiana*, p. 76.

[15] *Ibidem*.

Nathalie Grenon

Italian Design:
From the Ritual of the Espresso-Maker
to the Myth of the Mobile Phone

The look of objects is often twinkling, provocative, aggressive yet alluring, depending on the ways they will meet the user. It is an event that is repeated countless times in the space of a day, in different instants and places, according to how we divide up our time into different activities.

The intermediary between person and object is its use, which decrees the life of objects and products and which brings them to life. More, indeed, than for the individual, the use speaks for the social group as a whole.

We know and understand objects. They are ever-expanding in numbers, shapes and sizes. And yet without a *who, how, when* and *why* they are used, no meaning can be attributed to them. The sociological analyses and statistical investigation reveal preferences, tendencies, places and times of product consumption and even any important insights. By focusing observation on the pattern of Italian life, we notice that the activities making up the day take place with specific rhythms, features and cadence, in the relationship between place of work, the home, the street, and so on.

This chapter sets out to look at the material culture of this *fin de siècle* through the eyes of an archaeologist of the year 3000. We will try, therefore, to examine the findings that are, to a large extent, constituted by the objects of use.

A study of the findings, like in the 1965 novel by George Perec entitled *Les choses*, favours the eye for emphasising the visual consumption which has taken over one of content with the advent of the new society of mass consumption. The literary device of the "journey" suggested by the novel as a pilgrimage between "things" to view and (possibly) possess in the form of "Big Bouffe", exemplifies not only the Italian phenomenon but also Italian curiosity. It suggests that aesthetic vision tends to get united with fetishism over the new values of status symbol that are implicit in the object of consumption.

In 1955 Marcel Duchamp said: "I considered painting to be a means of expression and certainly not the complete purpose of life; at the same time, I considered colour as being a way to express oneself through painting— not the ultimate goal of painting itself. In other words, painting should not only be retinal or visual; it should be about the grey matter of our comprehension instead of being purely visual... By 'retinal' approach, I mean the aesthetic pleasure that depends almost solely on the retina without any auxiliary intermediation... The way *Alice in Wonderland* [the young artist of tomorrow] will pass through the mirror

Massimo Morozzi, pasta set, Alessi, 1985.

of the retina to reach deeper mines of expression... to discover new clashing values that are, and always will be, at the foundation of a revolution in art". At the basis of such assertions, we can perhaps also consider the *eye* and the visual reductionism of the complexity of reality (as far as the production and consumption of the object of use is concerned) as protagonists in this cognitive foray into material culture.

It is easy to note that the appearance of so-called "Italian design" on the world stage in the glorious '50s sprang from a style of understanding the highly distinctive form-function relationship. Vittorio Gregotti wrote: "As an overall judgement, Italian design seems above all very successful under the formal perspective. It is capable of making up for the gaps of a production that still displays large consumption imbalances (which are broadly still undergoing technological and organisational development and frequently improvised on a methodological level) with the single leap of a brilliant aesthetic solution. It is necessary to recognise that the international results of Italian design are really connected—even if in an apparently contradictory way with respect to other more industrialised countries—to its experimental and pioneering condition as regards industry, which often confines design to a wholly improvised and sideline activity or, on the contrary, sometimes raises it being responsible for fully individualising the product. On the whole, however, it makes it possible to work (under favourable circumstances) in a free space and with a greater freedom of action".

I shall begin with Carlo Mollino (1905-1973), an architect based in Turin who, of this experimental and pioneering condition, constitutes the perfect prototype. Indeed, his incredible mixture of artistic quality and techniques with an experimental and eclectic nature set him apart both in the inter-war period and, explosively, also during the '50s.

For Italy, these were the years of accelerating post-war reconstruction when everything was entrusted to the often intuitive creativeness of an entire generation of improvised new companies which—with the art of fending for themselves without any infrastructures or much planning—contributed to an instantaneous development of factories large and small particularly in the north, where imported raw materials were transformed with versatility into frequently innovative products that interpreted and changed the behaviour and rituals of a society which was optimistically projected towards so-called modernity.

"From spoon to city" was the slogan coined by Ernesto Nathan Rogers, then director of the magazine *Casabella*, to sum up this varied and all-embracing appearance on the market of such a wide range of products that were found in all aspects of daily life—from mobility on wheels (the car and scooter) to communication (radio and television sets) to habitat (the office, home, meeting places centred on the Italian *bar*, and equipment for hobbies and sports).

The inborn passion of Carlo Mollino for speed, the legacy of a Futurist mould, led him to an investigation, in a book published in 1950 under the title of *Introduzione al discesismo*, on the aerodynamic behaviour of the human body in its trajectories and forms on descending ski slopes.

The fields of experimentation were the high altitudes of the Matterhorn where Leo Gasper, one of the pioneers of modern skiing, practised this activity. Mollino, who was also a photographer, created a simulation in his own home in Turin—immortalising himself in photos that became symbolic of this technique which was full of insight—with the much more challenging real-life experimentation, where his more skilful friend is immortalised in as many frames.

It matters little that such simulations

Carlo Mollino tries the movements of a descent on skis in his own apartment. Carlo Mollino Photo Archive, Turin. The architect Carlo Mollino, due to his very fertile talent and his inexhaustible will for experimentation, is one of the figures that best represent the concept of Italian "creativity".

Top right: Photo by Carlo Mollino showing Leo Gasper during a descent. Carlo Mollino Photo Archive, Turin.

did not use a wind tunnel, which would have allowed much more precise experiments to be conducted: what matters was the intuition.

But Mollino's interest in speed was not limited to this endeavour alone. Here he is on the plane, painting acrobatic figures, and on cars, racing cars, like the 1954 Osca 1100 prototype, the 1100 Millemiglia, and the related aerodynamic research in modelling a car all round.

To follow, in 1955, the twin-bodied Damolnar, which he designed and built with Da Monte and Nardi, and drove. It was a revolutionary car with dual asymmetric bodies that was put to the test in international races for prototypes, including the 750 cc.-class Le Mans 24 hour, which it won two years running.

These accomplishments, which took in the most various of disciplines, were part and parcel of Mollino's architectural vision and which thus came through in his expression of indoor furnishing. Curved multi-layer tables, chairs, armchairs, lamps— essential structures which, once freed from immobility, preserve an unstable condition and emit a dynamic signal by means of the elastic tension of their forms, modelled according to the logic of force separation. These furniture

Bisiluro and Osca, two car prototypes by Carlo Mollino. Carlo Mollino Photo Archive, Turin.

items are the answer to the declaration by Francesco Cangiullo (1920): "Non avete mai osservato come sono immobili i vostri mobili?" (a play on words between *mobili*, furniture, and *immobili*, immobile: literally "Have you never noticed how immobile your furniture is?").

The Moment of Early-Morning Awakening
The moment of early-morning awakening is one in which day-to-day objects come to life. Emerging from the darkness, on contact with the gradually intensifying daylight, they too begin their day—starting with the alarm

clock, once characterised by a noisy tick-tock (Veglia-Borletti, 1938) but today synonymous with an electronic wail. Two memorable examples of alarm-clocks are the one by Lorenz, designed by Richard Sapper, and the Cube, which broadcast the world news and which, with its loudspeaker (model TS 502 designed by M. Zanuso and R. Sapper for Brionvega, 1964) separated from the main radio, acquired a dual personality: an inert cube shape is produced upon closure, whereas once open it reveals its real function.
The bathroom, whether modern, old-fashioned, clinical like a dentist's surgery or cosy like a living room, is not

lacking in design features: taps, bathroom fixtures, mirrors, bathroom scales, soap dish, toothbrush rack, towel rail, shower mixers, floor tiles or mosaics.
But of all the early-morning rituals, coffee making reigns as undisputed king. Italians drink coffee above all at home in company, and in a whole variety of ways: *ristretto* (extra strong), long, black, *macchiato* (white, with more or less milk becoming cappuccino, milky-coffee), *corretto* ("corrected" or fortified with grappa), with or without sugar, hot or cold. There are not only numerous product variations but also numerous different ways of making coffee: a real sampling for all tastes, from the most unbridled kitsch to the most fundamental design, from Neapoletana Delizia (produced by Verni, 1979) to the Thermos Express (produced by Meazza and Masciaroli, 1969), from Lavazza's Carmencita (M. Zanuso design, produced by Balzano, 1979) to the Nova Express (produced by Irmel, 1953), from the Cimbalina (R. Bonetto, produced by Cimbali, 1979) to the ever-popular Moka Express (A&R Bialetti design, produced by Bialetti, 1945), or to the latest edition Cobàn (designed by R. Sapper for Alessi, 1996), for "bar coffee at home" with E.S.E. (Easy Serving Espresso) technology. After soluble and decaffeinated coffee, E.S.E. technology, patented by Illy Caffè—with its use of "serving" individual doses of ground coffee, pressed and contained between two sheets of filter paper—was the most important innovation in the coffee sector in the '80s.
The irreplaceable aroma of bar coffee was thus also brought to unprofessional hands, ready to bring delight to those brief breaks that only the *tazzina* (little cup) knows how. One thousand five hundred chemical substances—800 volatile and 700 soluble—contribute to giving coffee that unique full and pleasant aroma. For a single cup of espresso coffee, about fifty perfect beans are needed: just one flawed is enough to

alter the taste of the blend. The evolution that began in the '80s was one of converting the espresso-maker into a home appliance: the new ritual of the "good coffee at the cafe" has been replaced by that of the "home-made coffee".

The first model which interpreted the mass psychological phenomenon of the Italian bar at home was the Cimbalina.

The Street

On leaving home, Italians encounters the objects of the street which eloquently throbs with the Marinettian legend of speed, turmoil of engines and noises, and whirling trajectories.
"Vehement god of a race of steel, automobile elated with its space, that chafes and quivers with anguish gnawing at the bit with strident teeth. Formidable Japanese monster,
with furnace eyes,
fed by flame
and mineral oils,
hungry for horizons and sidereal prey.
I incite your heart which thuds diabolically,
I incite your gigantic pneumatic tyres, for the dance you know how to dance away, along the white roads of all the world! ..."
On the road vehicles pass, lights flash, sounds clash, passers-by meet, mopeds zigzag: there were about half a million mopeds in 1970 and six million in 1980. Will they reach twenty million at the threshold of the year 2000?
This is a long history, full of innovations and models that have followed one after the other from the end of the war to the present day: symbolic of this development is the Vespa, born in 1946 as a "utilitarian motorbike", designed to "make sure all the mechanical moving parts were covered, that the rider could mount it easily, and would be protected with a front shield, with an ample foot plate and a smooth curve rearwards to the engine housing".
Half a century on, the shape has remained unchanged despite the vast

technological evolution taking place in the interim. Today the latest Vespa—the model ET4—is as similar to the first model as ever.

Off to Work

The factory job is the one that has undergone the most global revolution with respect to the other types of work, where the relationship between man and machine still leaves the man in a position of supremacy. In effect, the daily encounter with the object has practically vanished; the identity is one with the work space rather than with work's product itself.
The true protagonist of work in industry is no longer man. It could be the robot to some extent; but more than anything else, it is the machine used for measuring precision.
At first sight it is surprising to note how the need for increasingly more precise industrial measurement goes hand in hand with advancements in the automation of production methods. Yet in order to take account of this necessity, it is enough to think how less versatile a robot is with regard to the human operator it must replace.
The robot performing a given task in a production process is expected to receive objects almost identical in nature. It does not know how to repair a small imperfection from an upstream process with, say, the tap of hammer.
This is why precise measurement, frequently covering all aspects of the product, becomes essential at every phase of production: not only does it serve to guarantee the quality of the finished product, but also to single out and reject those articles which robots cannot deal with in subsequent processing.
The great measurement machines, fast, versatile, and capable of a level of accuracy that was inconceivable just a few years ago, are today the core of totally automatic manufacturing centres. The centres, with integrated testing facilities, resemble more a laboratory in their construction and

A table by Carlo Mollino. Carlo Mollino Photo Archive, Turin.

The Vespa ET4, Piaggio, 1996.

Richard Sapper, 9090 Espresso coffee machine, Alessi. This model won the 1970-79 Compasso d'oro Prize, and has been added to the MOMA Permanent Design Collection in New York.

operation than a workshop typical of the industrial revolution age.

Behind the wonders of an industrial production of goods that are useful or even only pleasant for daily life, there is the work of men and robots. The role of robot "inspectors" is fundamental, for instance, in the automobile sector. These machines are capable not only of rejecting defective pieces at the end of the production cycle, but also of stopping them from being built in the first place, such as the flexible "on-line" robot used for dimensional inspection (Bravo). Inspection off-line cannot be any less accurate: this is the job of another automated measurement machine for the dimensional inspection of mechanical parts, with a control unit, printer and a smart graphic work section (Jota 1203).

In the office, technology progress has generated an attitude that is exactly the opposite to that of the factory: the identification of place has lost its meaning, and has become dispersed in an environment where the daily encounter with the object is very free and diversified, but with relatively little specificity.

Once the myth existed of the "corporate image" which put every communicative element of the business message together: from the company's organisational efficiency to the appearance of its secretaries, right through to its executive offices, operational stations, cafeteria and archives. The list of designer products that interpreted this philosophy is long: Pianeta Ufficio, designed by Mario Bellini, produced by Marcatrè, 1974; Olivetti Syntesis, designed by B.P.R., 1955; Model TC 800, designed by Sottsass, produced by Olivetti, 1974.

Finite and Infinite Market
Again in the street, from fruit and vegetables seller to the grocer's store, from the market to home. And during the day, the revenge of the pedestrians: in the marketplace, the customer is sacred. From one umbrella-shaded stall to the next, of forms unchanged (market model, produced by Scolaro, 1982), which oversee extensive and multifarious fruit and vegetable landscapes: from pyramids of Amalfi lemons to cascades of Pachino tomatoes and mountains of Vignola cherries.

Yellow, red, fuchsia, are just some of the dazzling colours that explode into full view.

In the distance, the last noises in the street clatter before the break for lunch: the pop and crackle of the moped-cum-delivery van (model Ape 50 Piaggio) as it takes away the last goods; the pulling down of roll-up shutters (model Onda, "wave", produced by Pastore, 1982); and the click of the padlock (produced and patented by Ala). The appeal of many objects is first, of course, simply functional. In this regard, Bruno Munari wittily suggests a "golden compass to the unknown" in his book *Da cosa nasce cosa*, and justifies it thus: "Before the term 'design' was used to define a correct production of objects that perform necessary functions, such objects were already in production and are continually improved in their materials and technology. They are objects used day to day in homes and workplaces and people buy them because they do not follow the fashions, they do not entail problems with symbols and class. They are just well-designed objects and it is of no importance who they are made by. This is the true design".

The padlock for roll-up shutters is one such example.

Lunchtime

Lunchtime shopping or working has not yet succeeded in taking a hold over the working day: the ritual of stopping for a break to eat lunch is still very much alive. Except for some rare exceptions, shops in Italy shut for about three hours on average during the lunch period, and the market stalls are dismantled after two o'clock. The city is "affected" by all this and the pace slows noticeably. The background hubbub

Ettore Sottsass jr, personal computer M 20, Olivetti, 1981. Olivetti's model has been considered as almost the prototype of rational design, with added aesthetic elements, as in the case of the famous Valentine typewriter.

Mario Bellini, Divisumma 18
portable calculator, Olivetti,
1973; Marcello Nizzoli, Olivetti's
Lexicon, 1948; Ettore Sottsass jr,
Valentine portable typewriter,
Olivetti, 1969.

abates and the voices and sounds of people going about their lunchtime preparations are audible.

Eating is a moment to be shared with friends and acquaintances: at a bar, a restaurant with guests, or at home with one's family. The home becomes the place where a daily ritual is enacted around the central shrine of the table, which is rigorously laid with tablecloth and the other necessaries for a proper lunch.

"From the spoon to the city" could be interpreted in so many ways. Certainly it is meaningful that all the great designers and architects of the 20th century practised the design, or redesign, of cutlery—from Gio Ponti to Carlo Scarpa, from Carlo Mollino to Marco Zanuso, from Luigi Caccia Dominioni to Alessandro Mendini, to Enzo Mari, Joe Colombo, and Achille Castiglioni.

Tableware

On the subject of cutlery design, the writer Umberto Eco made the following memorable remark (in his writing for *Italian Re-Evolution, Design in Italian Society of the Eighties*):

"Frequently anonymous design corrects the mistakes of brand-name design. Indeed, among the causes of the crisis of utopia in design during the '50s, there was also an unconscious betrayal of the object's true function. Paradoxically, with the intention of realising functional objects, designers tried to accentuate the communicative functions of these objects; and instead of producing objects that communicated the way they could be used, they produced objects that communicated the philosophy of design.

"In other words, the object did not say 'I can be used in this way or that' but

Piaggio's Ape Car.

Three instances of design in household items. *From the top*: Philippe Starck, fruit juice squeezer, Alessi, 1974; Italdesign/Giugiaro, Levissima water bottles, 1986; Richard Sapper, kettle, Alessi, 1984. Design applied to small household objects has often consented great creative freedom.

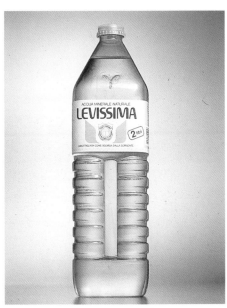

stated 'I am a perfect design object'. To make a very simple example, among Italian cutlery, the long-pronged fork was created as a result of anonymous design: it is a pretty object that resembles a hand. Once Bruno Munari designed a whole book in which forks 'spoke' by moving their prongs rather like the fingers of a hand (forks can do these things because Italians, as is well known, are very expressive gesticulators). At a certain point, designers tried to make forks more attractive and functional, inspired by the Danish design model, and produced very pretty forks with short prongs. For many, to buy these forks meant being trendy: the fork said 'I'm modern'. But unfortunately, whereas the Danes eat a lot of peas, in Italy spaghetti is the big thing. While the short-pronged fork can also double up as a sort of spoon for scooping up peas, it cannot wind up spaghetti, which demands one with long prongs, to spear the tangled mass and then to turn and wind it into a more manageable mouthful.

"If designer forks were fine in the homes of the affluent, who tended to eat more meat and less spaghetti, among the not quite so well off their limited usefulness made them a flop. And the same applied also to restaurants, where even the rich invariably order a plate of spaghetti—the speciality of the house.

"I expect that for some designers the choice was intentional: they tried to design forks to encourage new eating habits in a more affluent society. But designers alone were unable to influence people's meat-eating propensities and their designs have produced some beautiful museum pieces—but some rather useless restaurant forks.

"Thus anonymous design came back with a vengeance, correcting the mistakes of designer brand utopia, to repopulate the country with good old 'ordinary' forks, which went hand in hand with the operative words of

efficiency, comprehensibility and 'real-people oriented'.

"I believe that the history of Italian design must not be viewed as a linear history but as the story of these contradictions, these trial-and-error processes. In this sense it is an interesting history, even for those who are not Italian".

In Italy few meals shun pasta: 58% of the population eat pasta every day, divided by broad geographical region as follows:

in the North: 55 kg per capita per year;
in the Centre: 79 kg per capita per year;
in the South: 129 kg per capita per year.

Also, or rather above all, when it comes to recipes, the number of pasta variations is truly bewildering (no hard statistical data is available since, in addition to industrial production, home-made production by millions of housewives luckily persists). There are certainly over a hundred types, though, which when combined with as many different sauces, multiply into endless permutations for all palates.

For all its permutations, however, not many designers have tested their skills in recreating pasta forms. Among them was Giorgetto Giugiaro, with his Marilla model for Barilla, Italy's leading pasta maker. When addressing the appearance/quantity theme, he designed a tubular shape that increases in size greatly when cooked while actually losing approximately one third of its specific weight. Now that's what we can call a product to satisfy the eyes of eaters while respecting their diets!

As to the variations of utensils used to make and eat pasta, these are numerous: from the technological pasta machine (the Pastamatic, designed by A. Cavalli for Simac) to the traditional one (the Dalia, produced by IMB, 1962), from the essential grater... to the mechanised one... the automatic one... the elegant one for the dining room table (produced and designed by Cleto Munari).

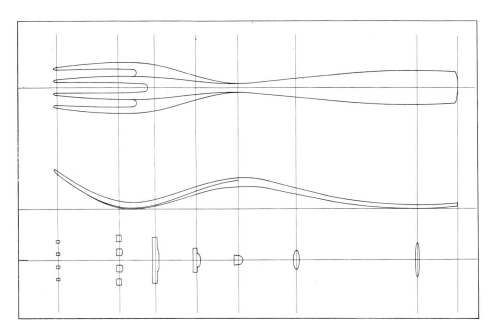

Left: Marco Zanuso, design for
a fork created for the Reed &
Barton contest, 1959.

Below: Giorgio Giugiaro, Marilla
pasta, Barilla, 1983.

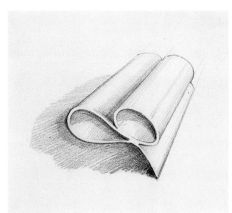

Early Afternoon. A Brief Interval
The shutters are pulled down and the traffic is subdued. In Italy, the lunch break extends well into the early afternoon, with shops generally opening again at three thirty or even later in the summer. Towns and cities slumber, the decibels drop, and only the incessant chatter of water breaks an otherwise relative calm as it flows from the fountains in the squares and streets. It is nearly time for the second coffee ritual of the day, and the proper place for its consecration can be nowhere else than at a bar, equipped in its unmistakable way, with its characteristic decor, coffee cups and sugar bowls, and its steam coffee machines for 4, 6, 8, 12 or 24 cups at a time (made mainly by Cimbali, Faema and Pavoni).

The Italian bar is, in itself, a social institution of no slight importance. It is "a phenomenon unto itself, more akin to a French café than an American coffee shop, certainly, but sweeping summaries, as always, can only paint a paltry picture of reality. In Italy the bars are mainly for drinking a quick coffee while standing up. Patrons who take a seat usually do so if they have time on their hands. Otherwise, one enters, orders a coffee, drinks it in a few minutes and leaves. But in this short interlude, standing at the plush polished stone- or stainless-steel counter, the topics for discussion are wide open: the day's business in retrospect, the decision to sell up and move home, the day's world news, the end of a love affair. As to the consumptions themselves, a coffee or aperitif (before mealtimes), a croissant, toasted sandwich, or maybe even a *bistecca* (steak).

"Italian bars belong to no one and to all: their domain lies at some blurred but pleasurable point between leisure time and working time. They are frequented by people who decide to play *totocalcio* (football pools) and so they are also a place for betting and discussions about wagers and sport. They are places where social class distinctions largely pale to insignificance, except for some areas of big cities where there are blue-collar and white collar employees' bars. The bar is also where a Managing Director of a corporation discusses the fate of ten thousand workers while, standing only two steps away, an accountant chats to a friend about how to spend the coming weekend.

"This cultural situation reflects, of course, also on design. Bars are the places where something is ordered, but also where one chooses and takes something with one's own hands (a roll or sandwich, a betting card, some

Bruno Munari, *Le mani parlano*, 1983.

chewing gum). Everything in the bar must therefore be 'legible', and every object designed so that customers can use them quickly, immediately, easily and autonomously.

"Without this human background, one would not even understand the espresso coffee machine." Espresso coffee is the symbol of Italy around the world but the real Italian coffee is exemplified in the method developed in Naples. This coffee is slowly infused, metering water, heat and time, with love and almost religious care, and without hurry, in small coffee pots. There is a splendid scene describing this in *Questi fantasmi* by Eduardo De Filippo, which describes

are indeed whole categories of workers (civil servants) for whom afternoon work is largely unknown.

It is by no mere coincidence that mobile telephony has developed at such an overwhelming pace—in 1998 there are already 15 million users—since it has allowed people to be "virtually" at work while physically they can be almost anywhere. In terms of brand name design, this small object is a formal descendant of the Grillo or rather of the UR-TYP archetype, a form that introduced a new way of conceiving, manufacturing and using telephones in the '60s. As recalled by Marco Zanuso, who, along with

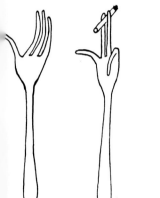

the custom of coffee and use of the *cuppiello* (a paper filter to apply to the spout of classic Neapolitan coffee pots). "Therefore the espresso machine found in bars is Italian to the same extent that Malinowski decided that certain bicycles used in African countries but manufactured in Japan for the African market were no longer objects of European civilisation, but new native objects of African civilisation. Espresso coffee belongs to the civilisation of the Italian bar. And the same can be said of the cups, sugar bowls, and the sliding-door glass cabinets which keep the pastries warm" (from *Italian Re-Evolution*).

Afternoon Work

Historically, work in the afternoon is rather variable in terms of timetables and type of work carried out, and there

Richard Sapper, designed them: "Although there was a fairly precise theme, the non-existence of a detailed briefing favoured my proficiency in clearing up problems by following the logic of ideas. But the general briefing was clear: to get rid of fixedness and facilitate mobility, restrained solely by the length of cable connecting the telephone to the wall socket—thus the addition of extra sockets in the space. The merging of body with receiver, however, posed some difficult problems. To start with, that of reducing the diameter of the dialling device, which was a constraint to the object's width. The solution was to divide it into only 10 sections instead of 11 (the 10 numerals from 0 to 9 plus the step of 'rest'), that is to make the finger making a turn plus one step in order to select each number. This

reduced the diameter by about 9%, to not bigger than 6 cm, at last a manageable object for one hand. The other constraint was the two angles: the first between the loudspeaker and the plane of the selection dial, and the second between the latter and the plane of the microphone, to optimise the fit against the ear while giving the right distance and angle for the mouth.
"With this arrangement, the challenge lay on the one hand in giving the object a compact shape when not in use (while allowing all the devices and parts to be housed), and on the other in giving it a different, ergonomic form when it would be actually used. The solution of course was the idea of the hinge. The problem of accommodating the mechanisms was solved by transferring a part of them—the bell basically—to the three-pin wall plug: thus came about a new sound for the ring and a new name for the object: *Grillo* (cricket), a name that was invented—and which aptly stuck—probably because of its resemblance to an electronic insect hunched up against the wall".

The Enchanted Shop Window
In Italy, the twilight hours dim the streets and squares to become the stages for people to see and be seen. Shopping on clothes gets the third largest slice of the family expenditure cake, immediately after those on food and the home.
Self—decoration and elegant dressing, generally considered in North America and other similarly puritanical countries as being part of the transitory, has in Italy been raised to the sublime status of being considered an integral part of the proper way to live.
The fashion system plays witness to a sophisticated creative process that draws on a huge wealth of all formal arts and constitutes the symbol of dreams that are often only realisable in that sort of body-art which is the great aesthetic monument of everyday life—and which is above all concentrated

in appointed town-centre sites.
A confirmation of this expressive Italian phenomenon happened in September 1914 with the Futurist manifesto of *Anti-Neutral Clothing* in which the bleak, neutral colours which were in vogue at the time were condemned and scorned as being "pedantic, professorial, and Teutonic". If mourning clothes are no good even for undertakers and good taste is a "mediocre-loving equilibrium", the intention of Futurism was thus to introduce new flexible elements, "dissonant and asymmetrical in form and colour", with brilliant lines to "colour and rejuvenate the crowds in our streets". "One thinks and acts how

one dresses. Since neutrality can sum up traditionalism, today we Futurists show off these clothes which are anti-neutral, and strongly warlike."
The Futurist wardrobe was expressed as much in fabric design as in male and female garments in all their elements and accessories, until it reached the maximum expression of stage costume. Beginning in 1913, the dynamic bright matches and multiple colours of his fabric designs, in which volumes and surfaces were entangled in motion, exploded in the notebooks of Giacomo Balla.
For man, the Futurists proposed a garment which on one hand had to be provocative, a testimonial to the breaking away from conventional models, while on the other hand it will have to be adaptable to the movement of the body. We can cite Balla's designs

Cimbali coffee machine, model M 30 Classic.

Fortunato Depero, *Dancer for the "Chant du Rossignol"*, collage on cardboard, 1916. Modena, Galleria Fonte d'Abisso.

dating back to 1914 and the "household clothing" of 1925, and Ernesto Thayaht's proposal for a single piece "overall" of 1919.

But the Futurists of course turned their hands also to designing accessories: for example, "Futurist shoes will be dynamic, with one different to the other in shape and colour" according to Balla; in 1932, Mino Delle Site worked out variations on the theme of ties: on an asymmetric collar, a band with no knot, and with geometric metallic plates. On the same theme, Balla decided that the tie was a plastic object or—better still—a plastic "complex". Headgear was given variable shapes to favour movement by using shifts of the sunshade visor and of its extension, from vertical to horizontal. Hard as it may seem to believe, the female garment was a minor source of inspiration for Balla. Crali and Thayaht shaped detailed and fanciful patterns in the fabrics and composition, while Del Monte and Balla chiefly developed the active role of colour. The freedom allowed in the creation of stage costumes also gave for the greatest expression of creativity in Futurist fashion. By exploiting every mode of sensorial expression, Depero, Prampolini and Pannaggi surprised up with mechanical fairytales where the ghosts and projections of Futurism were built in plasticism.

Home. The Illustrated Self

When speaking about rendering domestic space more personal, there are no questions raised regarding the obvious and unavoidably industrial origin of mass-produced consumer goods; yet when one speaks about furniture, be they sofas, armchairs, lamps, furnishings and/or various equipment, the artisan aspects of design and manufacture dominate.

It is not by chance that out of 99,000 Italian furniture companies, only fifty have a personnel of more than one hundred. Family firms and workshops scattered in the Brianza-Northeast-Marches triangle make up a broad network that allows for super flexibility and amounts to what can only be described as an incredible prototype design laboratory.

Since furniture items are produced industrially in only limited numbers, the true wealth of ideas and experimentation is collected entirely in the design phase which precedes production times and methods: this phase uses manual intervention and many craft skills. Objects allude to the behaviour and define membership of social groups. In a word, the status symbol is fundamental, at least in the living room. Lamps and sofas continue to be the grounds for experimentation in big-name design, from the lamps by Achille and Livio Castiglioni for Flos to those by Gio Ponti and Daniele Puppi for Fontana Arte, by Gino Sarfatti for Arteluce and by Richard Sapper for Artemide, and from the sofas by Marco Zanuso for Arflex and by Vico Magistretti for Cassina to those by Mario Bellini and Antonio Citterio for B&B.

The Design of Champions

After covering the activities that mark the phases of the typical day in Italy, let us now turn to the leisure activities—those which have no precise timetable and of which many are concentrated into weekends and holidays.

Italians are true sport enthusiasts through the cult of the champion and the feats of their own team seen at the stadium or on TV. The national sport is football.

Sport tends to be experienced above all on the record performances of champions, whether they be Formula 1 drivers, cyclists, soccer players, sailors, or skiers.

In this section, I would like to talk about the great feat of Francesco Moser, who in 1984 broke the world cycling hour record on a completely *ad hoc* bicycle invented simultaneously with the preparation of the "Galileo Ferraris" atomic clock. A measure of time

increasingly on the outer edge.
Italians have a truly ancient tradition in
research into the measurement of time,
whether speculative or technical,
starting from Giovanni Dondi's
Astrarium (Padua, 1364)—a complex
mechanical clock which, together with
the time, provided a whole range of
astronomical information—through to
Galileo's discovery (Pisa, 1582) of the
laws governing the movement of
pendulums. And indeed for nearly four
centuries, accurate time measurement
was based on the pendulum.
From this long tradition was born the
magnesium clock, an instrument
capable of measuring a single second to
thirteen figures, an accuracy that is
from a hundred to one thousand times
superior to that of the best existing
clocks.
For research and advanced
technological applications, quartz
clocks have been replaced by atomic
clocks. With the former, the oscillations
were measured of a pendulum or sliver
of quartz; with the latter, radiowave
measurements are taken that cause an
easily observable phenomenon to occur
in substances. These phenomena are
various (variation in transparency,
change of colour, and changes in the
way atoms travel), but they are all tied
to the properties of the substance. No
experiment has demonstrated that these
properties can change over time.
A radio wave is transmitted towards a
bunch of magnesium atoms, causing
the emission of a blue light from part of
them only if the wave oscillates
601,277,158,330 times per second. By
counting these oscillations, it is possible
to calculate the length of a second and
from this build a clock.
And in this context, the measurement
of time applied to Francesco Moser was
the hour record: a race against time,
against his thirty-two years, and against
the sixty minutes which whisked by as
his bicycle sped around the Olympic
velodrome in Mexico City. Moser rose
to the challenges and won, breaking the
record on 19 January 1984 covering

50.808 km, and going back just five
days later to break his own record, this
time crossing the 51-km wall to reach
51.151 km.
The bicycle he used was a record-
breaking marvel in itself: a winning
blend between consolidated craftwork
experience and modern technology:
solid, carbon-fibre disc wheels, the
front one with a smaller diameter than
the rear; the frame saddle pillar was
curved, and the time-trialer's handlebars
had shorter than normal grips.
Although the bicycle weighed more the
other used recently for record-breaking
attempts, it was specially designed to
exploit the flywheel effect generated by
the solid-disk wheels.
Moser's pedalling style was scientifically
studied using a dedicated calculator
called Elite (designed to elaborate
television images), capable of
calculating the spatial co-ordinates of
images in motion to infinitesimal
fractions of a second. It is "an
automatic eye" that reads, calculates
and stores all movements at a speed of
fifty images per second. With this

Mario Bellini, Area 50 lamp,
Artemide. Photo by Aldo Ballo.

Joe Colombo, the 4867 chair,
Kartell, 1968.

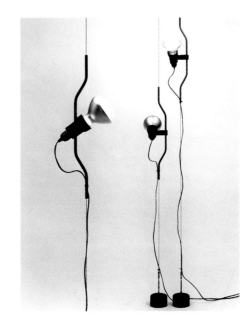

Ludovico (Vico) Magistretti,
Sinbad armchair, Cassina, 1981.

Richard Sapper, Tizio lamp,
Artemide. Photo by Aldo Ballo.

Achille Castiglioni, Parentesi
lamp, Flos, 1970.

Massimo Morozzi, Tangram
table, Cassina.
Photo by Aldo Ballo.

system it is possible to emphasise harmonies and disharmonies of motion, to correct erroneous movements and positions, and find techniques for improving co-ordination, thus enhancing the athlete's performance. Today perhaps the most precious footballing feet are those of the Brazilian "phenomenon" Ronaldo. The multinational sports footwear producer, Nike, chose the northern Italian town of Montebelluna to manufacture the special trainers that bear his name (model Ronaldo, designed by Max Zago, produced by Nike) and has established a special research centre in the Veneto region that follows the prototype design, production, experimentation and evolution of this sector. The reasons for this strategic choice are easy to uncover: concentrated in the area in and around Montebelluna are the most versatile and creative producers of ski boots such as Dolomite, Nordica, San Marco, Caber, Tecnica, and others.

Ecclesiastical Design

All across Italy, and to a much greater extent than elsewhere in Europe, a thousand-year religious and civic presence of the Church traces the emergence of every village and district. It is a strong sign of identity that accompanies the flow of every existence.

When we speak about Church affairs in Italy, we must always refer to "before" or "after" the Second Vatican Council (1962-1965). Summoned by Pope John XIII to bring the Church up to date, the Council indeed succeeded in updating every form of liturgical and pastoral communication in the Catholic Church, and therefore also ecclesiastical design.

The first document enacted by the Council, the one on liturgy, decreed that among other things liturgical rites should be praised in common language. But if Mass was to be recited in Italian, it was all too clear that a lot of other things were certainly in need of change as well. Since everybody was able to follow the service, it thus became necessary for priests to speak to their congregations—which meant addressing them directly rather than reciting with their backs to them. This requirement brought with it a revamp of how church interiors were arranged: the altar was moved and literally all spaces and the ritual objects needed to be moved to recreate a harmonious and proper setting (it was difficult for example to use Renaissance chalices in 20th-century settings) by replacing sanctuaries, paintings, sculptures, and giving them new forms. In a word, the Church was put to a process of redesign.

The redesign took in all of the most important symbolic items: the altar, ambo, baptistery and the baptismal font; the site of repentance, the Eucharist box, the monstrance and seat of the Ecclesiastical President. The Second Vatican Council was very precise about its indications for the details: "To the main criterion of truth may the criterion of sobriety be united, along with that of aesthetic coherence, and of a layout which is in keeping with the building and the enhancement of the artistic heritage".

From the point of view of overall image, two elements in particular stood out as conferring the immediate perception of new post-Council design: the sacred robes and the altar. The robe, or *casula,* evolved from an overgown of Greek-Roman origin: it sums up the early Church values of simplicity and fundamental essentiality, where form and substance are the current synthesis of them, expressed by the replacement of the ornate richness exalted in the Renaissance and Baroque periods.

The cultural aim of this chapter lies in attempting to lay bare just some of design's roots within the complex scenario of Italian life. We know that design's goal is broadly one of delineating highly standardised processes and results. But if this holds true in the most industrialised

Since the late nineteenth century, the bicycle has been a very Italian object, but lately it had drifted away due to the increased use of foreign technologies.
In recent times we have witnessed a return to bicycle engineering in Italy: a case in point is the bicycle used by Francesco Moser in 1984 to establish the hour record.

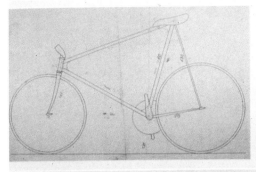
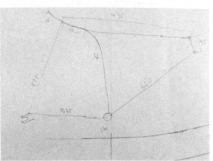
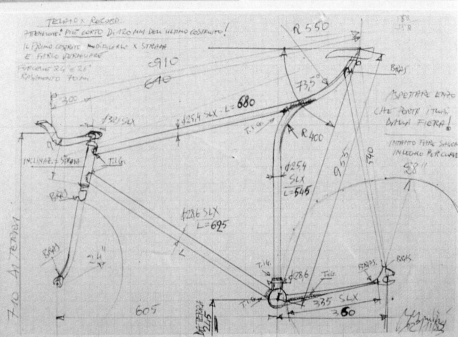

countries, in Italy the scale of industrialisation and repetition is such that product "diversification" seems instead to respond to the slogan: "to every citizen his personalised design". In Italy, indeed, the propensity to reject imported design models has created a situation whereby a recognisable identity and continuity of appearance with the past has been upheld over time. This explains why phenomena induced by mass civilisation elsewhere have had—and continue to have—a very different impact in Italy.

If the coffee ritual is as important as statistics reveal, it is hardly surprising to discover that the market offers an infinity of coffee-maker models and types to cater to the needs, whims and pockets of what is a highly developed market. If streets are to be used not just for transport but also for socialising, their anti-vehicle paving (bricks, flagstone, cobbles, etc.) is not surprising. As soon as the traffic dies down, the streets and *piazzas* turn into a playground for socialising—with seasonal ebbs and flows—and for restauranteurs to reannex, with small tables and potted plants, the spaces relinquished to the cars.

If food is an institution that induces countless trips to and from people's homes, the preparation of each meal requires ingredients bought in precise quantities to be carefully blended and cooked. On the stage of this play, pasta is without doubt the leading actor. Dozens of types are ready and able for matching with a host of different sauces.

If clothing is intended as an instrument of participation, the rapid adoption of the latest outfit by everybody—which is rendered personal for all—is not surprising. One only has to look at the explosive colour ranges (from pastel to fluorescent) of Italian jogging suits, originating on the American standard type which for years was entrenched in greys and blues.

And we only have to picture the explosion of different models of glasses on the market in the '90s. No matter if their function is sight correction or if they are sunglasses, they just have to look good on us! A long-standing tradition exists in glasses manufacturing which is concentrated in the Northeast and which has successfully managed—with companies such as Luxottica, Safilo, etc.—to ride the wave of a mass phenomenon dictated largely by fashion.

In a study of the early '90s, George Nelson photographed over 1,500 samples of road signs on the route from Venice to Palermo. By analogy, we can say that the structural complexity of the territorial features and framework, with its widespread differences, continually veers away from what we expected. Simple repetition and linear development are typical of industrialisation models.

On the basis of the above considerations, studies are directed towards following statistical indicators, intended as instruments for objectively noting, analysing and eventually interpreting, the nature, behaviours, rituals and taboos of Italian society. A complex and diversified society that is nevertheless boiled down by sociological analyses to a few model types which statistical data then translates into percentages, preferences, inclinations, customs and myths. Also artistic research—with its intuitions and anticipations—when entrusted to cinematography and literature, can of course influence products, and becomes one more reference to those changes and newly emerging features of production systems which, in overwhelming numbers, are expressed by industrially-made products. Technicians, experts, manufacturers and designers all contribute to work, whether it is conceptual, manual, mechanised, individual or in groups. And all of these inputs are part of the manufacturing processes.

All together, these observation points make up the picture within which the relationship between object and user is analysed.

The result, if we also include criteria that are not only aesthetic, amounts to such a cataloguing process that places objects of different stylistic extraction on the same critical plane where heterogeneity exalts quality, and lines of tendency, affinity and remoteness are created all at the same time. Brand-name products, anonymous ones, unique pieces or items manufactured industrially: all display the signs of the daily encounter with the user and thereby contribute to defining a model of Italian life.

This phenomenon reflects the Italian

The future of design foresees a new sector, the communication project. Here is an example by Pier Luigi Cerri for the "Italia '90" World Cup: a wall logo and a logo made of suspended elements.

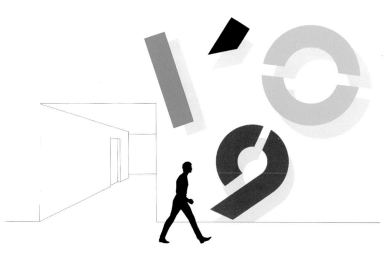

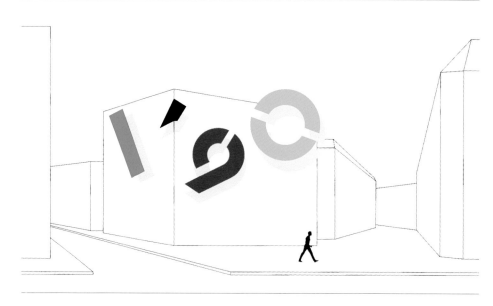

"Re-Evolution": a development model that avails itself of big leaps forward, and of situations and moments of a transformation which is great and yet at the same time also gradual—as if it believed that the objective should never really be reached.

What matters is the inspiration for change that this perspective generates in the present and daily life. And the same happens with design: the multiplicity of products and their appearance is more meaningful and conclusive than their particular specialisation, which can only be limited to certain sectors. And it is precisely this apparent non-specialisation that makes it special.

Three recent examples of ecclesiastic design. *From the top*: Studio De Lucchi and A. Micheli, altar, Stone italiana; Gabetti and Isola, altar, Sandri Leonello; Boris Podrecco, altar, Giardini Pietro.

Franco Zagari

The Italian Garden

The Italian Idea of the Garden

The garden is a typical form of expression of our civilisation, in some eras driven by original ideas, in others adopted from other cultures, acting as a precious area of hybridisation. Even today, the Italian garden continues to be an irrepressible component of the DNA of our creativity, with an unmistakable image of its own, even if not always easy to decipher. The fascination generated by the idea of the Italian garden, especially abroad, is due to the richness of the inheritance from the past which pervades the entire Italian landscape. It is an environment which has been strongly conditioned by the work of man, work which is recognisable in its creators' awareness of its ultimate effect, including at an aesthetic level. Even now, it continues to be the "bel Paese", the "garden of Europe" in spite of everything, in spite of us, its inhabitants. As in so many other creative fields, there are conditions prevalent in Italy that help maintain this continuity, such as the depth of historical tradition, a general well-being, a tradition of patronage which is still very much alive, combined with the natural association between art and the artisan, the variety of the natural environment and the generosity of the climate. There is also a kind of continuum between many different forms of figurative expression each exerting an influence over the other: design, fashion, stage design, cinema, the arts generally and, of course, architecture.

Between Past and Future

Many captivating images emerge from the past: the Roman synthesis of the oriental and the Hellenic gardens with its dense and mysterious *nemora tonsilia*, enclosures surrounded by frescoed walls depicting stylised landscapes, the control of water and its ostentation, the marvels of topiary sculptures together with the town garden of Hadrian's villa. Then there is the intimacy of the cloistered garden of the Middle Ages, the *hortus conclusus* and parterres of medicinal plants and spaces set aside for artistic gatherings and study, places for reciting the *Decameron* while awaiting the passing of the dark and the plague. This in turn was followed by the *Renaissance garden*, the great season of Humanism, leading to Mannerism and the Baroque, to the triumph of architecture and the age of enlightened patrons: Alberti, Bramante, Raphael, Romano, Ligorio, Vignola and Della Porta. This is the place of the classical garden "a balanced product of thought and action" (Giorgina Masson) which is defined in short as the Italian garden. It is the most extensive and sophisticated space acting both as a representation and a meeting

Pietro Porcinai, swimming pool in private Garden, Liguria.

151

place for the new society. It is destined for use as a public space, as was the case in ancient Roman gardens for the spas and forums, created in both the town and the country, one of the most extraordinary of man's inventions. The new rules of perspective govern the external space, widening the nature of the masses and the order of the buildings. It is a layout which re-interprets that used in Hellenic cities, set along *cardi*, straight axial main streets, crossed by *decumani*, secondary axes perpendicular to the first. The principles of architecture predominate and the spaces are defined by an entirely controlled plant life and vegetation: trees, hedges and parterres are for the most part evergreen, and cut like topiary sculptures. The rest is enriched by water systems and sculptured structures. It is a philosophical space, filled with great vitality and strongly interactive with the visitor, even if only playful, surprising one with tricks and marvels of water. It was also used as a space for experimenting with the most advanced scientific and technical discoveries in both agriculture and hydrology. These ideas, translated to a scale incorporating whole localities, were fundamental to the design of the royal gardens decorating the capitals of the new nations of Europe, from André Le Nôtre onwards: Versailles, Saint Petersburg, Schönbrunn, Caserta and Munich. Then it was the natural Italian landscape with its majestic ruins which, through the paintings of Lorrain, Poussin and Rosa provided the inspiration for a further great development, that of the landscape or English garden. From that time on, the Italian garden was to remain a crossroads, teeming with ideas and different cultural influences but without its own central focus.

At present, the Italian garden is at a difficult point of transition between the richness and weight of its past inheritance and the great contemporary themes such as town planning and the environment. The garden is not a manufactured object that can be defined

as simply another type of construction or building. It is a free form of creative expression that can be found wherever a synthesis between science, art and society is produced through a reflection of man on nature. It is less true than ever before to say that the present-day garden is only the (generally cultivated) external space appertaining to a particular house or villa, delimited by an unequivocal dimensional scale. The contemporary garden can be found expressed in any dimension of the external space, small, large or even very large, so long as the unity of the work carried out on it is recognisable as a reflection and representation of thought

The garden of Villa Arceno, Castelnuovo Berardenga, Siena. Photo by Mauro Tozzi.

in nature. It is a work of art, a unification of planned design and techniques, ethical purpose and aesthetic awareness. In this sense the concept of garden is more easily understood with reference to the English term "landscape" or the French "paysage". I do not believe there is a useful distinction to be made between garden art and architectural landscaping save in the prescription of limits for the sake of disciplinary convenience.

The exchange between politics, economics and society in Italy today in this field is often carried out in a way that lacks true communication. Different experiences are set against each

The garden of Villa La Suvera, Pieve Scala, Siena. Photo by Mauro Tozzi.

other both in cultural circles and in public opinion, but in many areas a conservative approach can be seen. It seems to me that there is a widespread failure of understanding which, from the start, finds itself in a kind of muddled limbo set somewhere between past and present, that is, between the historical inheritance and the vitality of the modern tradition. We need to define some areas of common ground where we can clarify what we mean by nature, and, in particular, our understanding of its susceptibility to change through our assessment of the value of the present (in which the past plays a pre-eminent role). We then have to decide how such an

assessment can be given aesthetic expression, and finally, how a differentiation will be made in the expression of this culture-nature relationship in the public and private domains. There are too many lovers of historical gardens whose idea of them has become static; they ignore the dynamic of time and human behaviour, and forget the extraordinarily vital function of gardens, archiving them like artefacts for a museum. This is all sacrosanct if one is considering an effective conservation campaign. For it to have either sense or future though, both historical judgement and a knowledge of the contemporary

figurative (and not only figurative) culture are needed. A similar lack of humour is shown by enviroment lovers. There is nothing more dynamic than the land, no corner of which has been left untouched by man. By the same token, there is nothing more impossible to control by the use of simple quantitative and negative prescriptions. Both groups of lovers have taken up arms against contemporary design, irrespective of where it comes from. This does not alter the fact though, that anti-modern criticism has also been taken up by interpreters of a more elevated standing , like the philosopher Rosario Assunto. He writes that the garden is "the presence of succession (in so far as it is the image of nature) and succession of presence (to the extent that it is the image of thought)... an object of life's contemplation, itself contemplating life—nature tamed by man, whose ideal is represented by the need to create art in nature, of nature and with nature aspires... a place analogous to poetry... the sameness of art and nature which in the service of other is bound to self-destruction". "Other" here is, for Assunto, use and consumption "both that of land-grabbing cupidity in the private sphere or that characterised in the public sector where flower beds are covered over and trees chopped down to create open spaces for use by the so-called 'masses'" (R. Assunto, "Il problema estetico del giardinaggio" in G. Ragionieri, ed., *Il giardino storico italiano,* Florence 1981). This aristocratic ideal of a place of pure contemplation has its fascination, but it is not easily found even in pre-modern times where the garden was always a place for both "dreams and power" (Pierre Grimal). The prince and the ruling classes used it as a form of self-ostentation and, at the same time, to create a place for congregation and theatre for their peers and subjects. Our problem, as for any historical era, is to understand which the values of contemporary expression are to be transmitted by means of the garden and

Renzo Piano, Auditorium, Rome (Franco Zagari and Emilio Trabella's landscape consulting).

what is the object and meaning of contemplation, without which, evidently, the garden will cease to exist as a garden.

The Tradition of the Contemporary
Contemporary design has created its own tradition in Italy over the last few years, but it is based primarily on fragmentary experiences. In this dialectic between past and present, the best ideas, those which allow us to continue to envisage a contemporary garden, originate from creators with varying backgrounds and training—indeed, they are often self-taught. They are largely made up of architects, landscape designers and artists. The landscape designers are those who, in Italy, have been pioneers in the adoption of a specific approach to the landscape—an approach which has already become well-established in many countries throughout the world. These are the descendants of "gardeners", who face up to the problems raised by external space in all their complexity. "The word 'gardener' indicates not only a garden lover but also someone who is responsible for ensuring its cultural and material well-being" (V. Vercelloni, *Atlante storico del*

giardino europeo, Milan, 1990). In this section I will try to touch on a number of the lines of research for the present day Italian garden. I will be using a few examples, individual works of garden designers who do not in any way claim to have exhausted all possibilities in a setting which is much wider and more complex than what I describe. My intention is to give emphasis to the approach involving garden and landscape, viewing them as a rounded and integrated work. I must apologise to the reader if I make too many references of an autobiographical nature, but this concrete approach helps me to explain some landscapes better since I am more of a landscape architect than an academic or theoretician.

Architects and Landscape
I start with an Italian architect, Renzo Piano. Nature represents a value of central importance to his work. In his *Elogio della costruzione*, a speech he gave on receiving the award of the prestigious Pritzker Prize, Piano refers to architecture as a human process originating from a changing of nature. From this he identifies the need to approach architecture as a service—it is a

listening art, not one that is imposed. Architecture does not only have a psychological impact, but also a physical and long-lasting one on the community at large. The architect has to listen to all sides, to explore social values, scientific thought and artistic expression. "Architecture... is an art which mixes things together: history and geography, anthropology and the environment, science and society. It is, inevitably, the mirror of them all." This is essentially a way of re-projecting the Vitruvian triad, *utilitas, firmitas, venustas,* through the modern lens of the fourth dimension of time. It seeks nonetheless a vision which continues to believe, with measured optimism, in the value of progress. Piano continues: "To really create, the architect must accept all the contradictions of his trade, between discipline and liberty, memory and invention, nature and technology. It is a contradiction which cannot be avoided. If life is complicated, art is even more so. Architecture is all this, society, science and art". There is no work by Piano which does not have a central reflection on nature. One of the latest of these, which I find symptomatic of

Carlo Scarpa, the Querini
Stampalia Foundation garden,
Venice.

Carlo Scarpa, Brion Tomb,
San Vito di Altivole.

his thought, is the new Auditorium in Rome where I was, with Emilio Trabella, commissioned as the landscaping consultant. Almost the entire building has a park as its roof, a dense hanging forest where the public can roam at large, and from which the three halls emerge like mysterious musical objects. Piano's intention was to create the new building as a seamless extension of the two background hills with their imposing masses of plant life and vegetation while, at the same time, extending the freedom of movement enjoyed by both visitors and local inhabitants, in this way setting up a new kind of polarity. The building does not disturb the spatial relations of place already in existence; it gathers them to itself and gives them new life. It internalises morphological interrelations in the same way as psychological tensions. All relations of scale are thus established with reference to the landscape and not on purely architectural bases. Dimensions are spacious, consonant with both the natural and man-made spatial order to be found in this part of the city of Rome.

This manner of thinking, which puts landscape and architecture in strict co-relation to such an extent that it affirms their identity with each other, lies at the base of what I have called the tradition

of the contemporary Italian garden. Going back in time, we can see how some works display the early symptoms of this tradition. I remember, for example, Carlo Scarpa who, with the Querini Stampalia Foundation garden at Venice and the Brion Cemetery at San Vito di Altivole, has left us two exemplars of high style. His magisterial attention to detail has found a happy synthesis in the garden, otherwise not expressed with such incisiveness in the exteriors of his other works. These two gardens create a strong feeling of the spaciousness characteristic of the Veneto villas, of light and colour in particular, a musical quality leading to a merging of their constituent elements. The architectural style of Wright is clearly ascendant here, together with the explicit reference to the contamination of contemporary Western art by the Japanese garden style—one of the richest sources of the abstract. One can also see his passion for museum art, with the sequential arrangement of the old and new architecture with absolute naturalness. In the context of this critical study of the modern and in the modern, I would consider Scarpa's gardens two of the most inspired origins of the contemporary Italian garden.

We are indebted to Gae Aulenti for another original and inspiring masterpiece in the Villa Pucci garden in

Fuksas, Jourdan, Fulcrand, and Zagari, Reception Centre at the prehistoric caves of Niaux, Foix. © Aki Furudate.

Massimiliano Fuksas and Annamaria Sacconi, Fonte del Diavolo park, Paliano.

Granaiolo, although when she created this work she was involved more than ever in stage design. A fourteenth-century villa is raised with great simplicity on a parterre, separating it from its surrounding woods. A rationalised section of stepped lawns both idealises and reflects the image of the terraced Tuscan landscape in the great tradition of the Renaissance garden.

We find other origins in the avant garde. Using the most rudimentary materials—tuff, concrete and railway sleepers—Massimiliano Fuksas and Annamaria Sacconi (at that time both almost unknown) transformed a wood belonging to a local authority in Paliano into a park of mysterious power: as Henry James might have put it, "a landscape in the form of a garden". In the Fonte del Diavolo park there are again a series of "objectives" arranged along a pre-set route. The narrative it embodies, though, is characterised by humour and poetry founded on an imaginary symbolism.

The traces and ruins of impossible architecture stand between flashbacks from the past and the imaginary world of childhood fairy tales. These same strange archetypes act, at the same time, as a medium for the conjuring up of new forms.

Fuksas is himself an example of an architect who, having passed from the Paliano wood to the glories of international success, has increasingly turned towards the concept of landscape in his creative activity. His most recent projects have often been concerned with the large-scale town and transformation of both countryside and townscapes. They show an insistence on both anthropology and geography. It is no longer a question of buildings and nature—even less of *genius loci*—but rather the evolving role of the place, separating out scales and systems, with interweaving and interchanging accessory features.

The Niaux Reception Centre (in collaboration with Fulcrand, Jourdan and Zagari) had to solve a highly delicate problem of environmental compatibility. It is a building situated in a monumental cave whose entrance looks out over a valley in the Pyrenees from half-way up the mountain side, giving access at its other end to one of a series of caves containing some of the most important pre-historic wallpaintings in Europe. The building has been conceived as one of the elements forming the landscape as a whole, a rusted metallic body in a vaguely zoomorphic form—a form from the most modern times which seems to have been waiting there for millennia... It has been designed essentially as a point of transit, intended as a moment of initiation and preparation for the entry to the deeper caves. It rests on the cave's sandy floor with a thousand slender feet, protruding slightly out of the cave mouth, overlooking the countryside. It is a panoramic vantage point as well as a great sign visible for miles around. Its function is purely that of providing orientation for the visiting

Fuksas, Grether, Roux and Zagari, Tremblay's "Atoll". France.

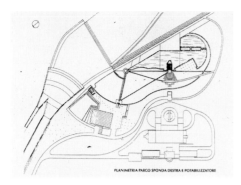

Benedetto Camerana,
Technological park, Turin.

Salvatore Dierna, project for the
Centocelle park, Roma.

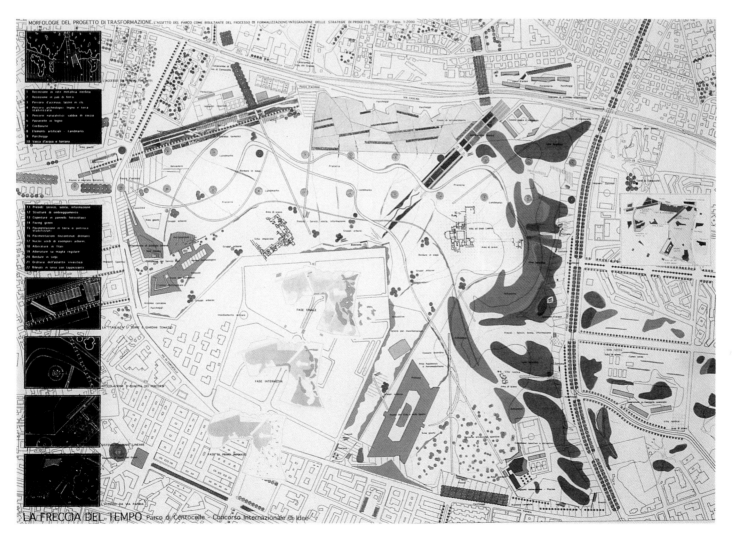

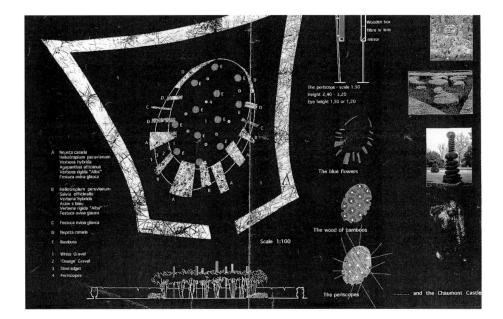

Fabio Di Carlo, Monica Sgandurra, *Le jardin du voyeur*, Chaumont-sur-Loire.

Gianpiero Donin and pupils from the Reggio Calabria School, *Garden in love*, Chaumont-sur-Loire.

Daniela Colafranceschi, *Shishi-o-doshi*, Chaumont-sur-Loire.

public. Passing through the building one progresses with great naturalness from the openness of the valley into the depths of the inner caves, while the facilities are given an accessory, almost casual function.

The town planning design for a large area of Tremblay en France (in collaboration with Grether, Roux and Zagari) situated next to the Paris Charles De Gaulle Airport, posed the same problems but over a whole locality. The key concept in the design was to leave a band of countryside intact round a historic village, forming a full circle, a great ring-shaped park of more than 200 hectares, encompassing and embodying a sense of purpose and unity for the whole complex urban machine. It is the image of an atoll, a purposeful discontinuity. It reflects the clear principle of identity and centrality in the uniformity of the *banlieue*. Interest is no longer so concentrated on analysing a single system, such as for instance, traffic movement, in a particular area. Instead attention is focused on the possibilities thrown up by the combination of a road, plus a wood plus a damn in the evolution of a whole landscape, and how they can establish their own recognisable characteristics and identity, providing a starting point for a process. Fuksas is indeed a past master of this technique of unifying and separating out different elements at a semantic (not figurative) level, diametrically opposed to the concept of "zoning". He has a clear sense of the institutional and economic purposes behind these processes, and hence also of their feasibility.

This approach is evolving fast within architectural thought. Many artists are involved in increasing awareness of landscape themes at the university level in Italy; to name just a few: Salvatore Dierna, Annalisa Calcagno Maniglio, Guido Ferrara, and Vanna Fraticelli. Benedetto Camerana, on the other hand, deserves mention as the founder of *Eden*, the excellent but short-lived Italian architectural landscape journal.

Francesco Ghio, park
of S. Antonio ai Monti, Naples.
Entrance from the "Eye
of the Mountain".

Valerio Morabito, design for the
Acicastello seafront.

Aurelio Cantone, private garden
in Catania.

Alessandro Villari, garden for
a pub in Acicastello.

Between Architecture and Landscape
We must now turn back to the more
intimate scale, traditionally appropriate
to the garden.
Chaumont-sur-Loire in France has
played host, for some years now,
to an important international festival
of the garden. It was originally set up on
the initiative of Jean-Paul Pigeat.
More than twenty gardens are designed
and laid every year by garden designers
from all over the world and the Italian
representation has always had an
important section devoted to it.
In the first presentation of the festival
Gianpiero Donin and the Reggio
Calabria School presented an original
garden design based on the idea of
pleasure. The garden obtained general
approval for the strength of its poetic
eroticism on the one hand and its
concern not to use grain to attract birds
on the other. Such a practice (however
involuntarily) seemed to be lacking in
respect for the political mood of the
time—being the beginning of the
summer of great protests by French
farmers against Maastricht—such is the
power of symbols!
Two Italian designers from the younger
generation made their mark at the
festival. They received important
accolades for their work based on the
senses and psychology of the public in
its relationship with place, fully

exploiting the interplay of architecture,
landscape and sculpture. Daniela
Colafranceschi designed a sound garden
around the noise of flowing water set in
a poetic, moving forest of *Shishi-o-doshi*.
She used elements typical of the
Japanese garden—waving bamboo canes
that emit a clear, dry sound as they fill
up with, and they empty of water. They
are normally used singly but here they
were in concert. On the other hand,
Fabio Di Carlo and Monica Sgandurra
created their garden around the theme
of inquisitiveness—a little wood where
first one loses one's way, and then is
surprised to find it again on the outside,
as in a labyrinth, where one's perceptions
have been defined by a group of
telescopes.
There is, however, a flowering of
designers which seems to me to be
symptomatic of this close identity
between architecture and landscape.
Francesco Ghio with his park of
S. Antonio ai Monti in Naples has
designed an original route climbing
vertically between the historic
Neapolitan town centre and the
Vomero, leading the visitor onto a cliff
which has been a fragment of
countryside within the city for centuries
(the central design was in collaboration
with Vittoria Calzolari). The following
examples also come to mind: Valerio
Morabito's design for the Acicastello

Russell Page, the park of Villar Perosa, near Turin.

seafront—inspired by the concept of public space and the "waterfront", using it (as one might say) as a pretext to give the town back its centre of gravity; Aurelio Cantone's private garden in Catania, a little "paradise" with an exemplary balance between tradition and innovation; Alessandro Villari's convivial pub garden set in a shady spot under the sheltering foliage of two pre-existing and mighty *ficus benjamina*, once again in Acicastello.

Landscape Designers
The work of the landscape gardener—which differs from the approach adopted by the architects though often in happy harmony with it—I would define as "pure". Let us now take a step back in time and begin by looking at ourselves with a critical eye and with the good taste of a foreign talent. It is impossible to talk of the Italian garden without remembering a great English gardener—Russell Page, who died in 1984. Having designed gardens throughout the world

he was asked to create many Italian gardens from the early '50 onwards. I recall two of these in particular—very different from each other—the park of Villar Perosa and the garden of Villa Silvio Pellico, both situated near Turin. At least they are apparently different from each other. Here, as in the rest of his work, Page is consistent in his eclectic choice of elements from the artistic repertoire of the past. He then abstracts them into their essential components and strips them of the echoes of past associations. In this way he is able to superimpose an elegant and many-stranded narrative on the setting, created entirely through plants and vegetation, with particular emphasis on the floral component. Villar Perosa is romantic in style, while Villa Silvio Pellico follows a decidedly classical model. Both gardens are Page's response to the requirements of a cultured and "private" par excellence patronage oriented towards a taste without risks, entirely estranged from the figurative

research characteristic of the times. Page's fundamental idea, as with so many English gardens laid in Italy over the past two hundred years, was to exploit the attraction of a particular theme and a particular context and to superimpose it with a light touch on his chosen motifs—history like a staff. This exploitation expresses a sensitivity that has been passed down from the last phase of the era of the landscape garden, like Payne Knight's "picturesque". It is above all the use of flowers which seems to bring together the chromatic range and wisdom of Gertrude Jekyll and Vita Sackville-West. But Page seems to have paused before an erudite culture and to have given his best, drawing from his initiatory gardener's intuition.
On a visit to Villa Madama one feels it is natural to search for and find a source "which has to exist" to understand the purposes behind that particular garden. Fascinated by Vignola at Villa Lante, it is impossible to disguise one's irritation with the continual references and

Russell Page, the garden of Villa
Silvio Pellico, near Turin.

Pietro Porcinai, the S. Ambrogio
churchyard, Zoagli.

associations made by sculptures and the
artifices of playing water. Russell Page's
fortune in Italy seems to be based on his
comforting and timeless classicism, his
mobile and "domestic" narrative thread
and the quiet and elegant colour changes
occurring over the different seasons. I
have devoted so much attention to Page
because he undoubtedly represents, with
masterly skill, an extremely widespread
idea of the Italian garden, as much
among the wealthy owners of wonderful
secret villas as among the public at large,
taking it up from their reading of
gardening journals. It is an essentially
private and self-contemplating garden
with generic sculptures and explosions of
vegetation in all its richness of different
species and colours. At the beginning of
the Italian Risorgimento the English
garden was used as a vehicle for
propaganda by intellectuals like Ercole
Silva, representing the ideal of liberty,
scientific innovation and social
liberalisation. The complexity and
richness of the plant life is one of the

most characteristic elements, a quality
which has been passed down to the
present day, though stripped of its deep
idealistic substrata. The English passion
for hybridisation, used by Page and
many other gardeners before him who
chose Italy as their elective homeland,
has become a stable characteristic of the
Italian garden and Page is its voice in the
re-expression of a deep and anti-modern
aspiration.

The case of Pietro Porcinai is entirely
different. He is the true great Landscape
designer of this century, if for nothing
else than the breadth and variety of his
experimentation, making his work into a
treatise dealing with almost all themes of
the contemporary garden. As one of his
students, Milena Matteini puts it, he
was guided by "an idea of the greatest
simplicity but nonetheless difficult to
pass on to others: harmony with
nature". Porcinai's work covers an
immense range. It is not without its
great failures, but never loses its high
originality. His approach is sometimes

Pietro Porcinai, Pietro Consagra
and Marco Zanuso, Pinocchio
garden, Collodi.

brutal, at others refined, moved by an extremely personal educational and cultural background, where his Tuscan origins were tempered by his early education in Germany and an assiduous attention to contemporary figurative trends. Porcinai is both modern and classical, following his intuition from theme to theme in a way that is free and unfettered by pre-conceptions. His attitude to his work has been described as "mystical", supported by a rare technical competence and an unremitting drive to experiment and create. Those of his works which are perhaps closest to my heart are the S. Ambrogio churchyard, at Zoagli, and a swimming pool built as a *trompe l'œil* against the sea in a private garden, as always in Liguria. He was arguably able to give his best when working alongside great architects. As proof of this one can cite two examples of collaboration with Oscar Niemeyer at Mondadori, Segrate, and at a villa situated in Cap Ferrat. How can one avoid making a

comparison with the harmonies and discords generated by Niemeyer's collaboration with Burle-Marx? Porcinai, when set against the creativity of Niemeyer, has the same autonomous creative force of his own. He draws on the strength of the architecture and gives it strength in turn, without for a moment falling into the temptation of mere choreography. Perhaps his work is even better expressed in the Pinocchio garden in Collodi, where he was again working with two other strong personalities—Marco Zanuso and Pietro Consagra. It is formed out of a sequence of individual settings, each different from the other, arranged along a circular route, each telling a precise moment in the story. The effect is like the leaves of the narrative weft of an English park. Architecture, sculpture and landscape are all moved by three kinds of artistic inspiration in extraordinary harmony with each other, bound together by their common use of the language of childhood.

Another Italian gardener who has played a unique role in recent years in his advancement of the cause of landscape design, to say nothing of his own work in the field, is Ippolito Pizzetti. Even though I know him personally, I have always found it difficult to follow his landscaping work because of his tenacious resistance to recounting and publishing it, because "a garden is difficult to narrate, and to get to know it one can only live it". Pizzetti is refined, he has a deep knowledge of plants and is highly receptive to the figurative arts. When he creates a garden his style is essentially open but tends towards the Anglo-Saxon and sylvan, with little interest in giving geometry and architecture in general too visible a role. Having started from the world of flowers where he is a master—*Il libro dei fiori*, Milan 1968, written with Henry Cocker, he has then moved increasingly towards the great themes of the contemporary garden in his impassioned work of polemicist and writer.

Arnaldo Pomodoro, project for
the Urbino Cemetery.

Artists and the Landscape

The reflections of the figurative arts on the landscape have themselves been an additional and important source of stimulus. Years ago, when environmentalists had not yet appeared on the horizon, Arnaldo Pomodoro proposed a work of "land art" as the basis for the extension to the Urbino Cemetery, giving rise to a veritable religious storm.

Pomodoro's design transferred the theme of his famous sculptures, erosions of taut surfaces from which crystalline lights shine, to the scale of a Montefeltro hillside. The burial sites are arranged in religious simplicity along tracts taken out of the hill summit, out of scale in a way which is highly appropriate to the place and the theme. What had upset Catholic sentiment in the cemetery's iconography was the strength of the natural imagery, seen as being too secular, or as expressing a latent Protestantism. The quality of the work of art itself only heightened this apprehension. As a consequence the design was never realised, so losing both an extraordinary garden and a unique opportunity for removing the ritual of death from our normal worn and figurative routine. What Lucien Kroll says is undoubtedly true: "Gardens are not innocent".

Niki De Saint Phalle, *Tarot Garden*, Garavicchio.

Richard Serra, *Open Field Vertical Elevation*, Celle Farm, Santomato di Pistoia.

George Trakas, *Love's Pathway*,
Celle Farm, Santomato di Pistoia.

Niki De Saint Phalle owes the opportunity to construct the *Tarot Garden* at Garavicchio in Maremma to the patronage of Marella Agnelli. This time she won out against ferocious criticism. It is another garden, fortunately persisted with, which is a true landmark of our times. A wood of cork and olive trees is animated by a dense concert of polychrome sculptures, each dedicated to a Tarot figure. The figures are typical of the work of De Saint Phalle. There is also a Kinetic sculpture by Jean Tinguely. The construction technique used, shells of reinforced concrete with mosaic coverings of ceramics and glass, together with their monumental dimension, evoke the architectural style of Gaudí or of Sam Rodia. As in a new Bomarzo, some of the Tarots are big enough to be lived in. Indeed, the sculptress actually

lived in the *Papessa* for the entire period of the construction. The Tarots, as they must be, are concerned with life, love, war, with birth and death. The whole garden has the appearance of a place of philosophical debate, inviting participation.

Celle

If the figurative arts and landscape are closely related with each other, and indeed, landscape is one of the most fundamental concepts which architecture has to assimilate, there is now a place in Italy where this dialogue is more clearly visible than ever before. The Celle Farm, designed by Giuliano Gori, situated in Santomato, Pistoia, is one of the most important and most visited sculpture gardens in the world, with a vast collection of sculptures arranged round a romantic park. What

makes the experience truly unique is that the works were not first created and then installed in the park. They were all conceived for the precise point in the park where they now stand, and were then effectively created in situ. This makes it into a laboratory of environmental art which acts as a sublime viewpoint to reflect on the contemporary garden. Its effect is impressive—to the original follies of the romantic park new ones have been added. These are not closed in upon themselves as simple objects; rather, they show themselves as spaces and situations with all the profundity and thematic richness of the garden. Few gardens can claim to be true contemporary gardens in the way that these are: Richard Serra's Menhirs (*Open Field, Vertical Elevation*), Dani Karavan's *straight line* (*Line 1-2-3*), George Trakas's double *Love's pathway*,

Richard Morris, *Labyrinth*, Celle Farm, Santomato di Pistoia.

Fausto Melotti and Denis Oppenheim's structures, Richard Morris's *Labyrinth*, Beverly Pepper's *Theatre*, Richard Long's *Grass Circle,* Ian Hamilton-Finley's *Figures* and many more, too numerous to mention. The whole collection then becomes an extraordinary work in itself.

Two "Italian" Gardens
I conclude this review with mention of two of my own gardens because, on both occasions, they were commissioned by ICE to be explicitly "Italian". The first was for the Glasgow Garden Festival of 1988 and the second for the Osaka Universal Exposition of 1990. In the final analysis the theme requested was precisely that of this review: to fix an image and an idea of a garden which is recognisably Italian. It was necessary to create this specific quality for a mass public—4 million people in Glasgow and 23 million in Osaka. In both cases the public to be visiting the site were cosmopolitan, from a wide range of backgrounds and, for the most part, inquisitive but certainly not specialists—typical of the great international trade fairs. In both cases I sought to

follow a variety of narrative threads superimposed one on the other and to make the key to their interpretation immediately accessible, enjoyable and spectacular. This was to cater both for the enormous flow of people just passing through as well as for those among them who wished to remain a little longer. For this latter group I wished to recount more intimate and secret stories which would reveal themselves a little at a time. The two gardens were very different from each other, even if arranged on the same basic plan—a straight main path with various small paths crossing at right angles. The axis has been the starting point for many Roman and Renaissance spaces, the focusing line of ordinary settlements transferring to the idea behind the basilica and then, to that of the garden in the Italian style. In the two gardens described here this style was adopted for its mediating character. This is because its significance does not imply a choice of a particular style, it is only the most eloquent evocation of the specific nature of the Italian garden. It incorporates the design of a palimpsest with its roots in ancient tradition.

Franco Zagari, Italian garden,
Glasgow. © David Hazel.

In Glasgow I approached the theme by recalling how the Italian garden has been interpreted and hybridised by the Anglo-Saxon culture over the last two centuries. As I have already mentioned with reference to Page, it represents an important exchange between the two cultures, an epic which unfolds above all in private places. It has a strong expressive character particularly in the richness and variety of its plant life with an absolute predominance of flowers. One only has to think of Villa Hanbury and Ninfa, to mention just two of the most famous gardens. So it was that in my garden, there were four successive enclosures arranged along the main path. Each was devoted to a different setting chosen from the Anglo-Italian garden repertoire: a garden from the lakes, from the Italian Riviera, from Tuscany and from the South of Italy. Everything was arranged with initial

simplicity, with four triumphs of resurgent plants and vegetation, each characteristic of the respective areas. The gardens were intersected by parallel walls of mirrors, dividing and multiplying the space. They were arranged at such a height as to allow the observers to choose between a position overlooking and dominating the scene or to lose themselves in a game involving the infinite multiplication of the plants, themselves and of images taken from the figurative heritage of historic Italian gardens traced on the mirrors themselves; a Bomarzo mask, labyrinths... As if this were not enough, each wall had its own voice, each different from the others. Thus, by going close to the wall it was possible to hear music by Paganini and Tartini played by Salvatore Accardo on the violin, Callas in *Sempre libera degg'io*, Petrarch's poems read by Elena Da Venezia and the songs of Italian birds.

Franco Zagari, Italian garden, Osaka. © Gianpiero Donin.

All this seemed an inspiration to the visiting public who, only a few minutes after the opening, had entirely understood the effects of their own movement on the voice of the garden. A number of messages were given clear expression through the popularising and somewhat joking character of the exposition, the tension between the different spaces separated by the perspective outlines and paths, and the picturesque and informal within the divisions clearly illustrated the points of attraction and difference between the two cultures. On the other hand the game in which the public were caught up between the visual and auditory clues and suggestions seems to me to have emphasised a fundamental element in the tradition of Italian gardens, the incredible theatrical vitality seen in human behaviour.

Osaka was another story. This time it was a garden which would remain as a public garden for the town. The setting is very beautiful, sloping towards the midday sun. Access is gained from the base of the plot onto a central longitudinal path running its entire length up to its highest part. It is a strip of land with wide shallow steps, flanked on the one side by a line of water and on the other by a line of fire. The first is a shallow rushing stream, hardly fourty metres in length, made from jets of water decorated with ceramics, dotted with reflected lights and erratically formed masses. The complexity of the design and arrangement of the individual pieces makes the whole into a kind of microcosm, to follow throughout its length, a short journey indeed but nonetheless demanding for that. The second boundary line, that of fire, is a long hedge of Italian azaleas. The azalea is one of the most loved and used plants in Japan. My idea was to plant the Italian species, apparently similar to theirs but in fact completely different, known only through books. There are six *decumani* arranged perpendicularly to the axial path, transverse walks with long seats and high

rose-covered espaliers. As for the rest, the beautiful cherry trees already on the site have been left as they were, the ground has been completely covered in loose bark, with erratic shapes and masses crossing the garden throughout, creating an effect recalling a little the abstraction of a dry Japanese garden. In the Osaka garden too, the arrangement of the paths in straight lines marks an important difference with Japanese architecture in nature—an exotic quality exerting, at the same time, an attraction precisely because defining the *other*. There are many themes however which put more emphasis on what the two cultures have in common—for example, the richness of the materials and the precision of the construction details. The ceramics come from the so-called "third fire" Maranello kilns and are the result of a lengthy and painstaking selection process, with many pieces having been designed specially for this occasion. The same quality of construction is echoed throughout the concreting work and in the wood and steel structures of the espaliers. This aspect also represented a retracing of steps for me. Scarpa was often in my mind while I was designing, and I was conscious of how much he had drawn on the model precisely of the Japanese garden in his highly Italian inspiration. Another theme was that of focusing on a syntax based solely on three great plant varieties: azaleas, roses and cherry trees, plants which are respectively Italian, stateless and Japanese—another design element specific to both cultures.

The Present

Against the background of a tradition where the great originality of stylistic periods has exerted an influence over the universal historical development of the garden, periods like the Roman, the Renaissance, the Mannerist and Baroque, the Italian garden still continues to have a clearly recognisable quality up to the present. The tensions between the past and present, between the international and the local are not unique to the garden, it is the "condition

of dual and dialectical cultural identity marking the salient feature of contemporary thought" (Fumihiko Maki). We are once again, in a period of lively cross-fertilisation of ideas derived from the interaction of other experiences with the main stem of our own tradition, continuing to produce an ability to interpret nature through tensions which are both innovative and forerunners of future developments. For the moment though we are still talking of a development taking place in discontinuous and somewhat isolated points. Otherwise, apart from these examples, the Italian garden has become a style which never tires of repeating the same old repertoire and following the same hybridisation. In the private garden demand is often limited to the search for choreography or plant collecting. In the public sphere, which in the present represents the main focus of interest, difficulties still arise because demand is often disoriented. In comparison with many other countries, the creative circuit of garden and landscape in Italy is not a conscious or broad-based movement based on the habits and customs of daily life, as it should be. It is still in a kind of suspense, in a hiatus.

Fashion Designers

Italian fashion returned to its status as an international phenomenon in the years after the Second World War, when the large Roman fashion houses found themselves involved in the film production that was concentrated in Cinecittà. The new Italian stars, but above all the American ones, were seen wearing creations by the Fontana sisters, Schubert and other ateliers that soon became part of the general public awareness through the pages of illustrated magazines. In the '50s, the star system was the model of a dream and what the stars wore amounted to an element of appeal in its own right.

At the same time, it was also true that Italy was becoming noted by America as an interesting country to visit. Thus, Americans re-enacted a sort of Grand Tour and travellers who were certainly less aristocratic and cultured than those of the past, and driven by memories of war or the cinema, swarmed to Italy's classic holiday destinations in search of sun, souvenirs and, why not, culture. Probably these factors went together to influence Gian Battista Giorgini in deciding that the right time had come to invest in fashion as a good production sector for exporting to the United States.

Basing his position on his professional credibility as buyer and the international image of Florence, on 12 February 1951, Giorgini organised the first international Italian fashion event at his own home, Villa Torrigiani. The success was such that for future occasions a less homespun organisation would be required—so, for the next two editions, the event was held at the Grand Hotel in Florence. But this also proved not enough, because in 1952 Italian fashion was well-known for the press and the American markets, and it needed to display an image of itself that was both strong and well-entrenched in the cultural tradition of the country. On 22 July 1952, the first fashion show was held in the White Hall of Florence's Palazzo Pitti, the venue that became from then on the official seat of the event. A collective exhibition was staged by the high fashion houses, the "sporting" ones, and the boutique fashion producers. The conditions for attending were very strict. All the fashion houses had to respect the same rule: that they could display eighteen creations, following on from one another according to a thematic ordering.

If the limelight of the show was stolen by high fashion, with its extravagant evening wear creations, the commercial success was concentrated on the so-called boutique fashion, which produced ready-to-wear garments in small quantities to sell mostly at holiday venues, and handicraft production such as bags, shoes, hats, and costume jewellery. Italy's reputation became increasingly connected to names like Gucci, Ferragamo, Pucci, and Roberta di Camerino, all of whom put forward top-quality and easy-to-wear items, and at places such as the island of Capri, Positano and Portofino, which had in the meantime also taken on almost a mythical significance for luxury holidays.

Given the economic and social situation in Italy at the time, it was probably no coincidence that the fashion concept upon which the Florentine events were founded was fundamentally pre-bourgeois. There was an aristocratic model that re-emerged in these Marquises who created—like they had in much older times—the fashions in their houses which, to American buyers, were imbued with the private luxury of a Renaissance court. The majestic old buildings or *palazzi* were opened to create the backdrop for the shows, in the artisan culture that had its roots in the workshops which used to serve the wealthy ladies.

Giorgini organised a type of modern version of the great Medicean party, whereby fashion proposals were brought together and compared, thus creating an alluring and highly involving spectacle that projected more the picture of an aesthetic environment than one of a string of products for sale.

It was a successful model: the fashion shows in Florence became a regular six-monthly date for buyers and journalists, and it mattered little whether it was competing with, or was complementary to, the one in France.

But problems were not far away over the horizon. In as early as 1952, some of the high fashion houses decided to abandon the Florentine stage, thus beginning a fluctuating behaviour of participation and defection that ended up by involving almost all the Roman ateliers. Indeed, in 1953, the Italian High Fashion Syndicate was set up and, in its by-laws, prohibited its members from taking part in the Florence fashion events. Despite these background manoeuvres, Palazzo Pitti became a fixed venue and stage from which Italian fashion was projected around the world by virtue of both its unique cultural and aesthetic backdrop, and of the way it stimulated the creation of new professional skills.

If this was the luxurious face of Italy seen in fashion magazines and repeated on the lips of people abroad, another, different Italy also existed at the time: an Italy that was in the throes of an arduous post-war reconstruction, an Italy that dressed itself at the local dressmakers' or, by following the American example, with industrially manufactured clothes. These were medium to low quality products destined to a market that could not afford to be overly interested in fashion, and made by traditionally structured medium- or large-sized clothing concerns.

It was this industrial sector that clashed with the social and cultural model sweeping the country during the economic boom. On leaving behind the subsistence years, many people became enthralled

Krizia, 1986-87 autumn-winter season. Photo by G. Gastel.

Krizia, 1984 spring-summer season. Photo by G. Gastel.

with the beckoning possibility of buying products with connotations of status symbols and modern comforts; the possibility of choosing from among the plethora of goods that industry was beginning to make available. In a word, a feverish climate of desire was created which, although lacking in good taste, tried to put on at least the appearance of luxury.

The clothing industry attempted to take up the challenge of this market and concentrated its efforts on the sizes and wearability. A clothing article could not be the same for everyone; it first had to adapt its characteristics to different sizes and shapes of the people. At last, the American templates were adapted to the Italian physical form, a result that was hailed as a success by the advertising of the clothing industries in the papers and television. But if it met with measured success in men's clothing—which was traditionally less sensitive to fashion trends—the female market was much less easy to satisfy. Ladies were adept at decoding the advertising messages which attempted to mask banal women's suits made in contexts stolen from the high fashion photographs or from those who spy on the life of the Famous in gossip magazines. But the real social phenomenon of the '60s was represented by the population of young people, a social group which has always been seen by fashion as an aesthetic model but without this ever amounting to a market in the real sense of the word. The young people of the post-war period represented a large slice of the population and they began to see themselves in an international frame of reference, made up of groups, cultural and political ideals, music, places to meet up in, and, last but not least, of clothes.

The clothing industry did not know how to meet the new demand. High fashion was simply ignored by the younger generation, which rapidly came to adopt what would soon be called styles, that is independent clothing behaviours that in many cases were self-sustaining.

Beyond the groups identified in a specific way, indeed, a new fashion exploded which was generally defined as pop fashion, from which the great clothing novelties of the decade were to emerge: the miniskirt and the male colour. In following the two different trends, England and France took on the challenge of the vanguard culture and adapted their own proposals to the new demand.

London became the symbol of youth culture: music, dance, cinema, photography, clothing, shops, everything seemed to find an enthusiasm and strength in opposing the century-old English tradition. And so it was in London that in 1965 Mary Quant launched a dress with a half-thigh-length skirt, a very infantile model to be worn with long tights in colours that could even clash with that of the skirt. The miniskirt was born as the uniform of an adolescent who refused to grow up and who wanted to stand apart from the adult model of mothers.

At the same time a similar phenomenon was taking place in the fashion of men, who began wearing their hair much longer with respect to the vaguely military cuts of the times, and favouring cloth which were more coloured, imaginative and varied. Shirts and trousers began to flourish psychedelic decorations while, as to their form, the clothes began to hug the body, thus creating an explosive effect against the bourgeois uniform that continued to represent the maturing to adulthood. The Peter Pan myth ended up by creating the first crack in a model that was 150 years old and which had seemed destined to never eclipse.

France's younger generation instead did not initially display the same anger and desire to break with tradition and so Paris fashion addressed the theme in different ways.

On one hand, *haute couture* proposed a fashion inspired on the wave of technology that was sweeping the West. The future, as projected in cartoons and science fiction, and put into practice by the Russian and American space projects, became the source of inspiration for a fashion made up of "architectural" clothes.

Geometry reigned supreme, and covered a feminine body that was slender, androgynous and vaguely infantile.

The mass spirit of the new era was backed up by flanking the high fashion collections with a ready-made clothing offered at lower prices, articles that conserved the same fashion value and which were available in the boutiques of the most important towns and cities. This form of democratisation, however, did not completely respond to the widespread desire to break away from a concept of élite fashion, and this was why a new avenue was explored from the start of the decade. An avenue which did away with the very idea of *couture* and spoke instead of the style to attribute to ready-made clothes. This idea became the focus of study for some young designers, who created lines of models which were connected by a strong and easily recognisable fashion idea. It was a procedure that characterised those who, from then on, would be called "stylists".

The reference market was less infantile and "angry" than its English counterpart, the models were a little more elegant and débutante in style, but the articles proposed by then were part of a list that amounted to a lifestyle model: mini dresses, miniskirts, coloured trousers, T-shirts, blouses, jackets, mini-coats, boots, low healed shoes, tights and naive lingerie.

Around this new type of production, a new distribution network was organised made up of "boutiques", a term that, immediately and throughout the Western world, defined the fashion shops for young people: lots of music and at high volume, a deluge of clothes arranged so that browsers could pick them up and try them on in front of a mirror, and only a few sales assistants who, incidentally, had to be young too.

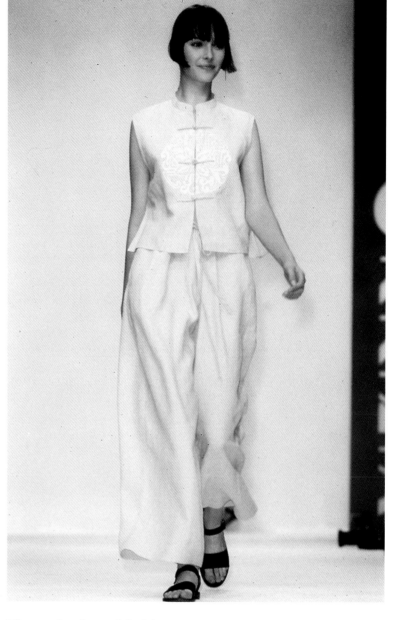

The youth culture of the '60s was highly international and, in Italy too, young people were listening to new music, seeking new grouping models, formulating new ideas, and dressing to the trends. In the big cities and holiday centres, boutiques began to spring up selling both imported clothes and small home-produced collections. It was around these apparently marginal creations that a transformation took place in the manufacturing system. To cater to the needs for these new articles, a new system was needed, one made up of people who could create models to a precise fashion idea, who could produce the necessary materials, who could

Krizia, 1994 spring-summer season.

Krizia, 1971 spring-summer season. Advertisement taken from *Vogue Italia,* February 1971. Photo by Chris von Wangen.

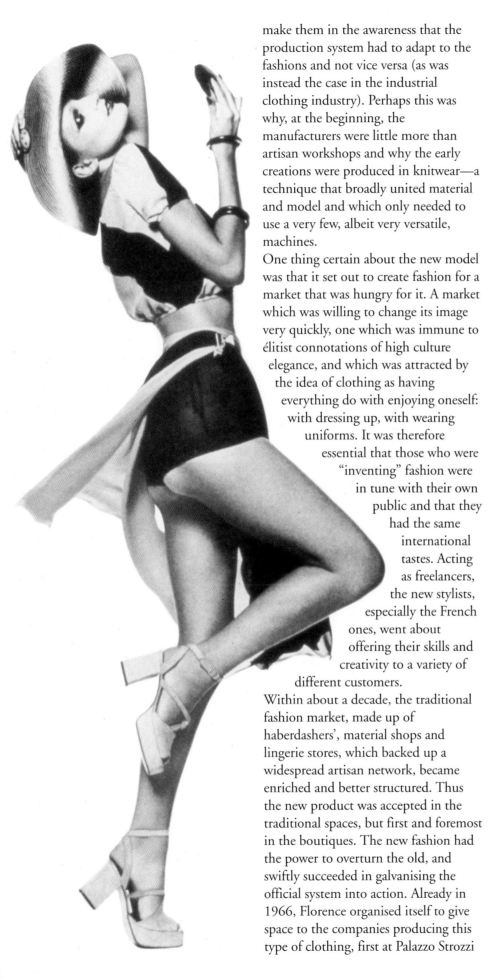

make them in the awareness that the production system had to adapt to the fashions and not vice versa (as was instead the case in the industrial clothing industry). Perhaps this was why, at the beginning, the manufacturers were little more than artisan workshops and why the early creations were produced in knitwear—a technique that broadly united material and model and which only needed to use a very few, albeit very versatile, machines.

One thing certain about the new model was that it set out to create fashion for a market that was hungry for it. A market which was willing to change its image very quickly, one which was immune to élitist connotations of high culture elegance, and which was attracted by the idea of clothing as having everything do with enjoying oneself: with dressing up, with wearing uniforms. It was therefore essential that those who were "inventing" fashion were in tune with their own public and that they had the same international tastes. Acting as freelancers, the new stylists, especially the French ones, went about offering their skills and creativity to a variety of different customers.

Within about a decade, the traditional fashion market, made up of haberdashers', material shops and lingerie stores, which backed up a widespread artisan network, became enriched and better structured. Thus the new product was accepted in the traditional spaces, but first and foremost in the boutiques. The new fashion had the power to overturn the old, and swiftly succeeded in galvanising the official system into action. Already in 1966, Florence organised itself to give space to the companies producing this type of clothing, first at Palazzo Strozzi

and later in various hotels. From 1967, with the defection of high fashion and its replacement with luxury ready-to-wear, also the White Hall of Palazzo Pitti opened its imposing doors to the creations of the stylists and newly emerging firms. This allowed the new exponents to leave anonymity behind and to feature in the specialised magazines of the day. And here the journalists played an important role in building the success of the various new fashion houses: names like Krizia, Missoni, Karl Lagerfeld, Walter Albini, Miguel Cruz and Alberto Lattuada began to ring synonymously with "new"—the first two also as company brand names, the others as stylists who designed collections for various companies while always leaving their wholly personal mark.

The first to capture the exceptional nature and ambiguity of the moment was Walter Albini: at a time when tailoring quality had to concede the limelight to fashion content, he thought it clear that the key figure of the process had to be the content's creator. Actually, while the production of high fashion was strongly personalised, ready-to-wear distinguished itself from its competitors by identifying itself with a company brand name, or the name of the boutique that distributed it. In 1968, Albini strode the catwalk of Palazzo Pitti as designer of five collections, but in the calendar of the fashion shows appear the names of Trell, Krizia maglia, Montedoro, Princess Luciana and Billy Ballo.

To make the name of the stylists emerge from anonymity also meant ratifying the existence of a third centre within the fashion production system. A centre that had an industrial output of small lines made on the ideas of a creative designer. To achieve this goal two paths were open, one contractual the other aesthetic. The first step was one of creating a same-level relationship with the manufacturer so that the designers were not mere external consultants and had the power and freedom to exercise freedom over the formal aspects of the collection. This was the goal that Albini attained by going into partnership with Luciano Papini to set up a small suit-making company by the name of Misterfox. The autumn-winter collection for 1970-71 unveiled at Palazzo Pitti in April 1970 was such a tremendous success that it severely strained the limited production capacity of the newborn company. The revival style, as exemplified by the articles and the press release, was soon found again in the pages of *Vogue Italy*, and became one of the key fashion elements of the times. The success went on to repeat itself in September at the Maremoda show on the isle of Capri, and in October, again in Florence. Nevertheless, in the same events Albini's signature appeared also in the collections by Montedoro, Paola Signorini and Diamant's.

It was at this point that the trend became reflected at a global level. The Florentine presentations had been designed by Giorgini as a function of high fashion—or anyway as a function of a system that was strongly artisan-based and which needed to position itself in an élite aesthetic frame to which it could anchor its image.

The new model that was developing did not seek ties with the illustrious pasts of the nations. On the contrary, it wanted to use such modern instruments as industrial production to sell to a mass market that was beginning to express its own taste.

Albini realised the time was ripe to depart from the old and attempt a new road that could immediately convey the idea of modernity, internationalness, and the future. Above all, his road would not scatter the stylist's fashion proposal into a thousand channels, but present itself on the market as a unique idea that was strong and recognisable and which could distinguish a huge variety of products. The solution, worked out by the two partners together with Ferrante, Tositti and Monti, the owners of Effetiemme, Italy's

leader in manufactured clothing distribution, addressed the different problems. They began by leaving Florence, with all its glorious past, to choose a new seat for their presentation: Milan, an industrial city with few ties with its past and absolutely no tradition of big fashion events. In the '60s, Milan had experienced an important boom and was the city which had experimented with new artistic ideas

Walter Albini, a pioneer of the Italian ready-to-wear.

Opposite: The advertising campaign of one of his designs.

and design. And, towards the end of the decade, it had also been the city of social turbulence. Choosing Milan meant turning towards a different Italy, one that did not live in customs but which was looking to play an active role in modernity.

The second problem was that of the relationship between stylists and the end buyer: rather than simply wanting a garment to wear, the mass market was interested in something more complex, something positioned in a central zone between taste, lifestyle and the cultural model of appearance. The youth cultures had by then indicated precisely that this was how they wanted to use fashion: by now for more than a decade, the way of dressing demanded that it signified a choice of belonging, a way of living, and an ideological standpoint. Albini arrived at considering the meaning of the profession of stylist after all this had taken place; after the hippie aesthetics had begun to make their breach in fashion and provoking refined ethnic choices; and after the revival taste had flanked the one that was strictly futuristic, midway through the decade. If the problem was a cultural and stylistic one, the task of the stylists was not one of designing individual clothing items; rather, it was to create a "climate of taste" in which the buyers could recognise themselves. This would only be possible by controlling a complete collection: in other words, all the clothes and accessories that could meet the requirements of the hypothetical buyers for a whole season.

On 27 April 1971 at the Circolo del Giardino, Milan, an autumn-winter collection for 1971-72 was exhibited. Made up of 180 models, it marked a watershed between past and future, and the garments, which were designed and signed by Albini, were made by five companies, each specialising in a specific merchandise sector: Basile for ladies suits, jackets and coats, Escargots for knitwear, Diamant's for shirts and blouses, Callaghan for jersey, and Misterfox for elegant wear and evening gowns. At the same time as Albini, Ken Scott and Cadette began exhibiting their collections again in Milan. Since they shared Albini's opinion on what the market wanted, it was with this dispersal that the real Italian ready-to-wear began in earnest.

Many aspects were still however unresolved, the first being the relationship between stylists and the manufacturing company. Again it was

Walter Albini who led the way, and in December 1972, in London, he presented a suits-only collection which, for the first time, bore his initials: WA. The price paid for giving birth to the stylist's *griffe* was the loss of four of the team's companies: only the faithful partner Papini went along with Albini into the new adventure. For autumn-winter 1973-74 two collections were unveiled, one in Venice under the brand name WA, the other—which became a sort of second line—in Milan under the name Misterfox. The same division was to be repeated also in the following season: Misterfox in Milan, WA in Rome. Finally, in January and June 1975, Albini presented two solo high-fashion collections dedicated to Chanel and to the great French fashion designers of the early decades of the century.

The path was not easy and was decided by the times: probably no-one was clear about the role the stylist as a figure should have in the new system. No models existed to which one could be inspired if not that of the fashion designer. In the attempt to invent a *griffe*, with all the cultural and above all commercial weight that it could have, Albini took a path of differentiating his products from the industrial ones. With a similar tactic to his idea of playing Milan off against Florence, he went in search of situations that were suitable for conveying the meaning of his personal fashion proposal, until he closed the circle in a direct confrontation with *couture*, upon which he tried to impose his own language and a new production model that could work without a fashion house. He limited himself to producing the prototypes, the models of which were sold to fashion houses, stores and boutiques specialised in then creating them "made-to-measure". The results, though, did not live up to Albini's expectations. The market was not yet ready to allow the *griffe* of a stylist to assert itself independently by imposing its own rules on both an industry

which, in many respects, still did not exist, and to the Rome high fashion scene, which was proving increasingly entrenched in its own old conventions. The second challenge was to fine-tune a fashion style that could be suitably presented to a public which was no longer composed of a restricted international élite able to confer success to a tailor or an idea. The population of young people had grown and was now much less homogeneous: it had a thousand different interests and was enacting huge transformations in the social fabric and lifestyles. And it was certainly no longer willing to identify itself with just one type of fashion, fed to it from "artificial" industrial sources. It had therefore become necessary for everyone to put forward a clearly recognisable style model and to pursue it consistently over time, so they could become identified with it, thereby creating differentiation from the competition and avoiding confusing overlaps. From the beginning of the '60s, Missoni had chosen to concentrate on the materials and colours of knitwear, reducing its tailoring research to a minimum. Krizia, after a period of self-identification during which it used the services of Albini and Lagerfeld, found an ideal situation in the association between Mariuccia Mandelli and Anna Domenici. By focusing on the fashions that were becoming increasingly popular (hot-pants, midi-skirts, maxi-skirts, kitsch, and revival), it worked out an ironic and "excessive" style that had close ties with the language of Pop Art and which appealed to an uninhibited and self-assured female customer base.

Albini instead chose the path of revival, by going about an extremely safe construction of a modern version of the fabulous and aristocratic atmospheres he had discovered in the fashion magazines of the early decades of the century.

Despite appearances, it was a cultural proposal that was wholly in keeping with the times. With the eclipse of the

Missoni, 1997 spring-summer season. Photo by Mario Testino.

Missoni, 1997 autumn-winter season. Photo by Mario Testino.

heady modernity of the '60s, the times were marked by a strong return to the past, which was souped up again in various ways. In just a few years, Luchino Visconti made three films like *Death in Venice* (1971), *The Damned* (1969) and *Ludwig* (1973) while the alternative Ken Russell made a film version of D.H. Lawrence's *Women in Love* about tormented sexual phobias. Across the Atlantic, Lisa Minnelli and Robert Redford rose to international stardom through *Cabaret* and *The Great Gatsby*. Meanwhile, Paris offered a spread of exhibitions that dwelt upon the art and fashion of those same decades. Even historical research enjoyed a moment of great fervour. It was as if people were suddenly rediscovering that the present had a past that could be turned to for an illustration of what was happening; a past that

it was necessary to come to terms with. Aside from the immediate phenomenon of taste that these events produced and which obviously extended to the world of fashion, Albini probably recognised that fashion too needed to take time out to reflect on its past if it were to find its right future. It was no coincidence, then, that he did not propose a re-vamp of his creations, but rather the images of a more refined and articulate lifestyle than the one contemplated by street fashion at the time. It was not just in his drawings, then, but also in his obsessive search for a "total look" that the desire emerged for finding a model of elegance and luxury which had no ties with the political movements or the high bourgeois rituals of *couture*.
It was as if Albini had understood that the market of the new fashion was positioned in an intermediate phase between these two extremes and that it

was made up of women aged about 25 who had traumatically broken with the traditional roles and who were now seeking an independent model of life and culture. The game of dressing up, which is a part of every revival, allowed a pause for reflection to experiment the possible meeting point between the different fashion proposals and the styles and life situations of the "new era". From the pin-up to the androgynous type, from the Lonchamps style to Marlene Dietrich, from the *femme fatale* to the blossoming girl—everything was brought to life again and experimented with in the space of only three or four years.
This went on until the arrival, in 1974, at a sort of "zero" fashion level: the blouse. Blouses, big blouses, nineteenth-century night-gown blouses, and so on began to invade the pages of the fashion magazines. As had happened in the

Picture taken from the "Giorgio Armani donna" advertising campaign from the 1990 spring-summer season. Photo by Jacques Olivar.

mid-eighteenth century, the non-dress turned its back on the past and on all its social and historical divisions, and opened itself to a new level of experimentation. Perhaps it was no mere coincidence that it was precisely in this moment that ready-to-wear finally made its way in Milan. In March 1974, also the fashion shows of Krizia and Missoni—unanimously acknowledged as the most solid representatives of ready-made fashion—were transferred to the northern industrial city. On 10 October 1975, *WWD (Women's Wear Daily)* was astounded that Valentino had decided to choose Paris as the venue for displaying his boutique collections and not Milan, which was by then considered "number one among the

capitals of Italian ready-to-wear". And perhaps it was again no mere by chance that this was when the names of three new stylists, who had not played a part in the pioneering phase, appeared on the scene: Versace, Armani and Ferré.

Gianni Versace had started out with Callaghan, taking up the place left by Albini, but he soon became the designer for Genny and Complice. Giorgio Armani, instead, after a long apprenticeship with La Rinascente and Hitman, established a company with Galeotti and was working for many different companies. He began to exhibit in his own right in 1975. As to Gianfranco Ferré, he had already made a name for himself by creating costume

jewellery and soon set out on his path as a stylist by clinching a contract with Sangiorgio to arrive at an association with Mattioli.

The second generation of stylists was to invent "casual", or, to use a term that was normally attributed to Armani, "destructurisation". The destructured object, however, was not so much the individual garment; rather, it constituted the whole of a society that had finally challenged the rights and roles used by the previous fashion styles. The idea was that fashion should not be related to states or fixed social roles: and this included a challenge to the classic differentiation of gender—the basic starting point of all Western fashion. So gender conventions were hotly attacked

Image taken from "Giorgio Armani donna" advertising campaign from the 1990 spring-summer season. Photo by Jacques Olivar.

Imagine taken from the "Giorgio Armani donna" advertising campaign from the 1984-85 autumn-winter season. Photo by Aldo Fallai.

by the feminists, but also by the adoption of trousers by women and by men's growing diffidence towards the formal suit. Despite the repeated economic crises of the decade, also the bourgeois work myth as the instrument for economic realisation and social climbing was replaced by a utopia that envisaged work as the realisation of the person and as a service to society. There were no bases, then, for a big expansion in traditional fashion since there were no "status" elements to represent or luxuries to show off. And it was precisely this that became the fertile ground on which a new type of fashion could flourish. The essential condition was that either the new fashion had no ties with the old, or that it would be able to give the previous

fashion a wholly alternative outlook. The experiment began with the most difficult clothing item and the one that most closely represented the male role on the one hand and tailoring wisdom on the other: the jacket. Armani worked on narrowing the sexual distinctions by creating a men's-style jacket with a soft cloth like those normally used in feminine fashion. He proposed it, with only minor differences, for both men's and women's version and, at the same time, he also engineered a revolution for the sector: by reducing the jacket to a single external "enclosure" by doing away with linings, padding, and reinforcements, he took away all of the shaping. Thus he effectively eliminated an absolutely fundamental operation for keeping a clothing item "fit": the long

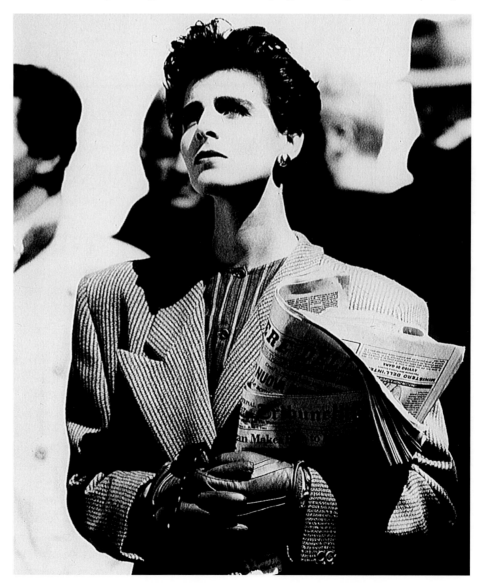

Picture taken from the "Giorgio Armani donna" advertising campaign from the 1990 spring-summer season. Photo by Jacques Olivar.

Image taken from the "Giorgio Armani donna" advertising campaign from the 1994-95 autumn-winter season. Photo by Peter Lindbergh.

Image taken from the "Giorgio Armani donna" advertising campaign from the 1992-93 autumn-winter season. Photo by Peter Lindbergh.

initial ironing. In this way, Armani took away a "tricky" clothing item from the tailor's know-how and offered it on a plate to the industrial clothing sector. From the cultural viewpoint, the operation was undoubtedly revolutionary: Armani had invented a jacket that was no longer strictly male or female and which, above all, had lost its formal connotations and, with them, its defining role. It looked rather like an old and somehow out-of-shape suit; certainly comfortable, it could be worn on all occasions and with all kinds of combination; it was a jacket that did not attempt to convey any particular significance but which did instead get across one explosive fact: that women no longer wanted to dress like "women" and men like "men".

The same cultural model also produced the Missoni cardigan, which, at a certain point, became a type of uniform for intellectuals and men from the world of entertainment—an item that went over a shirt like a jacket but which performed a different function because it was knitted, and took on a different

appearance because it was so rich in colour.

Within this framework, dressing "casual" took on a precise meaning: everything which was not formal and which did not require the day to be divided up according to pre-set rules; everything which could be used both at work and for leisure time. Dressing "casual" respected the body and its need for freedom of movement. So of course at this point the stylists threw their energies into creating styles, clothes and materials that could succeed in matching all these criteria.

The journey to the Orient, whether real or metaphorical, became a compulsory objective from which came light baggy cotton trousers, jodhpurs, long straight shirts, unusual widths, simple cuts, colours such as orange, saffron yellow, red and fuchsia. A similar journey to the Arab world brought djellabas, Bedouin-style coats, caftans and even attempts at chadors (or were these inspired from Italy's Red Brigades?).

But even the poorer clothing of the West was looked at again with a careful

Missoni,1996 autumn-winter season. Photo by Mario Testino.

Missoni, 1996 spring-summer season. Photo by Tiziano Magni.

eye, to glean new ideas like the use of heavy fabrics hemmed with simple wool overcasts; the overlapping of shapeless items which could be taken off or worn depending on the temperature; fustian or corduroy for trousers or "game warden" suits; the flower prints and folk embroidery; or the shawls and the heavy woollen tights.

These items generally had a very simple, tailored structure and one which could be easily reproduced on an industrial scale. But most of all they were items that had been "subtracted" or "de-localised" from their original contexts and they also had no predefined position within the public awareness of the West.

Together with the research into the style, the fashion business went ahead in its quest to create a new production model. Here again the innovative impulse was given by Armani, who succeeded in imposing his requests on a GFT which was suffering a survival crisis. The industry—and in this case the large-scale industry—took on the role of simple "dumb" producer of the collections which were signed by the stylists, who also dealt with their marketing and communications strategy.

The model was not destined for a general acceptance—as is borne out by cases like Max Mara, Genny and Complice, Basile, Callaghan, etc., which used an opposite type of model as their basis—but for the *griffes* that, in the next decade, would become the keys to Made in Italy, it was just this type of philosophy that would form the basis of success.

For Italy, 1978 was a year that represented a moment of deep crisis. The march of the culture of the Left was stopped in its tracks when the Premier, Aldo Moro, was abducted and later murdered by the Red Brigades. The public at large realised that 1968 had spawned a monster (the doubts and the various explanations would come out twenty years after).

The situation was extremely difficult also under the economic viewpoint, and the call to order was mandatory. Also the world of fashion heeded this climate and responded with a style that was dark, classic and somewhat military-like. Yet the industry was also projected towards the future, and adopted a new organisational system: in March, the first edition of Modit was held at the Milan trade fair premises, and in the following year the stylists began to attend the venue, presenting their collections at the *Centro Sfilate* L'Associazione Italiana Industriali dell'Abbigliamento e l'Associazione Magliecalze succeeded in co-ordinating all the parties of the system and creating a united image of Italian ready-to-wear. The end of the '70s was marked by the eclipse of their utopia: in 1980, Ronald Reagan was voted in as President of the United States with a decidedly conservative and liberal manifesto. In Turin in October, a rally attended by some forty thousand white-collar workers was held against the trade unions. The word "deregulation" was on the lips of the press and the people. The year marked the return of the new middle-class, of those who had become well off due to the economic upturn and who now wanted the pre-eminent role they felt was theirs, the jobs that had to produce wealth, and free time for ostentation and luxury.

The signal of Italian fashion's ability to cater to the newly evolving social scene was provided once again by Giorgio

Armani: in 1982, *Time Magazine's* cover story on him was the seal of recognition from America and a tribute to Italian fashion.

This recognition arrived, though, at a rather strange time. In March 1981 the fashion leaders turned up at the Milan trade fair with the new collections for autumn-winter 1981-82 vaunting an incredible enterprise. It amounted to the most creative re-working of ethnic themes ever witnessed. In keeping with the work method adopted, the top stylists unveiled spectacular collections inspired by the Orient. Armani had chosen Kurosawa's latest film *Kagemusha*, Krizia the Circus of Beijing, Ferré chose Japan, while Versace had taken models from the Western medieval life and "contaminated" them with eastern themes and icons. Marylou Luther, in the 30 March edition of the *Los Angeles Times*, dubbed the result as "fall fashion's spaghetti shogunate"). It was a "difficult" and extremely luxurious fashion, created using highly prized materials and with the kind of innovative work methods that had much in common with high fashion. And so too did the price tabs: in this period, Italian ready-to-wear seemed set upon becoming the clothing for the wealthy.

In the following March, two announcements broke at the same time: the first was of the cover story to be published in *Time Magazine*; the second was that Armani had decided not to exhibit his new collection—neither in public nor to the press.

Through long declarations published in the papers, he tried to explain his choice: "My decision is certainly not one moved by caprice or as a cheap publicity coup. Precisely in these last five years, our paths have divided for choices that are wholly respectable but nevertheless very different. Some of us have preferred to maintain a very high level and an atelier-studio dimension to our work, while others are concentrating on taking the path of industrial organisation. As a profession,

Images taken from the "Giorgio Armani donna" advertising campaign from the 1989 spring-summer season. Photos by Aldo Fallai.

Images taken from the "Giorgio Armani donna" advertising campaign from the 1987 spring-summer season. Photos by Aldo Fallai.

I have chosen to be a designer who supports the clothing industry, and this means designing thirty collections a year between men's and women's fashion; having nearly a dozen licences for accessories signed with my name; reaching 170 billion lire sales in 1982; starting up and guiding the launch of my first perfume produced by Helena Rubinstein, which will be presented on 30 March in Paris and then in New York, Dallas, San Francisco, London and Berlin; and managing the inauguration, from now until September, of fifty Emporio Armani stores (my production for young men) across Italy" (A. Mulassano, "Parte senza Armani la gara della moda" in *Corriere della Sera*, 14 March 1982).

And again, in *L'Espresso* of 2 May: "We must endeavour to produce clothes for the industry and the public that are reasonably ready to wear. Otherwise, we will risk having design only and of being like a designer who creates ashtrays that cannot contain ash".

In Armani's comment, clear reference is made to profession's taking stock of its situation. But there was a fact that provoked it: the flop of his winter collection, which had received as much acclaim from the fashion critics as rejection from the market. And in this light, both the self-criticisms and the plans for the future are justified. The temptation to devote himself to absolute creativity, almost throwing down the gauntlet to high fashion, had been too strong to pass up on. Like all failures, it hurt but, as the saying goes, every cloud has a silver lining. The problem in hand was to diversify the fashion supply according to the different markets and to then pursue the logic of the lines and licences. The first line—destined for an élite public— was given the task of image creation and experimentation: its presentation could be the occasion for transmitting the new ideas and trends and for giving scope to the stylist's creative research, both in the areas of design and of materials; it was an opportunity for attracting and/or rekindling the public's awareness and attention towards the name of the *griffe*. Thus, the creation of the first line was to have more artisan characteristics. As for the second line, instead, the assigned goal was one of large-scale sales and distribution, so it was characterised by more generally acceptable versions of the fashion ideas presented in the first line, with less innovative materials, and with a decidedly industrial production. Although industrially made, the young line had stronger and more unconventional fashion connotations and an advertising image that sought other communication topics.

But the move was not about simply production innovation. Rather, it reflected a very rapidly evolving cultural and social situation. The refusal of the political dimension and the so-called "return to private values" quickly took on the appearance of a new lifestyle in which the accumulation and flaunting of wealth were the prevailing values. Social climbing was back in vogue: the well-off of the '80s came mainly from the world of commerce or the high value-added service industry and lacked in tradition and culture. Back with a vengeance, they wanted simply to appear, to show off. People began talking of their "look", in other words a communication structure made up of clothes and consumer objects capable of building the image of things—or, better, people—that were not real. But the destructurisation of the traditional representation models had left a vacuum. Gone, indeed, were the clear rituals formerly available for flaunting one's wealth. Gone too, moreover, were the deep-seated and commonly-shared cultural values or instruments for creating new such rituals. By harking back to the old model of Sombart, they chose the path of ostentation and consumption. But also the choice of clothing and accessories to create one's personal look did not prove such an easy assignment, and a professional mediator was needed to ensure the conformity between the adopted (or desired) lifestyle and the clothing combination suitable for

Gianni Versace, 1987-88 autumn-winter season. Photo by Massimo Listri.

Gianni Versace, 1983-84, autumn-winter season. Photo by Richard Avedon.

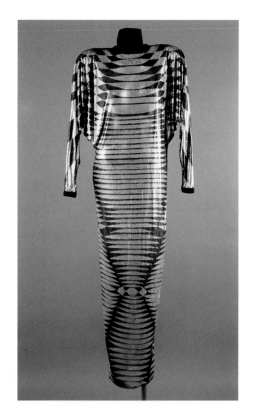

Gianni Versace, 1986-87
autumn-winter season.
Photo by Massimo Listri.

Gianni Versace, 1991 spring-
summer season.
Photo by Irving Penn.

conveying it. The Italian stylists were
ready for this task: they simply had to
put aside the research phase and move
on to a final identification of their own
stylistic message.

The collection for spring-summer 1983
marked the turning point: the excessive
references to the past were done away
with and everyone went about their
search for new ideas and a personal
language. Ferré came up with a fashion
that was sober, clear, and clean cut. One
intended—according to Pia Soli—"for
a cultured and refined" woman. Krizia
worked out a combination between her
experience acquired with ethnic
clothing and a love for the abstract, and
offered geometric forms, without
forsaking that sort of appointment
with her public of making
knitwear with large effigies of
animals.

For the time being, Versace
focused on translating men's
clothing, and its proportional
structure, into the women's field.
But above all, he presented the first
suit made of a metallic mesh, a
material that was to become the
symbol of his *griffe*.

And almost to underline the need for a
personalisation, many stylists
abandoned the Milan Fashion Show
Centre to stage their presentations in
different and more individual spaces.
The general view abroad of Italian
export production, which was already
held in high regard for its quality and
elegance, thus came to add many
different and well-defined styles.
The designer *griffe* therefore became
the aesthetic key of the new
consumption. And in the absence
of other elements that were
perhaps more certain but at the
same time more difficult to
decode, the *griffe* became a status
symbol. The new elegance was
aggressive and directly
communicated its meaning and
cost. But "fashion is in fashion" and
also in this brutal system the stylists
continued in their search, which

Gianni Versace, 1983-84
autumn-winter season.
Photo by Richard Avedon.

Gianni Versace, 1982-83
autumn-winter season.
Photo by Richard Avedon.

Gianni Versace,1994-95
autumn-winter season.
Photo by Richard Avedon.

became increasingly elaborate and refined.

There was however a concession that all, without exception, made to the heroine of the new era: the career woman. The proportions of the upper body took on the form of the sixteenth-century male torso, the shoulders became padded and the upper body exaggerated, overshadowing the legs. The jacket, which was the new uniform of working women but which was not worn as part of a woman's dress suit, was proposed as a basic garment, a clothing item that lived a life of its own and which went equally well with skirts, trousers or even Bermuda shorts. Every stylist interpreted it and varied it season by season, depending on their own models of taste and on the woman they wanted to appeal to: more or less emancipated, more or less aggressive, and with more or less sex appeal.

These were the years of great success: Armani, Ferré, Krizia, Valentino, Versace, Moschino, Fendi, Coveri, Biagiotti, Soprani, Venturi—among whose ranks Gigli and Dolce & Gabbana were later enrolled—became the new gurus of taste: their *griffes* sanctioned what was and what was not fashion, what had to be bought and what were simply use-objects, what made something a status symbol and what did not.

And the instructions were received as much by the career women as by the yuppies and the more modest orders.

The spread was total and it offered much scope for broadening the range of what to offer: in 1986, some stylists edged over to encroach on high fashion's patch, while a boom took place in designer casual wear, made up also of T-shirts, accessories, shoes, and so on. The most extravagant evening out and the most normal free time each required the same degree of attention if the "total look" was to be meticulously maintained.

So much power, however, was destined to end up by no longer being so

stimulating. The escape to high fashion perhaps represented a new professional challenge, also because the place of reference was Paris, where Versace measured himself with his own line and Ferré even went to work with Dior. Ready-to-wear, instead, was idly involved in producing mediocre items made with the latest discovery in materials technology: stretch fibre. The property of these materials' clinging to the body allowed two-dimensional clothing items to be made which took on the desired shape as soon as they were put on: it was to some extent the Italian answer to the new Japanese vogue which was making inroads in the Paris fashion scene. But the incessant demand for luxury coming from the market pushed producers to adorn much simplicity with applications that were increasingly more opulent and invasive by using sequins, precious stones, strass, coloured glass, embroidery and anything else that could be enrolled to bolster the new baroque taste.

Then 1987 came, and with it the crash of the New York Stock Exchange. A mortal blow was dealt to the Reaganian society: easy wealth and blockbuster careers went up in smoke overnight. The effect was like one of discovering a vacuum.

As if this were not enough, the fall of the Berlin wall and the war against Iraq did not engender the type of proud or victorious sentiments that might have been expected. Quite the contrary: they forced the whole of Western society to deal with a process of civilisation that had no reference values to offer if not those of selfishness, cynicism and appearance. It was no coincidence, then, that the spread of Aids was dealt with by using cultural instruments of a disgraceful modesty: from the attribution of guilt to the "positives", to the holy war against the categories at risk, to the point of abandoning Aids victims out of fear of contamination. All the removal forms of a social evil were dug up which should have been

considered by then as belonging only to either long-past or obscure centuries and societies.

The fashion world experienced this tragedy close up. It reacted as if to immediately register a change in customs that could cancel, together with the lifestyle of the '80s, an entire economic system. In Italy, moreover, at the beginning of the new decade the situation was worsening both on the financial and political fronts. The economic crisis and the discovery of a deep-seated corruption system brought to light a glaring fact: that the affluence of the '80s had been little more than a sick bluff. Internal consumption fell drastically and from various parts calls were raised for more uprightness and a return to many almost forgotten ethical values. The fashion business and the entire production system supporting it found themselves having to face these emergencies at the same time.

In 1992, perhaps the worst year of the crisis, they did this in an assortment of ways: by seeking new export markets in the Orient; rethinking the individual corporate positionings; looking for new merchandise outlets; investing more on communication; changing the women's clothes assortment; and, lastly, by giving an unusual amount of space to men's fashion. Those who, like Moschino, had maintained a critical relationship with fashion, directed all of their communication resources into announcing the change, while those who had a deep-rooted image in the consumption of more lavish items like Versace, broadened their horizons to less ephemeral areas such as the "homeworld" market, and backed up their strategy with unprecedented investments in advertising and communication. And again, those who had a more fluid image or who were entering the market at this time, like Prada or the Gucci revival, did away with all signs of opulence and replaced them with a style that was sober, modest; one made up of almost shapeless garments, which created the basis for a personal elegance that was more about taste and gestural expressiveness than about clothing in itself.

Italian fashion, however, no longer held the exclusive rights on minimalism, nor could it claim to be sole leader in that ironic, joking and intentionally exaggerated fashion which created a direct dialogue with the styles of the street. By now though, the Italian stylists had a very solid professional base and, in most cases, a reputation that would not be affected by simple variations in fashion. They took up the challenge through heavy investments in communication, projecting a different woman who was adolescent, slender, delicate and pale, and not aggressive; a woman to whom they no longer offered the "total look", but rather individual apparel items to be co-ordinated according to personal preference.

The new ideal woman had none of the classic characteristics of beauty: she was not very feminine, her body thin, emaciated, to the point of being anorexic; she carried a sneaking suspicion of the much-feared disease, Aids. This fascination in the sick, ailing and ugly, re-emerged from the symbolist culture and became a base for highly elegant and refined dresses with purely essential lines, made of materials which, although innovative from the technological viewpoint, harked back to the old and rather *fané* materials: printed or *devoré* velvets, washed silks, creased cottons, felted or teaseled wools. The appetite for luxury had not abated, and returned after the crisis with a vengeance, although this time it followed different principles. The luxury end of the market was now looking for a greater capacity by the stylists for discernment in terms of taste, and a culture of life that was more deeply-rooted. The elegant woman returned to wearing a straight dress which was not too short, a pearl necklace and well chosen accessories, much in keeping with the upper metropolitan classes.

Rather than being seen as aesthetic guides, stylists had become the guarantors of well-made products. And at this point, then, along with the personalised *griffes*, emerged the company labels. At first they paraded the names of fictitious stylists, but soon did away with even the sham that certain creative individuals existed. It amounted to a victorious return for big industry which, by depersonalising the product, made it independent from all "artistic" reference and transformed it into being what it is: simple merchandise to be sold and bought. And yet some doubt remains, as Miuccia Prada hinted at when she wrote: "I am convinced... that our secret lies in our controlling everything: creation, production and marketing. I have never believed in the 'look', for me it is an obscene word. I've always had it crystal clear in my mind that clothing is an object. Let's say that I pretend that creativity comes second, but then things could be no other way, after all. Here instead, it's taken for granted to some extent, as if the idea of the stylist in itself did not bring about any result while 'the hard day-to-day work' ..." (G. A. Stella, "Prada: 'Ecco perché abbiamo scalato Gucci. Nel mondo della moda noi siamo diversi'", in *Corriere della Sera*, 22 June 1998).

Moschino, advertising campaign for 1985-86 autumn-winter season. Photo by Sergio Caminata.

Moschino, 1984 spring-summer season.

Giampiero Bosoni

Myths and Figures of the Italian Architect

Looking at Italy from the outside, we can see that people widely tend to give an *a priori* recognition—one high in value and somehow mythical—of Italian artistic culture in general, within which architecture, of course, features. There is a certain ambiguity in this acknowledgement, which tends to overlook much of the technical and professional capacities of Italian architects. "Genius and disorderliness" is one of the world's most widespread stereotypes when considering Italian creativity, and it is applied as much to art as to craft work, or referred to architecture and design alike. In the case of architecture, though, the issue has always been more complex, since many areas of knowledge and experiences converge in this discipline: design, materials technology, decoration, construction science, spatial organisation, building site management, technical design, and client relations, to name but a few. But given these preconceptions and the profession's complexity, what is the basis for this common belief, which has been so well projected worldwide, of a mythical vision of the Italian architect who is something of a craftsman, an artist, a philosopher, a scientist and, in the same context, also creative in the relationship with technique and its management?

A Deep-Rooted Legend

To understand better a certain mythology surrounding the figure of the Italian architect, it might be useful to take, as the place where the myth developed, the rich northern European, in particular the British, literature devoted to Italy's extraordinary artistic history.

Indeed, it is from these continuous, broad and in-depth readings that certain recurrent historic formulas have gained in consistency. When translated into the mass culture of the nineteenth and twentieth centuries, they took on the character of stereotype models animated by a mythical aura. In this regard, one of the best known myths in western artistic culture is that of a new figure of *architectus modernus*, who assumed a particularly clear form in Italy at the beginning of the Renaissance. This new centrality of the architect in the public life and in the technical and humanistic doctrines, has often been particularly attributed to the primogeniture of the theoretical and construction work of Leon Battista Alberti.

Before this period, going back to the Roman epoch and passing to mediaeval times, the figure of the architect, however important and respected, was often—apart from rare exceptions— shrouded in demure anonymity

Adolfo Natalini (Superstudio),
Bahnhof Apotheke Krause,
Lübeck, 1976-78.

197

imposed by the prevailing social models. For example, Cicero included architecture among the *artes honestae*, but not among the *artes liberales* in that its practise brought money. Afterwards, the collective components of the mediaeval builders' yards, reinforced by the typical guild character, had mostly concealed the figure of the *magister fabricae*.

Nevertheless, also from this long and extremely important historical period—albeit less auctorial than others—derives much of the myth of Italian architecture if for no other reason than the revival, itself mythical, of Roman forms during the Renaissance, as also clearly shown by the role later taken on by the celebrated treatise *De Architectura libri decem*, compiled by Marcus Vitruvius Pollio in 27 BC, and officially rediscovered in 1414 in the library of the Montecassino Monastery and continually consecrated in the ensuing centuries.

In the Beginning, There Was Alberti

A complete thinker, a *universal man*, authentic champion and important symbol of *Humanism* in the widest sense of the term, Leon Battista Alberti stands out above all for his intellectual prowess among the most relevant personalities of the Renaissance. But the clarity of his contribution as a forerunner and founder of the great Renaissance themes is not expressed only in his rare and however exceptional architectural works or in his literary masterpiece, the *De re aedificatoria*,[1] fundamental treatise of the Renaissance architectural culture: it is expressed above all in his superb figure as militant architect who was intellectually active in society, devoted to study and to debating the widest range of scientific, philosophical, moral, religious and political issues. This character, who from then on would be acknowledged as a model of a certain type of Italian humanistic designer-thinker, was clearly understood by Vasari, the famous

biographer, when he recalled, "he was committed not only to trying to understand the world and measure the ancient works, but following his strongest bent, much more to writing than to putting his thoughts into practice".[2]

If above all in the field of architecture the Renaissance saw Alberti emerge as one of the main personalities, worth mentioning are the other eminent figures who worked with him or followed him in consecrating the new universal value: such important names stand out as Brunelleschi, Paolo Uccello, Piero della Francesca, Leonardo da Vinci, Filarete, Bramante, Raffaello, Giorgio Martini, Michelangelo and Palladio. These and others will be remembered as undisputed archetypes of genius in the fullest humanistic spirit, legendary figures of a new age when the study and exercise of artistic activity reach a role which was cultivated, independent and socially committed.

In that period, the new concept of the independent man in both thoughts and actions favoured the special connotation of the intellectual artist, who was fully conversant with the *trivium* and *quadrivium arts*, a model which all the most significant personalities of the Renaissance followed.[3] In some respects, it was a somewhat platonic inspiration which, as we will see later, would also influence all those architects who, in subsequent centuries, openly try to steal the limelight to this day.

From the Workshop-School to the School-Workshop

For a better understanding of the value, which today may seem obvious, of the revolutionary character achieved by the self-referencing of the intellectual architect, it is perhaps necessary to describe a few more relevant features of this fertile Renaissance period. In this sense, we must pause to analyse the passage between the thirteenth and fourteenth centuries, from the

Cristoforo Coriolano, *Portrait of Leon Battista Alberti*, xylography taken from the second edition of Giorgio Vasari's *Lives*, 1568.

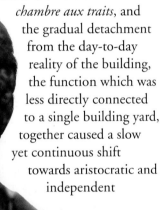

Daniele da Volterra, *Michelangelo*. Florence, Museo dell'Accademia.

fourteenth-century workshop-schools to the school-workshops of the Renaissance masters. This passage takes place also through the enhancement of human personality, which had already begun during the Carolingian Renaissance period. It would take too long to discuss here the path which led to the dissolution of medieval craft associations and which later fostered the rise of the intellectual aristocracy which found its proper environment in the workshop. It is certain, however, that the progressive distancing of the architect from the building-site workers, which had already begun in late medieval times with the creation of the *chambre aux traits*, and the gradual detachment from the day-to-day reality of the building, the function which was less directly connected to a single building yard, together caused a slow yet continuous shift towards aristocratic and independent

positions more open to the increasingly frequent working opportunities that the growing demands of society entailed. The model of the workshop remains, however, the vital and symbolic heart of that custom whereby the Maestro is elevated to the position of lay preacher, modern-day prophet. The figure of the Maestro can be epitomised in the expression *primus inter pares* (first among his peers) which would be taken up also by the twentieth-century master architects.

The myth of the *primus inter pares* architect was built day by day within the workshops of the Renaissance, as Luigi Vagnetti recounted well in his weighty work *L'architetto nella storia di Occidente*: "A gesture of deference or an act of reliance from the Maestro to only one of the helpers were enough to arouse jealousy, rancour, acts of rebellion, while it was common for group jokes—often rather cruel—to be organised for the youngest and greenest companions. But when the Maestro was in the workshop, his presence alone, his authority, and the esteem and respect which he gained from his group of helpers, were enough to ensure a serene and active atmosphere, one which was orderly, workmanlike and productive".[4]

In that period many of the canons for the modern architect were defined and in particular those of the model for the Italian architect, at least in the way they were handed down and fixed in the public's awareness. In this model, the intellectual approach to design appears repeatedly: it is the theoretical approach that gave rise to the rich Renaissance treatise literature, which was the cornerstone of western architectural culture. It is curious to observe that this approach finds a significant reflection in the characteristic exuberance of contemporary Italian architecture journalism. Another important feature of this model saw History as a design instrument, both in its reconfirmation through classical style and through its use for comparison and verification by the avant-garde. The latter, in turn, tried to work by using difference and contrast, yet enriched this patrimony by taking part in the development of this tradition. The centrality of the *polis* theme—and its superiority over that of architecture—was also confirmed, in that it corresponded more precisely to the material construction of the civil virtues; this value, within a broader scope, can also be traced back to the idea of context which, in the case of Italy, was characterised by a territory which was varied, rich in natural landscape and which, over time, has been prodigiously marked by the wise works of man. An expression of this is found in the classical architectural signs reproduced on a nationwide scale—hence, also the bucolic landscape with ruins as studied by the Renaissance masters—both through a new cultivated and refined project—and in this regard we can think of the birth of the Italian-style garden—and through the anonymous and vernacular work carried out in the countryside by common people who had only recently freed themselves from the dark period of the barbarian invasions.

The craftwork nature of the workshop remained constant, and to this day, especially in Italy, many maintain that a trade can only be learned through an apprenticeship, by working alongside the Maestro and upholding—albeit a little anachronistically—all the hierarchic rules handed down by that historical model; after all, one may also acknowledge a certain continuity in maintaining a social and political role connected to the prevailing power. This important role was achieved during the Renaissance through spirited determination, thus being allowed into princes' courts as "free thinkers" and "masters of art" being allowed, within the possible limits, a certain autonomous—and therefore respected—freedom of action. This feature seems to repeat itself today in the Italian model, often with decadent consequences, since clients the likes of

princes, who have a similar cultural and civil historical value, clearly no longer exist. Indeed, it is enough to remember that "no nobleman, no prince, no pope, would ever have dared to question an artistic proposal of their trusted architect, whose ideas were controlled only in terms of budget and never for any uncertainty of the aesthetic results".[5]

It is however true that this dialectic history between architect and client, which began precisely during the Renaissance, is studded with episodes typical of a role which has remained constant up to present times. This role was marked with frustrations and frictions between the two parties, humble and obsequious demeanours by the architects towards their coveted protectors, and the creation of a network of alliances among the artists, who were tied by this common fate of servitude, with the aim of raising their new social category as intellectuals to noble heights. Still a far cry from the power to which they gave such deference, these artists nevertheless succeeded in creating a clean divide between themselves and the rough and ignorant classes.

We can thus end our discussion on the creation of the Italian model for the architect in this important period of the Renaissance by noting again that starting precisely from that period, the architects (without forgetting that in those years architecture started to be considered a major art as it included the others), and so too the painters and sculptors began to find pleasure for being centre stage characters, isolated soloists even if deeply integrated in the system of their times and therefore interested in bequeathing the memories of them to the posterity: no longer only the works themselves but also the writings, chronicles, biographies and anecdotes. In this way the mythical figure of the modern architect was born, seen as the first among equals: this model has preserved its distinctive features—both positive and negative—

Iacopo Barozzi da Vignola,
*Regola delli cinque ordini
d'architettura*, title page, 1562.

Andrea Palladio, *I quattro libri
dell'architettura*, title page,
1570.

particularly in Italy, also through the somewhat promotional work started by some of the first chroniclers and art scholars amongst whom Vasari stands out.

Vasari's Lives

An important exponent in the group of court artists during the Manneristic period, Vasari (1511-1574) sketched the most meaningful traits of the "complete artist" during the Renaissance in his excellent and monumental biographical literary work *Lives of the Artists...* (Florence 1550). In these biographies, architectural thought often emerged as a process that summed up all arts, thus defining the artistic examples which, thanks to this rich and almost unique collection of biographies about exceptional artists, undoubtedly characterised the document on which the myth of the Italian classical artist was created and from which—as mentioned earlier—the mythicised figure of the Italian architect came forth.

But Vasari's work of consecrating the Renaissance arts does not confine itself to his already very important artistic historiography: his devoted erudition can be seen also in the first traits of the emerging art academies which would so strongly influence future artistic culture, starting from Italy and spreading throughout the world.

The Accademia Culture

With Mannerism at its peak, new artistic and educational institutions became established and flourished in Italy: the so-called *Accademie*. Initially a typically Italian phenomenon, the art academies were later reproduced in different models around Europe and in other parts of the world. As a direct result of the new Renaissance ways of interpreting and practising the craft of the artist, the academy represented the developed phase of the different forms of associative activity (a prime example being the school-workshop under

Leonardo da Vinci in Milan), experimented with as an alternative to the old medieval corporations.

After the spreading of the Renaissance treatises, the consolidation of the almost institutional form of the workshop and the renewed role of the architect in society (who was now independent from the court and bound with several clients), the birth of the academy appears as a natural outcome. The first was the Accademia delle Arti del Disegno (Academy for Drawing Arts), founded in Florence in 1563 on Vasari's inspiration; then, in 1577, the Accademia di San Luca was opened in Rome. Thus a new way of being an architect took shape which, from Italy, would spread throughout the western world to become a universally accepted practice. It is interesting to see that the main task of the academies in the early years of their activity was not so much one of teaching—which was carried out in only an embryonic form—as one of general consultancy on delicate artistic issues of public interest often related to large architectural projects. In this sense can be seen the request by Philip II Emperor of Spain who asked that the monastery to be built at El Escorial (near Madrid) be submitted for revision to the Accademia delle Arti del Disegno.

A further acknowledgement of the Italian artistic academies came in 1676 when, during the chair-principality of Charles Le Brun, the French court painter, the Académie Française was associated with the Accademia di San Luca in exchange for the high protection of Louis XIV. Then, at the beginning of the nineteenth century, a reform plan for the accademia statutes promoted by the Emperor Napoleon brought the great sculptor Antonio Canova to the presidency of the Accademia di San Luca. The prestige at European level of this appointment, confirmed for life in 1814, allowed Canova to go to Paris after the demise of Napoleon and the restoration of the monarchy to negotiate the restitution

201

of most of the artistic and cultural treasures plundered from Italy. Starting from the end of the eighteenth century, the academy model underwent a slow yet continuous regression that turned into a rapid decline in the eighteenth century: in those years, seen from the outside, the indignant isolation translated into those features of a blinkered and limiting vision which, from then on, would be considered typical of the conservative mentality of the so-called "Scuola Accademica".

Prestige and Nomadism of the Baroque Architects

The Baroque period, which in Italy saw such explosive personalities express themselves at the highest levels— amongst whom Bernini, Borromini, Fuga, Vanvitelli and Juvarra—watched as these geniuses passed unaffected through the increasingly restricted spaces of the academies. The intellectual confrontation between these restless souls and the rules set by the academy—which had not yet declined in Italy with regard to the most dangerous *principles of authority*— was certainly beneficial. But it was precisely from some of the limits set for the respect and continuation of the consecrated classical orders (as had happened in a different field with reference to the prevailing religious orders) that these architects managed to find out spaces for expressing their genius. Alongside these great lay architects, who were often participating in the official life of the academic institutions, such prestigious religious architects should be remembered as Guarino Guarini and Andrea Pozzo, whose training had taken place far from the art academies within the closed confines of the superior generals' houses and in the shadow of ecclesiastical hierarchies.

As Vagnetti well described, "the fame acquired by Italian architects during the Renaissance had brought then the high consideration of all the European

courts and already in the fifteenth and sixteenth centuries, journeys of Italian architects and craftsmen abroad were rather frequent as they were summoned by Sovereigns who wished to exploit their skills. Thus in the fifteenth and sixteenth centuries, whereas the European architects came to Italy to study the ancients, the Italian architects spread throughout Europe to work, and sometimes they remained. During the Baroque period, this outflow became for many a temporary and, for some, permanent custom: Bernini was called to Paris to provide consulting for the building of the Louvre, Juvarra travelled much through Europe and the same happened to several military architects who worked in numerous countries, to many civil architects (many of the famous circle of the Como architects) called to Russia by Peter the Great to build Petersburg or to Poland, Hungary, Austria, Czechoslovakia and so on".[6]

Piranesi's Suffered Freedom

It is worth taking time out to discuss Giovan Battista Piranesi, an exceptional artist, individualist and authentic precursor of the anti-academic architect, an emblematic forefather of a future line of intellectual designers torn between the need for practical exercise and the commitment to try out new spaces of architectural research. In his *Vedute di Roma* (Views of Rome; 1748) and more so in his sublime and disquieting views of the *Carceri* (Prisons; 1745-61), Piranesi opened a new intellectual dimension of architecture which aimed at placing emphasis on the fundamental value of free experimentation. This went decidedly beyond the late Baroque precept of "unity in variety" which tended towards research in the full autonomy of the virtual space of drawing, of an ideal solution which shunned compromises. With Piranesi, that slow yet continuous corrosion began—to be seen as the crisis of modern times—which would attack

Gian Lorenzo Bernini, *Self-Portrait*, oil on canvas, circa 1620, Rome, Galleria Borghese.

Giovanni Battista Piranesi,
Le carceri, pl. XIV, etching, first
stage, 1745.

the fundamental certainties of classic model. As correctly perceived by the great architecture historian, Manfredo Tafuri, "Piranesi did not possess the tools to translate the dialectics of contradictions into form: he could therefore only emphatically state that the new great problem was the search for equilibrium of opposed elements, which is particularly present in the city: the risk was the destruction of the concept of architecture itself".[7]

The Predominance of the Enlightenment Theoretical Architect
The pre-eminent and increasingly intellectual and theoretical role of the Italian architect was transmitted also to the Enlightenment. In that time the

rationalistic theories of Lodoli were highly influential which can be well summed up in his famous maxim "building and reason must become as one and their function must be representation", as well as Milizia's thought who, following Vitruvio, stated that "since architecture is born of necessity... beauty... must appear as necessary, as it is born of need". Also the position of Memmo, Lodoli's pupil, was honoured, who carried out the revolutionary rationalistic idea, by asserting that "through the outside.... the inside should always be expressed". All these personalities were critics, theoreticians, polemicists, scholars and historians, that is men of letters who, in those years, would reach an unexpected

203

Ignazio Gardella,
Antitubercolosarium,
Alexandria, 1938.

Studio BBPR (Lodovico Barbiano
di Belgiojoso, Enrico Peressutti
and Ernesto Nathan Rogers),
Velasca tower, Milan, 1950-58.

predominance in the dispute over architecture, often hushing the feeble voice even of the militant architects. From then on this typically Italian feature would mark the figure of the architect in society: on the one side the cultivated men-architects—who were only barely interested in the technical problems connected to construction—, on the other the building yard men-operators, with their mere performing role, who were largely unconcerned with philological disputes.

The Dark Years of Italy's Nineteenth Century
The English Industrial Revolution and the social revolution which began with the American declaration of independence and the French Revolution saw Italy at the margins of these ferments. The country found itself in a seriously backward position both socially and culturally with respect to the rapid technical and scientific progress of the nineteenth century. This condition was to weigh heavily on the education and development of the Italian architect, who, from this period on, played out a secondary role and one which, aside from some rare exceptions, largely followed in the wake of the international avant-gardes, above all in technical fields.
For decades a dispute went on in the

renewed academic body, instituted with the unification of Italy by the royal government which co-operated in attempting to define the characteristics of architecture teaching between the art academies and the new-born Polytechnics. The dispute would be a sign of the decadence of the Italian architectural culture of that period which would drag its heels also in the century to come and be incapable of properly responding to the lively initiatives and proposals put forward in the more industrialised countries. Ironically, though, it was precisely at the same time that the myth of Italian architecture was hailed abroad, embedded as it was in the "garden of Europe". And contained within this myth, therefore, was the Italian architect, idealised through the figures of the past. When seen in different lights, the Italian architect thus became a sophisticated reference to the essence of architecture in a period when modernity was overturning all the theoretical and constructional certainties which had been handed down to that moment in time. But it is clear that this was a defective and limited myth, one forced to act out a part that offered some sorely anachronistic lines, one chained to a contradictory role from which, in the nineteenth century only rare geniuses

Gio Ponti, Antonio Fornaroli and Alberto Rosselli, structures by Pier Luigi Nervi and Arturo Danusso, the Pirelli skyscraper, Milan, 1955-58.

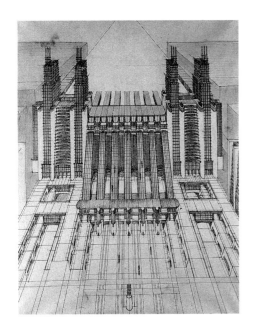

Antonio Sant'Elia, *Airport and railway stations with funicular and lifts, on three street levels*, ink and pencil on paper, 1914. Como, Musei Civici.

of design would emerge. People who would prove capable of climbing down from this ivory tower to unleash the most genuine aspects of Italian architectural culture for research.

Futurism and Sant'Elia's Shooting Star
It was only at the beginning of the twentieth century that another Italian architect became most admired at international level: in that period Italy won a key space among the historical avant-gardes by imposing itself with the impetuous Futurism movement. In the field of architecture Antonio Sant'Elia's precocious and ingenious figure stood out, a man characterised, both in his words and signs, by an inspired and foretelling language, as testified to also by his writing of the celebrated futurist architecture manifesto published in 1914. Sant'Elia became a real myth, not only for his pyrotechnical inventiveness in the fresh track of modernity but also for his premature death during the war, which left behind the idea of a promising man tragically stolen from the modern culture of the country.

The Maestros of Italian Rationalism
Sant'Elia remained however a source of inspiration for the maestros of the international Modern Movement and in particular for the Italians—especially those who, for their rejected ideas and ill-founded hopes, would come out crushed from the ever changing and tragic events of the fascist period. Their double overthrow expressed itself both physically in the extermination camps and morally for the defeat of man before his own destructive folly. Such was the case of Giuseppe Terragni, the celebrated architect of Italian Rationalism from Como and a follower of his fellow-countryman Sant'Elia. Terragni was however destroyed mentally and physically by his experience of the Russian campaign. Instead the extermination camps never gave back the lively personality of Giuseppe Pagano and the young and

delicate figure of Gianluigi Banfi. A substantial loss was felt also in the field of theory and criticism with the death of important reference figures such as Persico and Giolli.
It would take too long here to unravel all the ideological threads and the crushed hopes of that young generation of architects who, in the Fascist interlude between the First and the Second World Wars, heroically trod the path of modernity. This idea of the hero is certainly a rhetorical expression, yet in our discussion of the myth we should reassert it as owing to the so-called martyrdoms of Italian Rationalism, this celebrating emphasis constituted one of the strong points for the re-creation of Italian architectural thinking in the post-war years.
At first this battle of the modern—so "heroic" and so tragically concluded for some—saw some important figures keep some light and ambiguous relations with the Fascist regime: then the fights followed against the Fascist Academy which was run by Marcello Piacentini, a refined and ambitious man. When the political defeat became apparent, a new awareness ensued of an impossible relation, followed by an increasingly condemned isolation and at a certain point by persecutions which saw the shattering of all reference points and hopes.
But from a closer distance, the modern project in Italy was deeply-rooted in history. In this light the confrontations can be seen of such personalities as Terragni and Pagano who set themselves in a dialectic context with architects and artists having a Futurist model, this movement being felt as a vigorous artistic expression of modern times, or following the metaphysical doctrine or the nineteenth-century trend, both seen in their research of the erudite spirit of the classics.
Since both these central figures (especially Terragni) were given several important international awards while alive and also after their deaths, it is worthwhile remembering the strong

Carlo Scarpa, Banca Popolare di Verona, Verona, 1973-80.

Giovanni Michelucci, St. John the Baptist church (known as "of the motorway"), Campi Bisenzio (Florence), 1960-64.

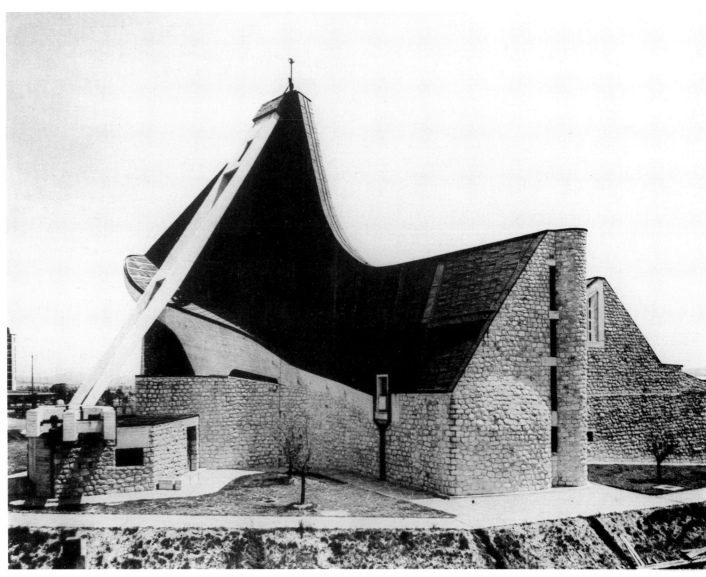

Ignazio Gardella, Vicenza theatre, plastics, 1980.

humanistic education which they brought into the Modern Movement and which found expression in its bond with history and the cultural and territorial context. These models were bequeathed to their fellow artists who, being slightly younger and luckier than them, survived the conflict and worked hard in the post-war years to rebuild the country.

Post-War Reconstruction
After the Second World War, new vigour was brought to the Italian architectural scene, but it was also a period subject to strong contradictions. "After the Liberation a difficult dialogue between knowledge and action was imposed—stated Tafuri—on those architects who were seeking new

solutions for the Italian reality."[8] Knowing and acting, thinking and doing, theory and practice, it was extremely difficult to ascribe these to the unity of the project. As we have already seen, after the golden period of the Renaissance, that mythical unity was slowly removed giving way, from the middle of the nineteenth century, to contrasting roles, theories and techniques, which would all cause considerable afflictions and difficult contradictions. What's more, the new experiences, the new myths and cultures, which were being overbearingly inflicted on the Italian

reality from abroad, were revealing the serious economic and political backwardness of the country; and against this dusty background, built of hope but also of serious misappropriation, the Byzantine theoretic sophisms and the unwanted academic formulas continued to be entwined.

However if we want to talk of the myth of the Italian architect, there is no lack of personalities in this period either. It must be remembered, however, that from this moment, in a new era of communications and consumption, the term myth loses a lot of its symbolic aura, to be transformed, especially in more recent times, in a sort of "hero of glossy magazines". Therefore it is necessary to identify, from now on, those personalities who deserve historic recognition, who have received a patina of legend thanks to certain events (perhaps they disappeared at the height of their career, or due to the rigour and originality of their work), and those esteemed intellectuals of architecture who have managed to successfully ride, with masterly determination, the so called Media Wave of the Global Village, and are therefore consecrated on the Mount Olympus of a certain international star system, but which is often an extradisciplinary position. Beware however, as it is not as easy as it seems to form such a clear distinction especially in contemporary architecture: the shades between the different situations can sometimes be very faint. We must also remember that today the process of "mythicising", even though it is encouraged by insistently affected roles and consequent attitudes, is in fact done outside the circle of each individual, in what is often an unpredictable manner, and can therefore involve figures who have no real interest in this sort of protagonism.

Two Poles of the Italian Model: Gio Ponti versus Ernesto Nathan Rogers
Returning to the historic traces already mentioned in the post-war

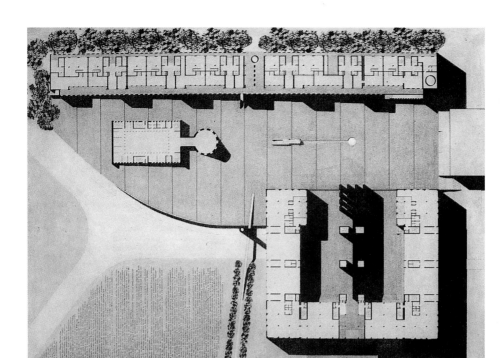

Aldo Rossi, Fontivegge project,
Perugia, 1982-89.

reconstruction period, two
personalities, Gio Ponti and Ernesto
Nathan Rogers deserve an initial
profile, based on what has previously
been said. It is important to remember
the effect that their work had
internationally, as has already been
shown, in their writings and teachings,
and in their projects and constructions.
They were very different from each
other in their cultural hypothesis, even
though they had certain curious points
of contact: Ponti was totally dedicated
to the reconstruction of the historic
and mythical "Italian model", the style
and decor of the *Bel Paese*, even though
he had a certain dialogue with
modernity; Rogers was involved in the
continuation of Italian Rationalism as
represented by the masters of the
Modernism, both nationally and
internationally, even though an open
debate was held regarding a certain
suffocating orthodoxy to try and find a
model that was closer to our history. It
is also important to remember that
Ponti was founder, in 1928, and
director for a very long period, of the
Domus magazine which was, and is still,
one of the most famous and
consecrated international architecture
publications, a real beacon of Italian
creativity in the world. For Rogers it is

fundamental to remember the ten years
(1953-64) when he was director
of the magazine *Casabella* (also founded
in 1928), another "official" voice
of Italian architecture, which was
mainly concentrated on the careful but
courageous debate on Rationalist
inheritance, which had been entitled,
in that period, International Style.
In this regard, we must not forget the
battle held by Rogers, accompanied by
some of his disciples, in sustaining an
Italian line in the CIAM meeting
(*Congrès Internationaux d'Architecture
Moderne*) held in 1959 in Otterlo.
The heresy which caused this
confrontation, along with the bitter
criticism, gave an unprecedented
success to the Italian alternative in the
modern scene, the effect of which was
a first official debate on the whole
monolithic system which had been
created in modern international
architecture. Paradoxically, the two
most emblematic works of Italian
architecture at that time, famous and
admired throughout the world, were
the Pirelli skyscraper (1955-58) in
Milan by Ponti, Fornaroli and Rosselli,
with the engineers Nervi and Danusso,
and the Velasca tower (1956-57) in
Milan, by Belgiojoso, Peressutti and
Rogers (BBPR), which represent two

Carlo Aymonino, sketch of the
Gallarate neighbourhood,
1967-69.

Paolo Portoghesi, Rome mosque, 1975-78, detail of the internal structure and plastic model.

contrasting faces of their respective research: a geometric and pure monolith for the "decorative" Gio Ponti, a "tower" with a "medieval" line for that awkward devotee of modern times, Ernesto Rogers and his companions. This apparent turnabout in their respective roles gave great witness to the cultural vivaciousness of these two masters, besides that class of autonomous and problematic thought of the Italian culture in that period. With respect to this consideration it is right to point out the importance that Italian architecture magazines assumed from this moment on throughout the world. Besides *Domus* and *Casabella*, an impressive number of other magazines were published, all representing different trends, many of which, for several years, held a leading role in the international panorama of architectural culture, holding an important position in the perpetuation of a certain myth of Italian architecture. One last point, although several could still be made, refers to the inheritance of these two consecrated fathers of modern Italian architecture: together with Rogers a group of young architects of the time formed a group called "the *Casabella* boys", and they were the editorial group of the magazine, they were all by now quite famous, and we will meet them again further on in our survey, Giancarlo De Carlo, Vittorio Gregotti, Guido Canella, Gae Aulenti, Aldo Rossi. On the other side with Ponti, we find a very mixed family, as the research by Ponti was unorthodox, giving birth to several "nephews" among whom should be noted the figures of Sottsass and Mendini, who were often closer to the world of design, both involved on several occasions in running *Domus*, of which Mendini had also been Director.

The Different Faces of the Italian Project
During the same period as Ponti and Rogers, other architects also deserve a mention, for different reasons because they certainly added to give recognition to a particular style of Italian architects. It is sufficient to remember the refined and sever mastery, the absolute tendency, of Franco Albini, the "masterly narrative" and the "museology inventions" of Carlo Scarpa, the "educated revisionism" of Ignazio Gardella, the brilliant existential and "organic" spirit of Leonardo Ricci, the audacious brutalism of the young Vittoriano Viganò, who pointed him out in international magazines, in the early '50s, as the prodigal son of contemporary architecture, and again the professional success abroad of architects like Luigi Moretti, Gianluigi Giordani, Marcello D'Olivo. A special mention should also go the prestigious figure of Pierluigi Nervi, excellent construction engineer, but also genial creator of audacious free forms inspired by science, which his consecration in the world of architecture is due to, in as much that, in the opinions of some, he represented the modern reproposal of the universal model of the Renaissance architect for his synthesis between art and science.

The Primate of the Culture of Italian Design
"To that frustration suffered during the planning experience of public building—Tafuri reminds us—Italian architectural culture has to confront the successes obtained in the design field, and, even more, those obtained in the field of museology."[9] If the peculiarity of the project for the "Houses of Art" has already been mentioned in the references made to the masters in this research (BBPR, Albini and Scarpa), a new and very special comment must be made regarding the international success given to the culture of Italian design. From the middle of the '50s the "Italian good design" exploded at world level. A growing phenomenon which was consecrated in 1972 with the famous exhibition *Italy: The New Domestic Landscape* held in the Museum of Modern Art in New York.

This special planning space which confronted the humanist culture of Italian architects with the techniques, but even more with the symbolism, of the industrial product and its environment of consumption, generated a renewed culture of autonomous planning, with a strong interdisciplinary character and, in certain cases, with complex and contradictory ideological appeals. As Vico Magistretti often reminded us in his public speeches, "in being architects we were designers who had studied Latin" and therefore only able to develop the humanist problems of an industrial product. Planning which was original and against the trend, which was known in the world, and which still holds a prominent position, thanks to that antique process which makes the planner first a philosopher, then a craftsman and finally a real and practical creator of his knowledge. Among the forerunners of this planning route was Gio Ponti, who in his kaleidoscopic research could not miss this chance of producing modern and industrial items filtered through the spirit and mastery of the "Italian style". But apart from his alternating results as industrial designer, it was basically his enthusiastic contribution to the design field, which, thanks to the work of his magazine *Domus*, quickly managed to attract important international audiences. Many, too many, are the figures to remember, each one for his own special way of thinking and planning, but we must mention, be it briefly, in this text dedicated to the myth of the architect, the undisputed success of protagonists of the international scene like Marco Zanuso, Pier Giacomo and Achille Castiglioni, Bruno Munari, Joe Colombo, Vico Magistretti, Ettore Sottsass, Enzo Mari, Mario Bellini, Gaetano Pesce, Andrea Branzi, to mention some of the more representative among them. In particular Marco Zanuso, who without doubt represented the most consolidated figure in the '60s and '70s

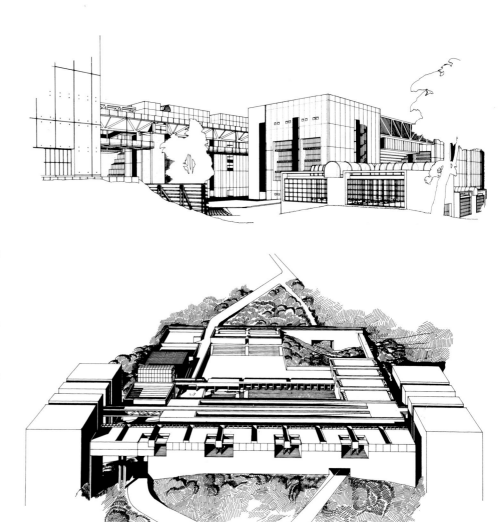

as architect and designer, a new *deus ex machina* of industrial design, both on a territorial and a utility item scale.

The Paradigms of Pluralism
Different languages and different design philosophies compete for the rare and uncertain spaces of planning in the period from the '70s to the '80s. After a season which lasted right through the '70s, in which the worrying political problems of our country were reflected in the withdrawal of the architects into the areas of theory and research which was then defined as "designed architecture", in the '80s a class of architects reappeared in society, characterised by a euphoric desire to appear, to become famous. In the field of architecture there was an irrepressible desire for hedonism, held up, in many cases, by

Vittorio Gregotti, University of Calabria, two drawings and a photograph of the complex, Cosenza. Photo by Mimmo Jodice.

an able promotional activity, and which gained fame and went beyond the theoretic positions, being more stylistic and much less interested in comparison, unlike the Italian society of those years.

Great mention was given in that period to one city which had historically lived through all the more important seasons of modern Italian architecture, Milan, the chosen home for the publishing world and for many of the protagonists of the history of contemporary architecture who have been mentioned, like the "Milan to be drunk".

In the middle of this ferment, which caused many to daydream of taking Milan to the centre of Europe, the figure of the Italian architect found new princes of politics and finance, in both Italy and Europe, who elected him as a man of modern culture, well integrated in the consumer machine, as

the ideal creator of the collective imagination.

It was a condition which touched almost everybody in the '80s, for better or worse, but which luckily diminished with the recession of the early '90s, bursting the bubbles and straining the dregs, giving way to a desire for order and quality which, not by chance, found its highest reference for coherence of principles, and not just decadent formal imitations, in the ancient mythical models. We could celebrate the personalities of our ambassadors of the Italian model in architecture, but their notoriety in Italy and the best part of the world is by now so well consolidated that they need no further presentation. The names of Aldo Rossi, Gae Aulenti, Vittorio Gregotti, Gino Valle, Giancarlo De Carlo and above all Renzo Piano, recent winner of the Pritzker Prize (1998) are

Francesco Venezia, Gibellina
Museum: the Riposo and the
inner courtyard, 1980.
Photo by Mimmo Jodice.

Pierluigi Spadolini, restructuration of the Salimbeni Fortress, seat of the Monte dei Paschi di Siena Bank, Siena, 1963-72.

Luigi Pellegrin, restoration project for Turin's Lingotto. The project was not carried out.

sufficient for confirming the primate maintained, on numerous occasions, by the ample and complex dimension of Italian architectural culture.

However we have already mentioned, at the beginning of this historic survey, how all these important affirmations are symbols of a distorted image of the Italian realty. Continuously impoverished of its identity and devalued in its cultural roots by the unwieldliness of the mass university, by the serious administrative shortcomings, by the striking regression of the relationship with the consumer, by the loss of direction of the professional Order which was clearly breathless when facing the urgent appeals, and weighed down by an excessive number of students.

Each of these protagonists, of which four (De Carlo, Gregotti, Aulenti, Rossi) matured alongside Rogers in *Casabella* during the '50s and '60s, is a carrier of personal and autonomous research, but in all of them, and others not mentioned here, like the emerging figures of the young generation of Italian architecture, we can recognise the historic constants of thinking and making Italian architecture: the theoretic research based on the critical reading of history as a planning instrument, the fundamental recognition of the cultural and physical context as a indispensable information in the project analysis, the spirit of the ancient renaissance workshop as the ideal forge in the laboratory of planning research.

If these, and other, strongholds of the training of the Italian architect are shown, beyond the mythicised rhetorical figures, as being at the height of the immanent and apocalyptic future prefigurations of towns and territories, we do not know. But we hope that the universal spirit of "good construction" and the quality of living inspired by the Italian model may return to fill all those spaces in the towns and country that have been abandoned for too long—and above all, it is sad to say, those in Italy.

[1] Already known in 1452 as a manuscript but not printed until in 1485 in Florence.

[2] *Le vite de' più eccellenti Architetti, Pittori e Scultori Italiani da Cimabue insino a tempi nostri descritte in lingua toscana da Giorgio Vasari pittore aretino, con una sua utile e necessaria introduzione alle arti loro, Florence* 1550 (Eng. trans. *Lives of the Artists*, Harmondsworth 1965).

[3] "In Medieval times, the so called *artes sermocinales* were called arts, or also the *trivium* sciences. These were: grammar, dialectics, rhetoric, alongside— and distinguished from—the *quadrivium* ones (also called *artes reales*), which were arithmetic, music, geometry and astronomy. All of them made up the so called *artes liberales* and they were used as the basis for school teaching." From L. Vagnetti, *L'architetto nelle storia di Occidente*, Teorema edizioni, Florence 1973.

[4] *Ibidem.*

[6] *Ibidem.*

[6] *Ibidem.*

[7] M. Tafuri, *Progetto e utopia*, Laterza, Bari 1977.

[8] M. Tafuri, *Storia dell'architettura italiana 1944-1985*, Einaudi, Turin 1986.

[9] *Ibidem.*

Umberto Eco
Il nome della rosa

Romanzo Bompiani

Ugo Volli

The Best-Sellers Business, Italian Style

1.

Italian people do not read a great deal, something which is exemplified by the figures of daily newspapers sales: for decades, the number of copies sold fluctuated from 5 to 6 million. At a mere 10 to 12% of the population, this proportion is at least four times smaller than the figures of the most developed countries in this field. In Japan, for example, 51 copies of newspapers are sold for every 100 inhabitants, while in the Scandinavian countries this proportion is about 40%. In Italy, instead, people tend to buy a lot of weekly magazines and "consume" a lot of television—on average almost 4 hours per person every day.

Perhaps the most disappointing statistic, however, regards the Italians' preferences for reading books. A Doxa survey published in 1996 in the daily paper *Il Sole 24 ore*[1] showed that 50% of all Italians say they have not read one book in the past year, a figure that is somewhat alarming also because this topic, which can entail an element of embarrassment, leads people to exaggerate their claims: probably many of those interviewed said they had read at least one book although this was not true. The modesty in regard to culture and its privileged—and somewhat fetishist—subject which is the book, holds strong in Italian culture, even if a qualitative survey conducted at the same time as the Doxa one and conducted by the Associazione Italiana Piccoli Editori, also painted a picture of an Italy which is partly hostile towards reading. There is indeed a growing faction that looks upon reading as a "waste of time" and an activity that "creates detachment from reality". This group favours television, for example, which is revered as portraying a "real window" on the world, or the collective pleasures such as discotheques or just simply socialising. Some non-readers—mainly middle class, young urban people with reasonable educational backgrounds—are even proud of their status, and claim it is a voluntary choice and not something to be ashamed about or a result of poverty and ignorance. Most people would honestly like to have read more, partly because of the social status associated with it, but tend to overstate their literary exploits when questioned on the topic.

Perhaps also for this reason the figures derived from surveys on the nation's reading habits have proved highly variable over time and therefore result as somewhat unreliable. In 1984, for example, the Istat (Italian Central Statistics Institute) estimated that only about 46% of Italians could say they had read at least one book over the previous twelve months; in 1987 in a survey by

Umberto Eco, *The Name of the Rose*, Bompiani. *The Name of the Rose* is the first example of great international editorial success from Italy. Indeed, in a few years more than ten million copies of the book have been sold and it has been translated into practically all the known languages.

Multiscopo, this figure appeared to fall to only about 37%. By 1995, according to another survey by the Istat, the proportion rose to nearly 50%, which could be considered a noteworthy improvement, even if, by default, this means that the remaining 50% of Italians probably did not have any contact with books or reading since leaving school. A new study by Multiscopo, published in 1997, reported the figure to be less than 39%,[2] thus depicting a somewhat dismal fluctuating scenario. Whatever the exact figures, the picture emerging is one of generally poor reading habits that are influenced by levels of income.

If we look at the overall figures of monthly family spending—again from the Istat[3]—we can see that from a monthly consumption of about 716,000 billion lire (equal to 2,857,000 lire per family) 48,000 billion lire were devoted to "recreation, shows, learning and culture" (192,000 lire per family). Of this amount, only about 11%—21,230 lire per family per month was spent on books (including the compulsory expenditure on school books) compared with almost 25,000 lire spent on papers and magazines, 11,000 lire for the television licence and 46,000 lire for recreational activities such as cinema, theatre, etc. Although people's spending on books is meagre, it does display a high elasticity to price. Indeed a veritable explosion in sales ensued from the initiatives by publishers to offer sizeable price reductions. Examples of this in recent years are the *Oscar* line of discount books and the generation of paperbacks that followed in the '60s; then, in the '90s, the *Millelire* (literally "thousand lire") cut-price paperback series. However, for catalogue constraints, publishing-cost economics or perhaps simply boredom among the public, these expansions were quickly withdrawn and the products too became deprived of their innovative characteristics. After only a couple of years, the *Oscar* series left the paper stands and their average price more than

doubled while the *Millelire* editions were quickly forced out of the market.

Some consolation can be found in the fact that most non-readers—i.e. those who have never opened a book in the last year—are older rather than younger people. As many as 70% of people older than 54 read less than one book a year, 50% from 35 to 54, 40% from 25 to 34 and only 25% from 15 to 24, even if the Istat survey explicitly excludes school books from the figures. It has also emerged from the same study that women read slightly more than men: 48 compared with 53 non-readers out of 100, with a widening gap among younger age groups where traditional gender discrimination about education is less felt. Moreover, and that people in the South read less than those in the North, who in turn read less than those in central Italy: 56, 48 and 44 non-readers out of 100 inhabitants respectively; data on the average readers (those who read from 2 to 5 books a year) and the more avid readers (over 5) are broadly in keeping with these figures. This geographical division corresponds to the *per capita* spending figures on books gathered by the Istat according to another method: 24,400 lire in the North, 25,406 in the Centre and only 16,407 in the South[4].

An obvious yet particularly marked correlation exists between education and reading habits. There are only 14% of non-readers among graduates and 29% among school leavers, 47% among those who left after secondary school and 77% of those who left after junior school. These figures also show how the amount people read is strongly connected to their educational level. The statistical analysis also indicates a very strong correlation between family income and their inclination to purchase books.

A certain degree of optimism on the future of books—as is confirmed by the figure on the greater inclination to read among younger as opposed to older people—can be partly justified when consulting sales figures from the publishers: from 1992 to 1995, the

Umberto Eco, *The Name of the rose,* covers for the Japanese (*above*) and Arabic (*below*) translations.

number of books published overall by Italian publishing houses rose from 42,000 to 49,000, and overall circulation rose from 223 million to 289 million.[5] In a word, more books are published although it cannot be taken for granted that this corresponds to a greater overall readership.

2.

What do Italians read, then? Data in this area is very confusing. The public library system is too inefficient to provide reliable figures on loan preferences. Smaller libraries are certainly used for reading, and re-reading, yet it is impossible to know what people read and how much. More reliable data is available on what people buy rather than what they actually read. The national newspapers print lists of the week's best-sellers, but since these are compiled using very different sampling criteria and calculation methods—from the opinion of individual book seller's through to the statements by the publishers and sampling analysis—they are invariably contradictory and thus unreliable.

Since the retail sales outlets are also very fragmented and specialised bookshops cover only a small fraction of overall book sales, the figures are uncertain and these statistics, which are made up using different methods, are suited not so much for a reasoned comparison as for polemics and suspicion often ventured by unsatisfied critics and writers.

Of course, many objections are raised on principle to the very idea of best-seller lists. Giovanni Raboni wrote in this regard: "I have never concealed my diffidence towards this instrument of cryptopersuasion according to which the books which sell more than others carry on in the same vein for the very same and tautological reason that they are selling more than the others".[6]

What all these lists do have in common is a poor sensitivity for books that carry on selling for long periods—the so-called long-sellers—and for the alternative channels to the bookshops:

supermarkets, newspaper stands, postal shopping and book clubs, and of course school books. To this last point we will return in due course. On the other hand, the data from the publishers are in turn somewhat unreliable for different reasons and therefore, to analyse consumption of books, it is best to use the classifications found in the daily papers.

A summary of the last twenty years of its best-seller lists, with the hundred best-selling books, was published in 1996 by the supplement of the *Stampa*, *Tuttolibri*, to celebrate its twentieth anniversary. It is worthwhile following it, if for no other reason than to observe the uniformity of its measurement criteria.[7]

A rather surprising starting-out figure is that despite the general conviction that Italian readers love all things foreign, which is backed up by a policy among the largest publishers of plugging the international best-sellers for fifteen of the twenty-one years examined, the best-selling author was in fact Italian (and in a sixteenth case, it was an ancient philosopher, Epicurus, for the launch of the *Millelire*). Considering all of the 101 authors present in this super-list, the preference for Italian authors, although slightly fallen, has prevailed: 61 of the authors featuring in the list are Italian while the other 40 are foreigners. If, lastly, we consider the list presences—which are often several in the case of certain authors, who occupy more than one place, both when they refer to books that have been in the list for several years and when to authors who have had success within different titles at the same time or in succession—the result is not very different: out of 210 positions, 139 are Italian (66%) and only 71 are non-Italian. The bottom line is therefore that if we make allowance for the heavy marketing emphasis in the Italian best-seller market of American action novels and the hype surrounding them, this is truly a surprising result.

Instead a negative figure, yet predictable, is the poor attendance by female writers.

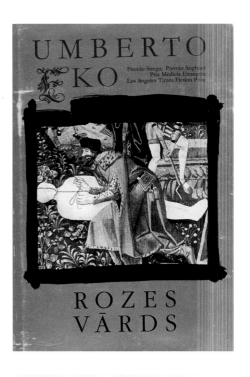

Umberto Eco, *The Name of the Rose*. Cover and back cover for the Chinese edition; cover for the Latvian edition.
Below: cover and back cover for the Hebrew edition; cover for the Albanian edition.

Only 22 of 101 big-time authors were women and of these only 8 (out of 40) were non-Italian and 14 (out of 61) Italian. So the world of books, and in particular the world of successful books, is a prevalently masculine domain, even if it is noticeable that women are taking up a growing proportion of readers. In this regard, there is a cultural as well as commercial divide that should be given due consideration.

3.

The secret of this prevalence of Italian writers over the outsiders, that is the Folletts, Crichtons and Smiths of this world, who although international best-seller "machines", with works churned out regularly by the British and American publishing industry, lies in the fact that in Italy the best-selling books—or rather, as we will see, those sold with the greatest continuity—are mainly not fiction novels, but non-fiction (generally popular in nature) or so-called "miscellaneous" books which, in latter years, have largely been by comedians (from the famous *Anche le formiche nel loro piccolo si incazzano* by Gino and Michele and so on). Actually Italians read a lot more fiction novels than other types: in 1966 71% of books in the best-seller lists against 15% for fiction and 12% of miscellaneous. But these last genres show sales that are more concentrated on fewer titles whereas the demand for novels is distributed across a much broader number of titles, so its real popularity is to some extent hidden. Not that an élite non-fiction does not exist: for example, we can mention the output connected to the universities, which is sold at relatively low prices and is therefore not included in the best-seller lists. However, this quality non-fiction dealing with history, sociology, philosophy, anthropology and so on, which is sold in such relatively small amounts as to rarely feature in the best-seller lists and is still enough to support companies such as Laterza or Mulino, is often by non-Italian authors. The fact that almost no foreign non-fiction

publications are present in the best-seller lists bears out that, rather than not existing, quality non-fiction finds it difficult to drive inroads into the Italian market. On looking at the culture-based publishing houses, we can instead easily see that, among its western counterparts, Italy is the readiest importer of foreign cultural products (and above all the books market): French history, German philosophy, American sociology to name but a few. The fact that these publications do not feature in the best-seller lists shows that, aside from certain exceptions, there is a general divide between university non-fiction and that of large-scale consumption.

The non-fiction works capable of achieving big commercial success—mainly politics and journalism related, as evidenced over the last twenty-thirty years, or on esoteric subjects that have recently established their popularity—are relatively few and invariably concentrated on the same names (Biagi, Bocca, Vespa, Pansa). Tending to be largely predictable, they are often backed up with carefully planned press campaigns. It is also worth noting that the successful capacity of these authors for selling is based not so much on the single product as on consistency in their output. An exemplary case in point is the journalist Enzo Biagi, who every year, at the best moment for book sales—Christmas—unveils his new book, which may or may not be a secondary fruit of his television work. He has a loyal readership who waits to read it or often gives it to someone as a present. It is clear that, in these cases, the television and newspapers perform an essential function of legitimisation and support, not only in the sense that, for all authors of journalistic non-fiction, the previews and presentation interviews on the leading newspapers and magazines are an essential part of the course, but that also the journalistic or television activities of the authors, which continues with regularity throughout the year, constitutes a sort of implicit and ongoing legitimisation—a sort of long-wave

Still photograph from the Luigi Comencini film *La ragazza di Bube*, 1963, adapted to the screen from the novel of the same title by Carlo Cassola.

Still photograph from the Francesco Maselli film, *The Years of Indifference*, 1964, adapted to the screen from the novel of the same title by Alberto Moravia.

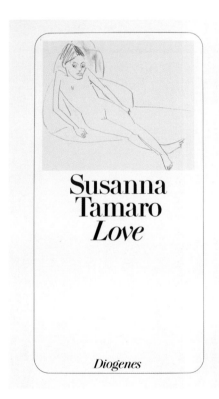

Susanna Tamaro, *Per voce sola*
Baldini & Castoldi. Covers for
the English translation and for
the Swiss-German edition.

advertising campaign that is sanctioned and constructive. Books and journalism, then, bolster each other and feed a publishing output that is average, at least in terms of size, and continuous.

A typical case of this is also given by Luciano De Crescenzo, a graduate electronics engineer introduced into the world of television by Renzo Arbore in a show called *Quelli della notte* (The Night-owls), which can also incidentally vaunt the merit of making Milan Kundera known to a wide television-watching public. De Crescenzo has succeeded in carving out an unusual niche for himself as a plain-talking teacher of classical culture and ancient Greek philosophy in particular. It is a niche that he occupies regularly, coming out with books that are sometimes highly interesting and well documented, at others less so—but all share those aspects of his public personality (Neapolitan, humouristic, and *bon ton*). Not dissimilar in this regard is Piero Angela, prince of science and nature both on the television and in publishing. Another exception from among the best-selling authors of non-fiction writing is Francesco Alberoni, a sociologist with an unquestionably solid academic background who has become a national personality also thanks to his column in the national paper *Corriere della Sera*. He writes on popular topics such as personal relationships with a highly readable and communicative style—proof that it is possible to have a popular non-fiction writer who does not purely revamp other people's work.

With regard instead to the miscellaneous area of publishing, this is an area of more casual topics, populated mainly by various collections of funny lines, stories, anecdotes, texts and sketches and songs. From *Io speriamo che me la cavo* (quotes taken from the homework of young Neapolitan children) to the *Formiche*, to the books by Paolo Rossi (comedian), Vasco Rossi (singer raised by now to cult status), Giobbe Covatta and so on, are the fruit of careful editing and, above all, highly assertive marketing strategies. In

this regard, some critics have gone so far as to speak of "non-books", but perhaps this stance is overly critical. It cannot be denied, though, that the success of these products depends largely on promotional back-up from the TV stations.

Generally, the television plays a very important role in the publishing industry's economics, as we have seen for the journalistic type of non-fiction. Also the authors of fiction and novels—who are both Italian and often non-Italian—use the television as an essential step in their promotional efforts. The TV adds, and partly replaces, the old presentations in bookshops and interviews in the daily newspapers and magazines. From this viewpoint, the function of the talk shows, and in particular the late evening *Maurizio Costanzo Show*, has lessened in recent years but has nevertheless played a role not to be underestimated—especially during the '80s.

With regard to the books covering other topics, and in particular comedy, the importance of this media reliance becomes increasingly marked. The examples are many and varied: from the simple collection of cartoons published by daily newspaper cartoonists like Forattini (whose astute eye for political satire is welcome on television shows at the big election-night marathons and who does not miss an opportunity to show his face in bookshops, much like Enzo Biagi) to the texts of shows and stories already presented on the television, to literary exploits—some actually very interesting—of authors whose fame actually derives from the television, right through to the compilations of howlers scribbled down by southern children in their homework (*Io speriamo...*) or collections of witticisms (*Le formiche*), which, in themselves, although not particularly "televisual", are nevertheless plugged and made famous by TV presentations. Here too the *Costanzo Show*, with its regular nightly spot devoted to a comedian or cabaret artist, has played a key role in moulding the form and content of

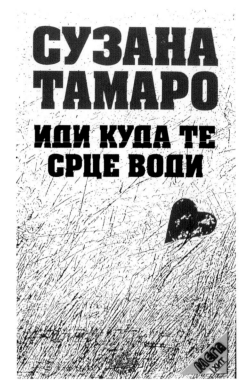

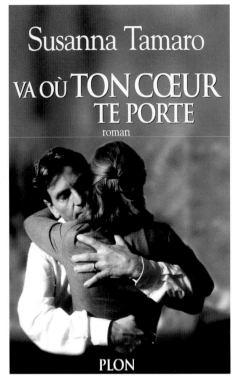

Susanna Tamaro, *Va dove ti porta il cuore*, Baldini & Castoldi. Covers for the American, Serbian, French, Chinese, Catalan and Finnish translations. Susanna Tamaro's has been the latest of the great international editorial successes from Italy, which surprised many observers because of its sudden and fast climb to notoriety.

material prior to it publication—and not just influencing post-printing success. A difference with respect to the case of the non-fiction writer should however be underlined. Although "serial" products do exist—especially in the form of continuations of blockbuster successes—usually the type of success enjoyed by miscellaneous entertainment publications is timely and also more explosive than popular non-fiction. Books on the mistakes, gaffes or howlers by kids from Naples or the witty lines by Gino and Michele are trendy and fly off bookstore shelves, yet their imitations, sequels or follow-ups tend to find a bumpy bandwagon to jump onto. Success tends to wane quickly, its latent energy diverted to another, newer idea.

4.

Italian best-selling authors, then, often have something unusual compared with the stereotype image of literature. On the other hand, this is a fairly general phenomenon, although the numbers do vary from country to country. In the United States, for example, an abundant output of "how to" books regularly jostles in the upper echelons of the non-fiction lists, but this type of publication is rather difficult to import into Italy's cultural context.

If we therefore return to the *Tuttolibri* super-list and look at its contents, we immediately find confirmation of the division between Italian and non-Italian authors and between fiction, journalistic non-fiction and miscellaneous writing. Indeed, among the most popular authors (who, in order, are Enzo Biagi, with 12 presences, Umberto Eco, 11, García Márquez, 9, Luciano De Crescenzo, 8, Oriana Fallaci and Milan Kundera, 6 each, Ken Follett and Cesare Marchi, 5, Francesco Alberoni and Giobbe Covatta, 4) only five—and three of these are foreigners—write fiction (but Eco and Fallaci are difficult to classify in this respect). All the others are authors of non-fiction or miscellaneous publication and all are Italian: these are the true best-selling Italian-style authors.

From our point of interest, few changes occur when we no longer consider the number of the positions in the list but rather the points accumulated by adding up these presences (and allocating to 100 the top name of each figure, as is the common practice in these classifications). In this scenario, Umberto Eco moves up to first place with 680 points, followed by Biagi with 618; then comes Gabriel García Márquez (487), De Crescenzo (485) and Fallaci (489). The classification follows with few variations: instead of Follett we find Gino and Michele, instead of Marchi is Goldoni (the journalist, Luca, not the Venetian eighteenth-century playwright, Carlo). On updating this chart to the period 1995-98, the only noteworthy addition is Susanna Tamaro, who with two and a half million copies sold of *Follow Your Heart* (1996) would probably unseat Umberto Eco and his *The Name of the Rose* (1981), at least when considering only the Italian market.

On browsing these charts, it clearly emerges how most of the literary authors who achieve success among the Italian public do so (with due account taken of specific cases) more on the model of miscellaneous than with non-fiction writing. Usually it is an isolated success, often preceded by interesting attempts that were not however appreciated by the public and only partly made up for after the explosion of the best-seller, and followed by other attempts which, compared with the first success, achieve results that often encounter at least some difficulties. Again, allowing for the due differences, this has largely been the case for Italo Calvino, Alberto Moravia and Giorgio Bassani, but in more recent times also for Umberto Eco and Susanna Tamaro. There are also authors who, whether by choice or destiny, practise an output based on continuity, from Bevilacqua to Fruttero and Lucentini, but these are in the minority with respect to the model of the explosion of a talent in the area of novels suddenly discovered by the public, often due to a word-of-mouth communication irrespective of the reactions from the critics and the publishers' forecasts. It is worth citing lastly some of the titles of novels (not very numerous, as we have seen) that appear high up in this list. In 1975 we find Leonardo Sciascia with *La scomparsa di Majorana*, in 1982 returned as leader (due to the effect of the paperback edition) *One Hundred Years of Solitude* by Gabriel García Márquez; for the same reason, in 1984 reappeared George Orwell's *1984*; in 1985 it was the turn of Kundera's *The Unbearable Lightness of Being*; in 1986 prevailed *Out of Africa* by Karen Blixen; in 1988 Joseph Roth's *The Legend of the Holy Drinker*; in 1989 Rushdie's *The Satanic Verses*. As we can see, there is much dishomogeneity among these titles, and so often their authors cannot feature in the general classification. It is worthwhile noting, however, that in many cases they are very high quality works, appreciated above all thanks to their publication in an economy edition.

5.

This effect of quality in the case of books that are sold in large volumes and over long periods of time, but not enough for them to feature in the best-seller lists, is underlined by a recent study devoted to the question.[8] On examining the data, it emerges that in 1996, for example, *The Leopard* by Tomasi di Lampedusa sold almost 25,000 copies, *The Cloven Viscount* by Italo Calvino more than 22,000, *The Tartar Steppe* by Dino Buzzati almost 17,000, *The Late Mattia Pascal* by Luigi Pirandello 16,000, and *The Years of Indifference* by Alberto Moravia only a few less. From among the translated texts by non-Italian authors, the record among the long-sellers is held by Hermann Hesse's *Siddharta*, which in 1996 sold almost 50,000 copies. In a nutshell, these classics of nineteenth-century Italian literature continue to sell year in, year out with the same sales figures as a reasonably successful fiction novel. In 1992, for example, *The*

Leopard sold 21,000 copies and *Il fu Mattia Pascal* 48,000. While it is true that school sales bump up the average, one can certainly not say that these are texts which are compulsory reading like Dante's *Divine Comedy*, Manzoni's *The Betrothed* or Verga's *The House by the Medlar Tree*, which are not considered in this classification. Even more interesting statistics are to be seen in poetry where, in 1996, a low-priced anthology by Eugenio Montale sold over 30,000 copies and another by Giuseppe Ungaretti over 27,000.

6.

If we consider, lastly, the more recent trends (the data referring to 1996) of new books on the market, we must start with the fact that, as already mentioned, there is a predominance of fiction in the best-seller lists (71%). This fact is a constant in the sales of books in Italy, even though it is subject to strong swings caused by changes in the social and cultural environment. During the '70s, for example, there was a considerable reduction in fiction with respect to non-fiction, a situation which was fully redressed however in the following decade.

In 1996 the fiction titles were two thirds foreign (for example, Ken Follett, Coelho, Sepulveda, King, Grisham) compared with a third Italian (Tamaro, Baricco, Brizzi, Bevilacqua), while non-fiction (14%) and miscellaneous books (11%) were almost exclusively Italian. Non-fiction was nearly all written by journalists like Vespa and Biagi, but also by intellectuals like Bobbio and Alberoni. The miscellaneous category belongs, as always, to comics like Giobbe Covatta, Forattini, Benigni and Greggio. The final result is that the two sectors obtain the same objective: 51% of books sold are Italian with 49% foreign. This trend was nearly confirmed in the first months of 1997, with 59% of foreign authors, who have entered the non-fiction field thanks to the New Age trend, and 41% Italian. Among the foreign authors are Stephen King,

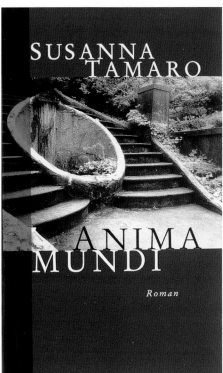

Susanna Tamaro, *Anima mundi*, Baldini & Castoldi. Covers for the Danish and Finnish editions (*front page, top*), and for the Spanish and German translations (*this page*).

Michael Crichton and John Grisham; among the Italians there are Antonio Tabucchi, Claudio Magris, Dacia Maraini and Giorgio Bocca.

7.

What we have said so far regarding the complicated and difficult relationship between Italian publishers and their public and the more prevalent reading habits in Italy, should help us to better address the question as to what makes a novel successful in Italy, leaving aside the vaunting and self-damaging prejudices that often reign in these circles. First, is it possible to create a classification at all? Perhaps the only person who tried to, and only for the foreign best-sellers which were successful in the first half of the '90s, was Filippo La Porta in an essay in the 1995 version of the very useful *Tirature* annual by Vittorio Spinazzola.[9] La Porta lists first "the novels which belong strictly to the genre and those which freely use certain stereotypes and codes, to then violate and mix these with others". Here we have the spy-stories, the legal thrillers, etc. Then we have "exoticism" (by which we mean certain Chinese or Japanese successes like Banana Yoshimoto). The third category is the group of "guaranteed or evergreen" authors who range from García Márquez to McEwan. Then comes the group of novels to do with "humour and comedy", and then there is the series of "books which follow, in one way or another, in the wake of successful films". Then there are the "philosophising and moralistic" (and those which try to be initiatory, which have become very popular over the last two or three years), those characterised by the "TV effect", and finally the "totally eccentric", unclassifiable books.

Such a generalised *ad hoc* classification, in which a book could easily fall within various different categories, only goes to underline the difficulty in classifying literary successes, both in Italy and probably abroad. It is also difficult to apply this classification to the great best-sellers by Italian authors. For example,

exoticism is missing, naturally, but where are the spy-stories (if we do not consider, that is, *The Name of the Rose* in this category...)?

What do the complex plot and the refined historic references of the semiologic thriller by Umberto Eco have in common with the sentimental intimacy or the dry style of Susanna Tamaro? Could his work be considered "philosophising, moralistic", like the work of Paolo Coelho, for example? Is it possible to link *History: A Novel* by Elsa Morante with *The Ragazzi* by Pasolini or with *A Man* by Oriana Fallaci? Of course not. What connections does the elaborate story of *The Leopard* have with the family intrigue of *The Garden of the Finzi-Contini*? It is clear that there are two completely different ways of relating to historic material.

We could debate these contrasts at length, but there are certainly some common elements. For example, it is clear that the *Bildungsroman* (the character-moulding novel) is quite a common theme in the greatest literary successes, but not however in the adventurous and individualist sense of the *Bildungsroman* by Goethe, by Sterne or even Flaubert. Rather, it is education as adaptation or rebellion with respect to a social scene, which is above all familiar, thus being the most important factor of the human landscape of these texts. Moreover, this familiar environment is damaged, degraded with respect to its model, but through this shortcoming or its silence, we can retrace our need to command it and, in a certain sense, its authentic form, which is rooted in the family history. This archaeological operation seems to be the fundamental gesture of many main characters in novels—the authentic content of their adventure. But perhaps this content should be looked at above all in an anthropological rather than in a literary sense; first it speaks of the Italian society, then of literature.

On examining the biggest successes of modern Italian literature, the biographical information which has

229

already been mentioned would certainly emerge (and which is relevant for a future biography of the book, besides that of the author), showing that Italian best-sellers are not the product of specialized craftsmen, like their American counterparts; they are instead the work of intellectuals who like to be called writers, but who often make their livings doing something else—perhaps in the fields of journalism or publishing or university teaching—and they prefer to carry on with this dual activity (also for the promotional reasons of which we have already spoken). Of course they are not complete outsiders, who would have little chance of recognition in the Italian literary scene (examples spring to mind of Morselli, and the difficulty Tomasi di Lampedusa had in selling his *Leopard*). The successful Italian author is therefore a professional intellectual rather than a professional writer. His encounter with success is overwhelming but often occasional. His work is not continuous but often interrupted by long pauses of silence or of other work. His relationship with the public is always rather precarious, and precisely because of this at the moment of success the public moves so easily to enthusiasm and the consecration of a *maître-à-penser*. The cases of Pasolini and Calvino, who are so different from each other, have at least this aspect in common.

Another consequence is the relationship between the best-seller and "high" literature. Certainly, today, it is not possible to give a precise scale of values to those books which do not have sufficient historical substance, to the extent that each attempt at this type of evaluation is followed by a series of discussions on the exclusions and the assignment of the positions. It is thus difficult to decide if any of the best-selling novels of the last decades will enter the best-seller lists of Italian literature and, if so, what position they might take up. After all, it often happens that the successes of one generation are forgotten by the next, which revives authors who were otherwise ignored in

their time. This has been the case, in our century, of Pitigrilli and Svevo. Yet on the other hand the concept of success in literature is nowadays subject to severe criticism from literary theorists. Moreover, before any classification can be made, the literary society exists, with all its rites, hierarchy, schools, and capacity of co-optation. It should be noted that in Italy not all the products of the literary society, nor even all the more prestigious works, enter the best-sellers lists, but more often the opposite is the case: the authors of successful novels want to belong to the literary society and usually they already do (even though their best-sellers usually undergo more or less violent attacks depending on their success). In short, whilst the Crichtons, Kings, Grishams lie outside literary society and—with a few exceptions—this division is fixed, in Italy the opposite happens: the authors of best-sellers, including Bevilacqua, Bassani, Tamaro, definitely belong to the literary society, which has excluded only those explicitly genre authors, like Liala. And it is not by chance that the only serious "political" attempt to separate the "simple and consumer" literature from the "high and experimental" one was made by the Gruppo '63 using the slogan "today's Liala" to the detriment of Bassani and friends. On the other hand, the same thing happens to books as to newspapers: in Italy the Nordic separation between quality papers and the tabloids does not catch on. This is the limitation, but also the fascination of the Italian best-seller.

[1] See P. Attanasio and E. Carfagna, "I figli leggono più dei genitori", in V. Spinazzola (edited by), *Tirature '96*, Baldini & Castoldi, Turin, from which some data cited below are taken. For a general history of the relationship between books and the public, in the period we are interested in, see G. Turi, "Cultura e poteri nell'Italia repubblicana" and G. Ragone, "Tascabile e nuovi lettori", both essays contained in the useful book edited by G. Turi, *Storia dell'editoria nell'Italia contemporanea*, Giunti, Florence 1997.

[2] See P. Attanasio and E. Carfagna, "L'enigma dei lettori", in V. Spinazzola (edited by), *Tirature '98*, Il Saggiatore, Milan.

238

Dario Fo, study for the show
Coppia aperta by Franca Rame,
tempera and marker, 1983.

[3] *I consumi delle famiglie*, Istat, Rome 1993. See
P. Attanasio and E. Carfagna, "Il consumo di
libri e altri consumi", in V. Spinazzola (edited by),
Tirature '94, Baldini & Castoldi, Turin.

[4] *I consumi delle famiglie*, ISTAT, Rome 1993.

[5] Source: *Tirature '98*, pp. 234-240.

[6] For a summary and bibliography on the most
recent disputes on the old chestnut on best-seller
lists, see L. Clerici, "Best-seller visibili e invisibili",
in *Tirature '98*.

[7] See L. Clerici, "Vent'anni di made in Italy", in
Tirature '96, from which some figures used below
were taken.

[8] The study dates back to 1996 and is published
in M. Brambilla, "Best-seller, le vere classifiche",
in *Corriere della Sera*, 26 April 1997. For these data
and other later figures, see L. Clerici, "Quando il
pubblico premia i libri giusti", in V. Spinazzola
(edited by), *Tirature '98*.

[9] "Best seller stranieri per il pubblico italiano", in
Tirature '95, edited by V. Spinazzola, Baldini &
Castoldi, Turin.